MASKED INTENTIONS

NAVIGATING A COMPUTER EMBARGO ON CHINA

WRITTEN BY

Allan Joseph

Contents

DEDICATION

This work is dedicated to my wife and family. This book would not have been possible without their enthusiastic support.

PREFACE

Memoirs of this nature require a prodigious memory or a record of some kind to provide the details of the events portrayed. In my case, I have an extensive photographic record that helped to prompt the more intimate recollections. Contrary to public belief at that time, my Chinese hosts not only allowed me to photograph but helped me do it as well. For that reason, I am eternally thankful to the Chinese people mentioned in this work.

On a more recent note, there are several people who provided assistance in tracking down the many facets of this story.

Kudos must go to John Chou who inveigled me to return to China in 2001. The facts I gathered during that visit with him provided the incentive to write this book.

Charlie Swift deserves special thanks for all the efforts he made to verify the parts of this story I was not personally involved with.

I will be eternally thankful to George DuBois for his herculean editing efforts. Were it not for George, the world would see how poor a grammarian I am.

Chapter 1 – In the Beginning...

London Times, Oct. 30, 1976:

"US AGREES TO SALE OF ADVANCED COMPUTERS"...(TO CHINA)

I stood at Chairman Mao's feet, his statue rising into the night, his cast face obscured in blackness. It was snowing; big, wet flakes. Even though I kept my face buried in the collar of my coat, the flakes felt wet and cold against my neck. The flakes were so large they should have made a noise as they hit the ground around me. Instead, total silence magnified the black night. I put one foot down and heard the "squish" of compressed flakes. Then I put the other foot down. "Squish." I kept doing this as I slowly marched about the circle. Although I had a cast-iron stomach, my head was sensitive to Chinese liquor.

Chairman Mao's big shadow loomed against the pale yellow light of the little street lamps. When I looked up, I could see the snowflakes against Chairman Mao's shadow. I looked again. The snowflakes weren't white! The snowflakes were grey and dirty. I realized the snow was coming down through the smog I had seen that afternoon. The falling snowflakes were actually cleaning the air, collecting particles of soot and smog as they floated down. I was in northeastern China in a city named Shenyang. It was 11:20 PM Tuesday, February 17, 1978. We had just said good night to our Chinese hosts at a welcoming banquet.

What am I doing in this God-forsaken place on the edge of the planet; in the middle of winter walking around a statute of a Communist dictator?

Let me tell you.

I was trying to walk off an industrial strength bout of drinking with my Chinese hosts. Although the popular concept of a Chinese banquet is lots of good food, it also includes lots of drinking. Perhaps my hosts were taking advantage of a company-paid (in this case, the government) drinking bout; perhaps it was normal genial hospitality in a strange land far from my own. Whatever the reason, the results were the same; a head disemboweled from the rest of my body. The Chinese have a secret weapon for these affairs; it is called "Mai Tai", a clear liquid drink that comes in a little square opaque white bottle. It was about 200 proof; one drink was enough to put a non-drinker under the table. For me it took about three.

By the mid-1970's China was in a period of turmoil. Chairman Mao Tse Dong was increasingly ill, and his previous unchallengeable authority over policy and practice was weakening. Occasionally a pragmatic faction lead by Premier Chou En Lai and his deputy, Deng Xiao Ping had quietly attempted to move China toward greater interaction with the West and to modernize China, but Mao and the Marxist hardliners had squelched such efforts. More than ten years previously, Deng Xiao Ping had been removed from his high office for espousing such thoughts and sent to the "country-side" for rehabilitation. He was restored to his former positions in 1974 only to be removed again in 1975.

The fierce ideological opposition of the Marxist hardliners was not the only obstacle to the modernization. After decades of relative isolation, China was woefully lacking in modern technology education, as well as the technology itself. The pragmatists knew that obtaining Western computers was absolutely essential to their plans.

By 1975, the Peoples Republic of China (and all other Communist countries) was under a strict military embargo clamped on them by the U.S. and our NATO allies. Mao Tse Dong did not give a damn; his view was China could go forward by herself. Chairman Mao, even on his deathbed, utterly despised contact with the West. Most "technologies", unfortunately for the pragmatists, had a military component. A scenario to obtain those "technologies" in spite of the hated embargo was required. The liberal view espoused by Deng Xiao Ping and Chou En Lai demanded China's entry into the world community as an equal, modern nation. The nation's future depended on it.

To jump start their modernizations plans, the pragmatists had to devise an immediate program to import significant Western "technology", specifically, computers and to surreptitiously establish a technology education center around it for all of China! A little subterfuge was necessary to mask these intentions.

The best solution would have been full diplomatic recognition of China by the United States. Although many western nations had full diplomatic relations with China by 1975, the United States was the sole holdout. Since 1972, when Nixon and Kissinger visited China, no perceptible movement toward recognition had taken place. Distractions abounded. The "Cold War" with the Soviet Union was on high heat and American elections were 18 months away. The results of those elections, in terms of diplomatic recognition of China, were difficult to foresee. The noisy protestations of a "one" China policy to include Taiwan in any mainland discussions clouded the issue. The influence of the "Anti-Communist" political block in the United States prevented any meaningful discussions.

Military-use computers were out of the question. Generalized computer education uses had never been an acceptable embargo exemption. Proof of civilian use of any modern computer might permit the export of a computer under the embargo. So, the plan used historical exceptions to the embargo that other Communist countries had used.

One idea was to buy a large-scale computer for a university. A university in Hungary had been allowed to bypass the embargo by NATO with a civilian research project and obtain a large computer. In 1974, the Chinese government tried to interest IBM in selling them one for Peking University but the Pentagon and senior IBM management shot that idea down. Another idea, in mid-1975, was to have the Bank of China purchase a computer; but IBM had not taken seriously a circumspect request made during a banquet for a visiting IBM executive. Still another idea was to have some civilian factory (a la the Russians) purchase a computer and programming to run it The Russians had obtained a computer for a truck factory; why not China?

Factories and the government, however, were indistinguishable in China; the central government owned or controlled everything. The selection of the specific factory needed to downplay that aspect. Since the factory receiving the computer was to become the technology education center for a good portion of China (like the university!), it had to be in a convenient location.

The hated embargo was also very specific about "dual use" products, i.e., civilian items used by the military. They were verboten! The factory had to be one that manufactured civilian products only. The products couldn't have any connection to the military. At the same time, the factory management had to be amenable to the direction China's emerging leader Deng Xiao Ping was taking. The factory had to need modern technology desperately. The factory had to have dynamic management as well as workers who demonstrated openness for change. Without saying, everyone had to be good Communist Party members. They had to follow orders from Beijing without question. All was state-owned and state run!

At the time, it was impossible to have a conclave of leaders to make these determinations. While Chairman Mao was healthy and active, his control was personal and ideological. He branded anyone even thinking of Western contact or modernization a heretic. More than ten years previously, Deng Tsao Ping was removed from his high offices for espousing such thoughts. Deng was ousted and sent to the "country-side" for rehabilitation. He was returned to his former positions in 1974, only to be removed again in 1975. As Mao became increasingly ill, his control diminished. Others tried to speak in his name. Until Mao died and his successor was firmly in place, advocacy of liberal ideas was almost politically impossible in China.

A conclave was unnecessary anyway; those believing China's future lie in modernizing knew exactly what do to. Deng's master plan was as intricate as it was grand. He needed large sums of foreign currency to purchase Western expertise and technology. Known massive natural gas deposits existed in China which could be used to satisfy domestic energy needs (remember China had few automobiles in the 1970's) freeing up oil for overseas markets. Foreign currency would flow into China. Whether that part of the grand plan was ever successful is problematical. The last piece in the puzzle was the problem of compressing the natural gas to move it around China.

Zhou Zhi Jen leader of the First Ministry of Machine Building, a modern thinker and a Deng loyalist, went into action. His Ministry controlled all the factories in China that built industrial products used by other factories in their manufacturing activities. More specifically, his ministry controlled the only gas compressor manufacturing facilities in China. Secrecy was necessary. The cover plan had to be implemented by loyalists who were not privy to the ultimate goals of the project.

The leaders considered and rejected an automobile plant in Peking. That plant produced dual use products, i.e., products used by the military and civilian sector. They considered and rejected a cable and wire factory. The management there was slow and cantankerous. An airplane repair facility for fighter planes was clearly military. The workers at an electrical transformer factory once demonstrated for better conditions; their factory was rejected. Those factory workers couldn't be trusted. The requirements produced a short list of factories consisting on one name.

The Ministry leaders finally selected the Shenyang Blower Works in Shenyang, China; the air compressors manufactured there were clearly civilian; their products required modern technology to build; the management was forward looking and it was located in the heart of the industrial northeast of China. As a bonus, compressors were essential to the oil and gas industry, a key industry in modernization plans. The selection was a win-win situation. The die was cast!

The Vice-Minister of Technology, Mr. Sun You Yu, and Director of the Bureau of Science and Technology, Mr Guo, knew that computers needed highly educated people to operate them. Early in 1976, long before Techimport (Mr. Wu) contacted IBM, the First Ministry of Machine Building Science and Technology Bureau sent orders to the Worker Bureau in Shenyang. Worker Bureaus existed in all cities in China, they were the nearest thing to a Western employment agency. They functioned a little differently. They were supposed to provide every worker with a job, or, if you prefer, every job with a worker, i.e., a government employment bureau, albeit a compulsory one. It was the same in Russia. You had to register and you had to go where they sent you. If you were sent to a factory that did not need you, the factory was obligated to give you work. It was a crime if you did not register after high school and it was a crime (for which you could go to jail) not to go where they assigned you.

The Worker Bureau in Shenyang, based on the requirements from the Ministry in Beijing, assigned and moved seven electrical engineers from a factory that built boats. They formed the Blower Works computer staff. I met each one of them later on. Not one of them ever was involved in manufacturing or designing a compressor or any kind. None of the computer center staff came from the compressor factory itself even though there were many engineers there. Everything and everybody came from somewhere else. When I found that out, I was amazed. I was astonished for two reasons. First, the Blower Works had approximately 75 working engineers any one of whom would have jumped at the chance to learn modern computing; and, second, why graduate <u>electrical</u> engineers. The job at hand was essentially mechanical engineering; there was no intention to design or manufacture computers. Or, was it? Who knows? In any event, we totally missed the significance of this choice when we found out about it.

The ability to move people around was and is, at least on a national scale, one of the benefits of centralized planning and control. In the U.S. when masses of workers are forced to move, it is a catastrophe. In Shenyang, every one of those electrical engineers was pleased at the opportunity. I have yet to understand the connection between boat engineering and compressor engineering. On the other hand, the Worker Bureau understood both were engineers, so that was that. Obviously, their choice was perfect for an computer technology school!

For timing, the last thing to consider was the degree of Chairman Mao's control over the government. He was deathly sick, but not sick enough. He had been well enough in November 1975 to remove Deng Tsao Ping from all his government posts yet again. The Deng faction members had to wait until they were sure that Mao or his minions wouldn't rise up when their plans became known. By spring, 1976 the time was ripe! Mao was on his deathbed and incoherent. His wife, Jiang Qing, a leader of the Marxist hardliners, was a problem but the liberals apparently felt they could control her.

While all this was going on, Western contacts with the Chinese were increasing exponentially. Everyone began to see that China was getting ready politically to make its peace with the rest of the world; more particularly, with the United States. More and more politicians and executives went to Beijing to meet with their counterparts. It was part of the conditioning process necessary to eventual permanent connection. Although there had been some contact between IBM and the Peoples Republic, policies and politics prevented any permanent linkup. Prior to 1939, there had been an IBM subsidiary operating an equipment rental business there. The war and subsequent activities had wiped that business out. Since the Communist takeover in 1949, there had been a vacuum for more than twenty-five years.

Not all, however, was that smooth in Beijing. Right after the riots and pitched battles in April, 1976 Deng Tsao Ping was removed from all his party posts again. The Marxist hardliners won that day! Then Mao dies in September 1976. Political instability was the order of the day until a new Chairman and leader was selected. Hua Go Feng, a compromise candidate, was named Chairman on October 6, 1976, the very same day the four leaders of Marxist hardliners were arrested.

By late 1975, Congressional committees had been to China and even David Rockefeller of the Chase Manhattan Bank had made the obligatory visit with Chinese leaders. In fact, his Chase bank had organized a consulting arm to enable businesses to begin connecting with potential clients and customers inside China. The head of that consultancy firm, Ken Morse, was making calls on both sides of the Pacific to initiate business. One of the telephone calls he organized was from David Rockefeller to Frank Cary, the CEO of IBM.

The result of that conversation was twofold. Cary called his Senior VP Ralph Pfeiffer almost immediately.

"Ralph, I just received a call from David Rockefeller. He wanted to know if we are interested in getting involved in Red China. He said he had a young man who is head of their China consulting arm that could be very useful to us. What the heck are we doing in China"?

Pfeiffer answered, "We're watching and waiting for the right time to jump in".

"I don't want to be just watching and waiting! I don't want any other computer company to get in there before we do, Ralph. Check with my secretary to get on my calendar for a review of what we are going to do."

"Right, Frank."

Ralph Pfeiffer hung up the telephone and immediately picked it up again. He called Charlie Swift, his VP, whom I mentioned earlier.

"Charlie, Frank Cary just called me. He wants a presentation on our planned activities in Red China." There was a pause while he listened to Charlie's response. "I know we haven't been doing anything there, but that's all changed now. As of now, we <u>are</u> doing something. Come by my office and we'll lay it all out."

Two weeks later, before the Christmas holidays in 1975, they made their presentation to the CEO. First, Charlie said, we will not repeat the mistakes we made in our Russian operations. There, a permanent staff of close to 75 people serviced two contracts. The IBM Russian operations lost money almost from day one. Second, we will hire the Chase consulting firm to pursue an invitation to the People's Republic aggressively in order to bid on possible contracts yet unknown. Three, we will assign no more than two mature professionals to follow up any leads. Moreover, we will not allow any other computer maker to get ahead of us in China.

Frank Cary listened. When Charlie was finished, he turned to Ralph. "Ralph, just make sure we don't come out second best"! The meeting was over. The WORD had come down!

Ken Morse and the Chase consultant firm were hired. The Chinese respected Ken as an agent of the Rockefeller name and bank in China. The Chinese remembered that the Rockefeller family built the first hospital in Beijing back in the early 1920's.

During one his many trips to China in early 1976, Ken spoke to officials in their foreign trade organization suggesting that they contact IBM if they were interested in purchasing computers. Maybe he was not aware of the computer embargo! The Chinese person he contacted was Mr. Han Li Fu, of the China National Machinery Import Corp. However, Han was not the one who actually made the contact, nor was Han's bureau, yet another mystery. Why did the Chinese move the contact point from Mr. Han at China National Machinery Import Corp. to the

China National Technical Import Corp? This bureau (called "Techimport") would make the contact. Could it be because of Han's negative history with IBM? On the other hand, could it be the embargo-busting cover story needed a technical image? Who knows?

Mr. Wu of Techimport telexed IBM in the late spring of 1976. He asked that a delegation come to Beijing to have technical talks with them. Mr Wu never defined who "them" was; he never defined what "technical talks" meant. Because of the Cary dictates, the request went directly to Ralph, as the CEO of IBM subsidiary for the Americas and Far East who immediately passed it along to Charlie. Rather than sending a high executive as others had, Charlie had his marketing staff prepare a plan for a series of lectures from technical people. Charlie defined what "technical talks" meant. They would outline the IBM computers and software catalog to the Chinese. After some preliminary messages, and a delay due to the death of Chairman Mao, October 1976 was scheduled. I note here that there was no unanimity on the plan, some thought it the proper thing to do; others thought not. IBM was just like the government; there were people who wanted to recognize the Communists as well as people who wanted nothing to do with them.

News of this contact with China and the plans to send a technical delegation to Beijing raced around the IBM establishment. Everyone volunteered to go. Frank Cary, our CEO, had already ordained that IBM was to have a consultant for these activities. Lower down the executive ladder, my guess of the necessity for a consultant was to have someone to blame if things went wrong again. Ken Morse, its leader, and Mary Wadsworth, their Chinese experts, came to help. I believe that the marketing consulting arrangement which, for IBM was a first, was a two edged sword. On the one hand, we had to have someone who spoke Chinese; Mary was fluent. On the other hand, as I noted, if something went wrong we blame the consultant. At about the same time my experience with Communist's bureaucracy in

Moscow caused Charlie to contact me. Unfortunately I could not join this group because of commitments in Moscow. I would join the project several months later.

John Ryan was the head of the technical delegation that went to educate the Chinese in October 1976. IBM was ready!

The Ministry was ready. The Vice-Minister of Technology, Sun You Yu, was ready. The plant director, He Ju San was ready. Three men at the factory carried out this plan. All three were unaware of the grand objectives their leaders had in mind. They were only aware of the dictates they had received. "Get new Western machine technology for your plant; modernize your operations as quickly as you can; purchase as big a Western computer as you can .... Lead the new revolution!"

Our relationship with these three ordinary revolutionaries began in 1976 in Beijing just after Mao's death. We did not know them at that time since they were nameless individuals sitting in an audience to hear about wonderful IBM computers. We had heard that a compressor factory in north China wanted to computerize its operations. The questions "why that factory?", or "why that place?" never entered our minds then. We "negotiated" the first computer contract with them by an American manufacturer in The People's Republic of China over the next twelve months, In a Cold War environment we slowly peeled away layers of mistrust. Ultimately, we created personal bonds that crossed the cultural and political divide and helped to open China to the new world economy.

That little computer deal exploded into the greatest industrial metamorphosis the world has seen since the Industrial Revolution! We also created one of the largest markets for IBM in a long, long time. By the end of our discussions across the negotiating table, we developed friendships lasting more than thirty years. The People's Republic of China embarked on a journey towards modernization that is still not over.

Two of our three Comrades across the table were born and raised in Shenyang, a large industrial city in northeastern China.

The province borders both Russia and Korea. In the decades preceding our contact with them these men had endured Japanese occupation, communist takeover, an influx of Russian "advisors" as well as the Chinese Great Proletarian Revolution (the Cultural Revolution), and finally war in Korea (which was never, never mentioned!), Chinese troops poured across the border into North Korea from this province during the Korean War. The shadows of this rocky history mark the people's attitudes to this day and touched our discussions. The Japanese aggression in the 30's, the feelings of betrayal when the Russians abandoned the area in the 50's and the elation with the Communists' ability to get food on the table was mentioned repeatedly.

Notably absent from our conversations was any reference to the then current turmoil in internal Chinese politics. The "Gang of Four" was desperately trying to succeed Mao. The appellation applied to three former leaders under Chairman Mao and to Jiang Qing, Mao's widow. The "Gang of Four", Marxist hardliners, wanted to continue the closed society Mao espoused. When our contacts began in October 1976, we had little or no idea of the intense struggle going on in China for leadership of the country. In fact, while we were speaking from the podium that week, the "in" government arrested the infamous "Gang of Four" to put them under house arrest. Our meeting room, however, was very isolated from the events on the streets of Beijing that week, and every other week as well. We were in a self- contained space capsule in the midst of intergalactic political upheavals.

Communication was always a challenge. Some of our counterparts spoke a little Russian. Some spoke some English, but did not want us to know. None of the American principals spoke Chinese. We had to work through inexperienced translators supplied by the Ministry of Foreign Trade. It took us months to find out the factory name and the positions of the people we were talking to. Even though they were not particularly secretive, gratuitous information was absent. In the United States, after a few moments of introduction most men would be pounding each other on the back and showing pictures of their wives, girlfriends or children and grandchildren.

Ultimately, after three months of contact, we discovered our counterparts were Xu Bingxian ("Mr. Shu"), a planning manager and a mechanical engineer with Shenyang Blower Works, Mu Reilin ("Mr. Mu") a mechanical engineer with the Shenyang Blower Works and Mu Chengzhen ("Big Mu"), an electrical engineer newly with the Shenyang Blower Works. Although they shared a common geographic background, each of these men emerged over time as unique individuals, brought together by circumstance and persistence to see their mission through to completion.

Mr. Shu was a scholarly looking man, with newly graying hair at the temples and sad eyes. His expressions rarely changed and it was difficult to gauge his feelings. Although he did not talk much, when he did speak, people often asked him to repeat himself just to hear what he had to say. There was nothing of chitchat about him; when he said something, it usually was important. Back in 1976, he wore his faded blue Mao style jacket and pants with dignity. Mr. Shu was medium height and had an aura of physical strength about him.

Mr. Mu, on the other hand, was rather slim. You could see all his bones. Except when a serious subject came up, his eyes twinkled, and a little smile always creased his face. He was about the same height as Mr. Shu, but he appeared to be much smaller. His hair was black, standard Chinese black. His hands were very wrinkled and calloused. It was obvious he had been working with them for a long time. Nevertheless, his fingers were very long, like a piano player's. His eyes, however, gave him away; I always thought they mirrored his responses and feelings. Nevertheless, as the saying goes, looks can be deceiving. I think Mr. Mu might have been a proactive member of the Red Guards during the Cultural Revolution but I am not sure, even today.

Mu Chengzen, "Big Mu", was quite different. He was much younger. He stood far above all the other Chinese-hence the nickname we gave him. Although the Americans pronounced his name the same as Mr. Mu's, the Chinese characters for their names were different. Although not heavy set, he gave the appearance of a long time basketball player, which he was. He had a ready smile that suggested he had not been in the business world for long. In fact, he joined the group right out of graduate school. Since he was the new man on the block, and the youngest by far, he never joined in the conversation unless specifically asked. I thought he was quite handsome.

MR WU

MR MU

MR SHU

BIG MU

Through a translator, Mr. Shu told me, "My father would never, never understand the work that I do. He could understand digging in the ground, he could understand shoveling dirt from one place to another, and he could understand planting things and making them grow. But he could never understand how I support my wife and children by working with pen, ink, and paper". His sad eyes mirrored his sincerity. He and his father had suffered through fourteen years of Japanese occupation prior to World War II.

Mr. Mu said, "My father couldn't wait for the Communists to arrive in Shenyang. Although he worked hard, sometimes it was difficult to feed us. When the Communists came, all that changed. If he worked, we ate." He pointed his cigarette for emphasis. Like Mr. Shu, he had lived through the Japanese occupation followed by the fierce battles between Communist troops and Chang Kai Shek's forces just south of the city in 1947 and 1948. The Communists had finally "liberated" the city in November of 1948.

Big Mu said, "My father worked in the railroad office in Dalien, a port on the Yellow Sea about ninety miles from here. My father started out as a fisherman on an island off the coast near Dalien, but when he couldn't support his family by fishing, they moved to the mainland. My mother never wanted to be married to a fisherman. She made him move off the island to Dalien."

"YOUR Mother made him move?" I said. I couldn't believe my ears. "I have never heard of a Chinese wife telling her husband what to do?" Unbelievable!

Big Mu responded seriously, "My mother wanted us all to be better off than she was. My sisters and brother all went to college." I thought to myself that sounds like a Jewish mother. If I had said it aloud, I was certain no one would have understood.

I had to leave it at that. Big Mu had lived through the daunting ten year Cultural Revolution and the infamous Red Guards starting in 1966. He told me that he was in school when the Red

Guards were in action in Dalien. He remembered a pitched battle outside his dormitory between the Red Guards and the teachers. He still remembers the ricochet of bullets through the dormitory lavatory while he hid under the sink.

During one of our breaks in the negotiation, Mr. Mu told me about Chinese public education rules. Though Chinese peasant tradition held that sons supported parents, Communist policy, at least in urban Shenyang and the surrounding province, was that all children go to school regardless of parental situations. Not only did children have to go to school, they had to stay until graduation from high school. That was not much different from American educational rules. After that, things were a little different. If your teachers selected you to take the competitive examination for higher education, you got the chance to move up. If not, the State created jobs for all, including their parents, to make sure there was always rice in their bowls in the summer and cabbage in their soup in the winter. These three men had stayed in school as required. Pre-Communism, they would be working as soon as possible to support their parents in their old age.

At the time of the modernization revolution Mr. Shu was forty-five years old, Mr. Mu was forty years old, and Big Mu was only twenty-nine years old. From modest backgrounds, to say the least, all three had attended public grammar schools, middle and high schools. The older ones had survived the competitive examinations for college which they remembered with great reverence. They had sat for these tests before the elimination of all such testing in 1966. I guess the theory was that since everyone was equal under Communism, there was no purpose to testing. The government announced the resumption of those examinations during the time we were negotiating. Someone made it a point to tell us. All three went beyond the first college level to technical educations; Mr. Shu and Mr. Mu were mechanical engineers, while Big Mu trained as an electrical engineer.

By the time I met them, the two older men had lived through at least three different upheavals. Mr. Mu told me that he had to learn Japanese when he first began school. At that time, Northeast China was a "colony" of Japan. The Japanese occupiers constructed the Blower Works. That was the first revolution. The Japanese occupation started in 1935 and lasted until 1945.

The next upheaval these men lived through was the battle with Chiang Kai Chek and his warlords. When the Japanese surrendered, a Chiang Kai Chek war lord took over. Within two years the civil war began. Mr. Shu told me that the battles between the Communists and the so-called "democratic" government of Chiang Kai Chek took place in the streets. The People's Liberation Army won that war hands down because of the total corruption of the warlord forces. That was the second upheaval. It lasted sporadically from 1945 until 1948

The Soviets came in the 1950's to re-industrialize the north but left in 1960. That was the third period of upheaval.

Mr. Mu told me, "You Americans can never understand our circumstances. When I was in college, the Russians were here 'advising us'. He sniggered. I instantly noticed his use of the words, 'advising us'. I think he meant that the Russians were telling them what to do, but his Chinese veil of courtesy prevented blunt talk.

"Then they left and took everything with them." He said, very sarcastically. His normal smile had disappeared. His eyes became hard; he was really living the story.

"The Russians took the equipment, the desks, everything. The schools closed, the factories closed. I'm lucky to have any education." Mr. Mu made it quite plain that he had no love for the Russians. The other men listening were shaking their heads in agreement.

Mr. Shu added, "We are all lucky to have educations." He was not smiling. He did not have any love for the Russians either.

When I heard this, I spoke the little Russian greetings that I had learned in Moscow.

Jokingly, I said, "Hello, how are you?" in Russian.

"Very well, thank you." Mr Mu replied in Russian. When he was in primary school, Japanese was the required second language; when he was in secondary school, Russian was the required second language. Although neither he nor I were able to go much further in a Russian conversation, he remembered enough to respond. Today, the required second language in all Chinese schools is English.

If the Japanese, the "democratic" Chinese, and the Communist takeover were not enough, the Cultural Revolution in the 60's brought the economy, and their lives, to another halt! The very same liberal faction engineering our revolution in 1976 were the same people agitating for modernization in 1965. Deng Xiao Ping, along with Chou En Lai, leaders in the mid 1960's were gently moving the country toward openness and modernity. Their agitation caused Chairman Mao to launch the Cultural Revolution in 1966. Chairman Mao dismissed Deng and called for return to core Socialist values. Why he did not dismiss Chou is a mystery; Chou remained Premier from 1933 to 1976, when he passed away. C hou was one of the very few leaders who lasted as long as Mao did. With Mao dying in 1976 however, Deng was coming back and the modernization he espoused more than ten years before was finally beginning. Because of the U.S. embargo, and the part that computers played in it, however, the modernization plan had to be a little devious.

The two Americans were long time employees of the international division of IBM. John Ryan had worked his way up the ladder to being a trusted advisor to mid level executives in the international division of the company. He had spent three years in Japan as Director of Organization. With no warning, he suddenly became the leader of the China effort. His boss, Charlie Swift, Vice President for Operations in the Far East, had called him in and told him that he was going to lead a technical group making presentations in China. Just like that! John asked, "Why me?" Charlie answered, "Because!" and that was that.

John was tall and rangy; he had a kind face. He was sensitive to people, one of the better types of manager in my I BM experience. Many times, promotion to a managerial position in IBM was the reward for doing well in a previous non-managerial job. The reward for doing a good job was getting a new one you knew nothing about. This was a disaster for many but not for John. He had a talent for gently guiding the people he was responsible for without the over-bearing attitude of many others. He was tough when he had to be. His father had been a doctor. Maybe that is where he learned how to listen. In my experience, listening was not a common trait of IBM managers. Most did not have time to listen. His greatest talent was providing a listening board for senior executives. They prized his ability to hear everyone out and then give them a concise objective summary. Given the risk of problems arising with a China connection, he was an excellent choice.

In my marketing role, I had most recently worked in the Soviet Union. My Moscow experiences with Communist bureaucracies somehow qualified me for the Communist bureaucracies in China. Like John, I had been in international operations of IBM for some time. I had served in Japan, England, and France before I went to Moscow.

While in Russia, I was managing of a group working with the state-owned U.S.S.R. tourist "bureau". We designed and installed a Russia-wide transportation and hotel reservation system for the ill-fated 1980 Olympic Games held for the first time in Moscow. The central planners in Moscow had set the grand policy of this Communist show-off without a thought about the impact a tremendous influx of visitors would have on their transportation and hotel infrastructure. When the tip of that iceberg had surfaced, there was a mad scramble for capitalistic Western (the enemy at that time) processes and technology to solve the problem. Mr. Zoloyev, my Russian counterpart, and I had many "discussions" about the problems of playing "catch-up" with so-called plans made in the absence of reality.

The cover plan to change the entire Shenyang factory process featuring new and different technology along with a computer was Mr. Shu's responsibility. His little piece of the modernization plan was to be the first in the country. He told me what he did.

"I asked the factory translation department to find any references to new compressor engineering techniques in up-to-date overseas technical journals," he said. He knew the people in the translation department could handle almost any language. He told me, "I don't know how they had access to all this information, but they did".

I asked myself the very same question. HOW did they have access to such a wealth of technical information? Moreover, how in the world did these documents get from the West to an out of the way place in northeast China? I never did get an answer.

They could and did handle English, French, German, Italian and Hebrew as well as Arabic and Russian (although there was not much input from those sources).

I said, "Mr. Shu, you are lucky. I don't think any American factory has a translation department."

"Every technical factory in China that has engineers has a translation department. It is essential."

A couple of weeks after his request, Mr. Shu and his planners received translated copies of many American, Italian and French articles. They had, in his words, "about a kilo of paper to go through". He held up his two hands, palms facing about six inches apart. Every single page was translated into Chinese. After examining all the articles, he and his engineers decided two compressor manufacturing technologies were appropriate. One was French; the other was Italian. The French one was actually American since it was developed by a subsidiary of an American company. The articles, however, did not provide enough information for a purchase. They needed much more detail and technical information before he could decide which one was best for them.

"First, I had to get the money, the budget. Then I could get everything I needed." He really liked telling this story in his dignified understated way. He was waving his arms about and smiling all the time. Although Mr. Shu would never have expressed it quite that way, he had just taken a first step in Deng's new industrial revolution. Little did he know at the time, money for this project would not be a problem for him. Secrecy concerning the ultimate purpose of a computer purchase required that Mr Shu be kept in the dark, not to mention the naïve IBM negotiators.

Mr. Shu went ahead and prepared his proposal based on what he had learned from the technical journals. Beijing accepted his proposal. He was, literally, ecstatic. He did not know his use of the computer to design and build computers was secondary to the ministry's scheme to establish a computer school to educate all the engineers in their factories in North China, a purpose completely at odds with the embargo. He did not know the authorities wanted an IBM computer because IBM could get a computer delivered in spite of the embargo. He did not know it but acceptance of his proposal was a foregone conclusion at the Ministry in Beijing. He told me, "For the first time in my life, I was doing something new, something different". He had to decide which "technology" was better and then make a deal? He had to talk, face to face, with both the French and Italian companies. He had to compare their offerings. Easier said than done!

After many years of experience, the Communist State, Russian or Chinese, had a way to handle this situation. Important organizations in China (and the U.S.S.R. as well) had a Foreign Affairs Bureau or department which dealt with foreigners and foreign companies. All outside contact funneled through this department. I might add these people were also very important sources of intelligence about the West. While in Russia, I understood the Internal Security Bureau (the KGB!)

interviewed our "Foreign Affairs" friends frequently. For this reason, people assigned to the Foreign Affairs Bureau were solid Communists and often on their way up the leadership ladder. Positions in the Foreign Affairs Bureaus were tests of loyalty.

Therefore, Mr. Shu went to the Foreign Affairs Bureau of his Ministry which told him to see Mr. Wu Xiao Xian of China National Technical Import Corporation (Techimport, in telex terms) in Beijing. At that time, in the summer of 1975, that was no easy task. A travel permit had to be applied for, guarantees to return to Shenyang had to be provided, and the explanation that his purpose in going to Beijing was in line with the political objectives of his factory was required. In due course he set out to see Mr. Wu Xiao Xian.

Beijing was an exciting place at the time. The premier, Chou En Lai, one of the authors of this modernization program, was incapacitated with cancer; Deng Xiao Ping, his deputy, lurked somewhere in the background. People were concerned about Chou, but his detractors were hard at work trying to halt this bud of modernization before it got too big. Sometimes, there were crowds in the streets, sometimes riots, espousing one view or another.

Mr Shu was finally able to get to the offices of Mr. Wu Xiao Xian at the China National Technical Import Corporation (Techimport). I will call him Mr. Wu. By the way, do not be confused by the use of the term, "Corporation". I certainly was when I first heard it. These "Corporations" were not companies that used the corporate structure for their work; they did not have Boards of Directors to set policy and they certainly did not have stockholders who invested in them. These "Corporations" were bureaus of the Ministry of Foreign Affairs, an arm of the government like our State Department. There were about 50-60 corporations at the time, each one handling a specific foreign industrial or institutional area.

Again, although Mr. Shu did not know this, the selection of Techimport as the importing corporation was pre-ordained. The head of Techimport was a solid Deng Tsao-Ping fan! Normally, a purchase of this machine would have gone to a corporation called Machimpex (China National Machinery Import Corporation); but not this time!

Mr. Shu told Mr. Wu of his plan and the budget that he had. He told him there were two Western firms with the "technology" he was interested in.   Dresser-Clarke of France was one and Nuovo Pignone of Italy was the other. Wu immediately contacted both firms by telex inviting them to come to Beijing to describe their offerings. Both responded quickly. Everyone outside of China at that time was mesmerized by the imagined potential Chinese market. By the spring of 1976, before any new attempt to contact with IBM, Wu and Shu had detailed discussions going on with these engineering firms in Beijing. Their representatives thought this magical Chinese "market" was opening for them. Like many others, they were only the pawns in the bigger chess game. When concluded, this sale would be their sole transaction in the China "market"!

The death of Chou En Lai on January 8, 1976 and the national mourning that followed interrupted their talks. Immediately upon the conclusion of national mourning, on February 7, 1976, the street celebrations marking the appointment of his successor, Hua Guo Feng, took place. Beijing was a jumping that month. In February the deposed President Nixon returned to China for a personal visit in apparent disagreement with the non-recognition tactics of the then President Ford. As he had in 1972, President Nixon again met with Mao. This meeting clearly showed the Chinese discontent with President Ford's pro-Taiwan stance since his visit to China the previous December. In April, outright battles erupted in Tien A Mien Square between the hard line Marxist followers of the "Gang of Four" and followers of the more pragmatic Deng Tsao Ping. Mr. Shu and Mr. Mu were in Beijing watching all the street spectacles. Adding to the political turmoil, there was a monumental and deadly earthquake in the Tientsin area on July 26, 1976 felt all the way in Beijing, a distance of over ninety miles.

I could never figure out the reason for Mr. Mu's involvement at this point. The technology was clearly in Mr. Shu's area of expertise. Big Mu's involvement was admittedly for the computer itself. Mr. Mu's area was the purchase of machine tools; no machinery was to be purchased, just "know-how". I now believe his involvement had a dual purpose; purchasing was one, the other was my belief Mr Mu was a leader of the worker's committee of the factory. That position would account for the deference all others showed him. In any event, at the conclusions of the discussions, Mr. Shu was able to define his technical requirements (the "specs"). Mr. Shu chose Nuovo Pignone, the Italian company. The "technology" step in Deng's new industrial revolution was on its way.

The Nuovo Pignone choice was unique, yet old fashioned. The Italian and Chinese governments had signed a commercial trade accord in 1975. Some Western governments (not following the U.S. lead) recognized Communist China at that time. Again, maybe it was because of the immense "market" mystique we all had about China. The Italian Ambassador held a banquet in the Italian Embassy while the Nuovo Pignone discussions were on going in Beijing. Nuovo Pignone was part of an Italian state owned enterprise. Italy was a quasi-socialist country. Mr. Shu and Chen So Min (Chen hereafter), a translator from the factory, Jiang Ze Min, Director of the Foreign Affairs Bureau at the Ministry, along with the Minister Zhou Zhi Jen himself, attended. All the Chinese were Deng enthusiasts. It was a very jovial dinner. The conversation was in English, even though most of the people couldn't speak English, but the Ambassador, Jiang and Chen spoke it well. According to Chen, Mr. Jiang carried most of the conversation; he was jovial and charming.

I should digress here to tell a little more about Mr. Jiang. At that time, he was the Director of the Foreign Affairs Bureau at the First Ministry of Machine Building. At that position and with his background, it is a safe assumption that he was aware of, if not a co-author, of the plan to get a computer in spite of the U.S. embargo. A long-time party stalwart from Shanghai, he was a "comer" in the national government. After his education as an electrical engineer, he had held various positions in the First Ministry in that field. Mr. Jiang worked in the First Ministry for approximately twenty-five years.

In the early 80's, (after this story) he became one of the leaders of a new Electronics Industries Ministry. With that background, it is easy to speculate that he either knew, or should have known, a great deal about western computers. In 1985, he moved on to become the Mayor of Shanghai. Still later, he became the Prime Minister and ultimately, the President of China. That's right; our Mr. Jiang became the head of the whole country! He was associated with Deng Xiao Ping right through the 80's. When Deng retired, the leadership role passed to Mr. Jiang. There were some very important people associated with this venture! Of course, we did not know any of this!

A few days after the banquet, a message attributed to Jiang came down through the First Ministry Foreign Affairs Bureau in Beijing to their Heavy Machinery Bureau in Beijing. From there, the message went to the Shenyang Factory Foreign Affairs Bureau to the Shenyang Factory Secretariat. At that point, the message (that the Italian company was the best choice) moved to the Shenyang Factory Planning Department. It takes longer to describe this path than it actually is. It only takes three or four phone calls between old friends to move projects forward. The Communist bureaucracy is just as convoluted as any other government bureaucracy.

A few days after that, Nuovo Pignone's technology was "found" to be superior to that of Dresser-Clarke. After all, a Socialist political party governed Italy and one of the first rules of Politics 101 is "Take Care of Your Friends".

During their discussions with the Italians, Mr. Shu and Mr. Wu found that all the engineering computer programs (the technical "know-how" they were purchasing) ran on IBM computers at the Nuovo Pignone plant in Milan! Was that coincidence or fate? Who knows? Mr. Mu also found out that the programs were written in FORTRAN (Formula Translation), a common mathematical programming language at that time.

Whether through intent or ignorance, the Chinese chose to ignore the fact that those programs would run on almost any computer, not just IBM's. There are no compatibility issues with FORTRAN. They could have set up a grand old competition for the computer purchase. That did not happen. We later learned of Mr. Shu's logic. If the programs ran on an IBM computer in Italy, they would certainly run on an IBM computer in China. Accidental or not, it was very convenient that not only did the central planners at the Ministry want an IBM computer, but the factory people wanted the same thing.

IBM or not, it became obvious to the planners (those people in Beijing!) that computers were going to be part of their process of modernization, if not the seed for their crop. It was a foregone conclusion that the Chinese understood that computers and computer software were at the heart of any modern economy. It was imperative that China get their hands on computers of any kind, of any size! They were, however, the tail of the dog and not the dog itself in the beginning.

The Chinese had no plan that I am aware of that dictated the purchase of a computer to make other computers. In fact, the U.S. and NATO never approved an export license of a computer to make other computers. Every purchase I am aware of was to perform some function in the Communist industrial network. Purchasing computers to make computers would come about 8-10 years later and would be brought to China by American companies seeking lower labor costs.

For the planners, the computer was merely a required tool; an embargoed tool, but a required tool nonetheless.. What better company than IBM could the Ministry find to work their way through the maze of computer embargoes. IBM had done it many time before. We had to write a contract with a country where contracts did not exist and export a computer to a country under a world-wide embargo.

Everyone (except us!) believed the Blower Works had to have an IBM computer to run those Italian programs. They thought only an IBM computer could eliminate all risks. That is where Big Mu comes in. By the time the deal with Nuovo Pignone was made, the planners in Beijing knew someone with a high-level computer education (as high as possible in China!) was required to manage a new computer department. This person also had to be involved in the negotiations for that computer. Again, through the Worker Bureau in Shenyang, the Beijing Ministry ordered Big Mu assigned to the Blower Works as soon as he finished his courses at the university. How he came to the attention of the planners or the Worker Bureau in Shenyang I do not know. The Blower Works and Big Mu had absolutely nothing to say about his selection. This was centralized planning and control at its best. This was Deng Xiao Ping's modernization program running full steam ahead!

I always marveled at this Chinese (or Communist) ability to plan events on a grand scale and have all the parts work together. The example I was involved in was relatively minor if compared with the Four Gorges Dam. Deng's plan was to use natural gas for domestic energy freeing up oil for export, and one thing led to another; new compressor technology was needed to move the natural gas; new people were selected to make the high pressure gas compressors required; a new building was built to house the new technology; new factory equipment to produce the zero tolerance parts was required and was purchased; and a new computer was ordered. All the pieces were put in place two and a half years ahead of the events themselves. Everything came together at the same time. Deng's program, implemented by some very intelligent people, aimed at nothing but complete success. If there is such a thing, this was a well-planned revolution.

Right after Big Mu met Mr. Shu for the first time, he had to ask him for some time off. It was a touchy situation. They were just getting ready to assign people to the IBM technical seminar scheduled for October 1976 in Beijing. Big Mu, the new person on the block, asked for time off to get married. Mr. Shu, as the kind and thoughtful manager that he was, gave Big Mu all the time he wanted so that he could get married. Nevertheless, he had to come to work right afterwards. That is not much different from similar situations in America.

We did not learn most of this for twenty-three years.

Chapter 2 - The World Around Me

By now, it is apparent three great opposing bureaucracies had to cooperate to achieve a result their leaders desired. China, with its vast centralized economy was the first bureaucracy. The United States, with its disparate politicized government was the second great bureaucracy. The International Business Machines Corporation (IBM), with its giant research, development, manufacturing and marketing units spread all over the world was the third bureaucracy.

In China, Chou En Lai (The Prime Minister, while he was alive) and Deng Tsao Peng (the Deputy Prime Minister) were the leaders of their political and government bureaucracy. In the United States, Jimmy Carter (the new President) and Zbigniew Brzezinski (his new National Security Advisor) were the de facto leaders of their government bureaucracy. In IBM, Frank Cary (the Chairman of the Board) and Ralph Pfeiffer (Chairman of the Board of the IBM World Trade subsidiary) were the leaders of their bureaucracies. Each leader, in his own way, and for his own reasons, wanted to move China, a nation of a billion people, into the modern Western world.

However, there was a major obstacle, i.e., the US and NATO embargo on the shipment of goods to China. The choice to either obey the embargo requirements, ask for an exception, or to ignore them, or to devise a way around them was apparent. Participants had to decide for themselves.

On October 1, 1949, the government set up by the Chinese Communists was a model of the government of the Soviet Union. The central planning apparatus and the industry control apparatus were duplicates of the Russian model. Ministries, departments, and bureaus organized as copies of their Russian counterparts. .

China withdrew from the family of nations in 1949 by order of Chairman Mao Tse Deng of the Chinese Communist Party. Every foreigner, regardless of position or title had to leave China. When Chairman Mao sent Chinese troops over the Korean border on November 1, 1950, President Eisenhower of the United States, quickly followed by others, imposed an embargo on sales of many essential products to China. The United States forbade the export of all military material, as well as dual-use products (including civilian and military computers). China, along with the Soviet Union, became the enemy.

The victors of World War II set up an international bureaucracy in 1947 to coordinate their embargo activities.. The 18 members (including the U.S., the U.K., France, Germany and other Western powers including the Republic of China (the predecessor to Communist China) agreed to a catalog of military and quasi-military goods on an embargo list. Originally aimed at the Warsaw Pact (Soviet Union) countries, President Eisenhower added China during the Korean War in 1950. This international bureaucracy, named COCOM (the Coordinating Committee for Multilateral Export Controls) ensured compliance with their embargo. The signatories to the agreement agreed to submit applications to the committee as a whole for the export of any goods on the embargo list. Exceptions built into the embargo rules allowed for specific exemptions when commercial non-military interests of members required them. If a French company received an export license for some exception to the embargo, the next English application would get one. Smaller computers (assuming a civilian application) were one of those exceptions. Educational use of computers was NOT an exception!

If international approval for export was not enough, the U.S. government had its own bureaucracy to satisfy. Within our government, there was a committee (yet, another one!) composed of members from the Commerce Department for administration, the State Department for international political considerations and, of course, the Pentagon for national security issues. Approval of this committee was required before the international committee would even consider an application for export. Any company desiring an export of an embargoed product or any product to an embargoed country had a daunting path to follow!

To obtain an export license, a company had to document many things. The most prominent requirement was to describe a non-military use of the exported product. COCOM, under U.S. leadership, translated that requirement into something called "old technology" computers only. If the computer were part of the manufacturer's current line of products, COCOM denied the license application. On the other hand, the purchaser usually wants the most advanced and current technology available. A conundrum!

Another troublesome requirement for computer export was annual reviews and visitations to the site of the computer to report on usage. In other words, you could get a computer exported for a non-military use; but you had to monitor that non-military use continuously. Viewed from the other side, the exporter would have to spy on his customer long after he delivered the goods.

Chairman Mao insisted China could and would live, breathe, and survive without any commercial contact with non-Communist countries of the world from 1949 to the early seventies. A crack in that ideological policy appeared in 1972 when Henry Kissinger and President Richard Nixon went to China to declare there was but one China. On the Chinese side, Chou En Lai, their Premier engineered that meeting. I do not doubt he had to convince Mao of the importance of meeting with the American President. Beginning in 1972, however, due to his sickness and his continued domestic failures, Chairman Mao's influence diminished in ebbs and flows. By 1975, China was one of the most backward countries in the world. The country had suffered significant food shortages caused by Mao's policies. At that point, groups of his liberal aides (subtly led by Chou En Lai and Deng Tsao Peng) advocated re-connection with the West, notably the United States. Scientific exchanges proliferated. Almost 100 countries had re-established diplomatic relations with China. All of the members of COCOM had re-established relations and trade; the U.S. was the only holdout. In September 1976, Chairman Mao Tse Tong died. The liberal advocates openly began activities aimed at restoring China's connection to the United States. Before that, most activities were surreptitious and quiet so as not to attract attention from the opposition. Many conservative Chinese openly called for continued isolation.

The government of the Peoples Republic of China, as well as the Chinese Communist Party, was a gigantic political bureaucracy. Led by a few forward-thinking scientists and political leaders, a modernization movement slowly emerged. In January 1975, the Fourth National People's Congress convened. Chou En Lai addressed the assembled delegates. He declared four modernization programs; agriculture, industry, science and technology and national defense. Immense improvement to Western standards was the new targets. The four modernizations became the battle cry of the liberals; their opponents openly criticized and ridiculed them.

A metaphor for modernization was a Western computer. A modern, American, computer became necessary! The general, run of the mill, workers had to have the opportunity of seeing and understanding how a computer worked. They had to understand how a modern factory computer was used. The factory management had to understand. Hundreds of factories making up the industrial base of Communist China had to understand computers and computer applications. The process of spreading this knowledge had to be jump-started! A plan evolved to purchase a computer and put it in the northern heart of industrial China.

The order may have come from the State Council (the governing body of the country) to the Ministries controlling industry in the country. After selecting the specific ministry where the first computer would go, the budget and the order went to that Ministry. The Ministry of Foreign Trade received their instructions. Foreign Trade was responsible for contacts and contracts with Western computer manufacturers. Finally, the specific factory selected to be the site of the first computer was informed. A very select group of bureaucrats who believed that China's future had to involve American computers became involved with the process. There were many in this chain of Ministries, departments, bureaus and factories who did not believe, and, given an opportunity, would gladly drown the plan along with those who participated in it. It was a deadly game!

The process at all these levels had one common component. Each government unit involved was led by a trusted and compliant Communist who believed United States connections and modernization were the essential to China's future. Rejected Ministries had leaders not considered politically safe, or who did not believe; rejected departments had leaders not considered trustworthy modern communists; individual factories had people in management not considered politically trustworthy, or, equally important, did not have the political friends necessary to the selection.

At the working level, local computer competence was not a factor; local electronic competence was not a factor; local education level was not a factor. The selection and transfer of the workers required to run the computer was a simple local matter. The local Central Labor Bureau (Worker Bureau) selected and assigned all factory workers to their jobs. The Director of the Labor Bureau received his orders at the appropriate time.

To satisfy the embargo exception rules, it was necessary for the selected civilian plant to come up with a plan, a cover plan, requiring the use of a computer in their civilian operations. Whereas, in Beijing, the overall plan was modernization and education; embargo considerations dictated a local factory level with a concrete, specifically civilian, plan. Senior Chinese bureaucrats in Peking were well aware of the specific COCOM requirement that a exported computer couldn't be used for military or educational purposes. They knew of the Soviet debacle when COCOM permitted the export of embargoed computers to a new truck manufacturing plant in Eastern Russia. A civilian use of the computer described in the application for an embargo exemption was flawless. However, on a subsequent May Day national holiday, trucks from that very factory appeared in Red Square as Red Army vehicles dragging rockets and artillery. The embargo bureaucracy in Europe and the U.S. went ballistic! The IBM people who wrote the license application had a lot of explaining to do.

The Chinese cover plan had to consist of purely civilian uses in a non-military environment to expect an approval for export to China. They could only dream about the opportunity for the factory to obtain such modern western equipment. In addition, as icing on the cake, the new equipment was to be the best offered in the United States; new American computer equipment required hard currency (U.S. dollars). Hard currency was in very short supply and normally not within the purview of a local factory. Therefore, it was a win-win situation at the factory, the lowest point on the Communist political hierarchy. Even a "no plan" might work; let the vendor dream up civilian uses for his computer. I think Lenin said, "Give the capitalists the rope and eventually they will hang themselves".

The plan bubbled up the central planning structure endorsed by the very same people who made the initial decisions selecting the ministry, department, and factory as the beginnings of computer modernization. Communism, Chinese style, was working!

The second bureaucracy was the government of the United States. Jimmy Carter, the President, took office in January 1977. Chinese Communism was a foreign policy ogre. The Chinese were the enemy under the Eisenhower (COCOM) sales embargo. The Chinese were a feared enemy in Korea. Regardless, Carters' predecessor, Gerald Ford, had continued Nixon's policy of detente.

Ford was the first "un-elected" Vice-President, and the first "un-elected" President of the U.S. He did not have an election mandate; he succeeded Spiro Agnew as Vice-President when he resigned and succeeded Nixon when he resigned. As such, he was content to continue Nixon's policies stewarded by Henry Kissinger as his Secretary of State. The "open China" policy engineered by Kissinger when Nixon went to China in 1972 continued. Scientific delegations crossed the Pacific every year to bring Chinese scientists up to date on Western advances. Ford's trip to China in December 1975 solidified the policy. There was no embargo on information, only on products. However, the policy was completely passive; but circumstances were overtaking any passive policy.

China was becoming a force in Asia. While Chairman Mao was involved with his domestic troubles, his Premier, Chou En Lai was busy bringing China back into the international diplomatic community as well as calling for modernization. By 1975, the U.S. was the only country (even within COCOM) without diplomatic relations with China. US Commercial interests were clamoring for recognition of the Peoples Republic of China (PRC) to prevent outright exclusion from the mammoth market perceived by businesspersons. The Chinese "market" mantra was reverberating all over the world. Nine hundred million people constituted a "market" that couldn't be denied!

In retrospect, this was an extremely shortsighted perception of the Chinese "market" Twenty-five years later, the Chinese "market" had become a Chinese manufacturing giant while the US had become the mammoth "market" for Chinese manufactured goods. The forecast was completely backward!

The time was ripe. For a change, the Chinese nationalist (i.e., anti-Communist), public relations movement in the U.S .was muted in 1975. Chiang Kai Shek in Taiwan, paired with conservative anti-Communists in the United States, dictated our Chinese foreign policy initiatives for decades. At the same time, The "Cold War" with the Soviet Union was raging on and on covered over by the appearance of "detente", or a desire not to enrage each other.

Carter's National Security Advisor Zbigniew Brzezinski walked into this morass filled with ideas of a double diplomatic shot. First, put the Russians on the defensive by removing their massive Far Eastern ally from the equation. Second, assuage American business interests by allowing them to do business with the Peoples Republic of China.

The appointment of Michel Okensburg, a Professor of Chinese Studies at University of Michigan to the National Security Council China seat put a focus on mainland China. He was an avowed pro-Chinese thinker. It took Brzezinski and Okensburg only 30 months after the Presidential turnover before they were off to China to begin talks on diplomatic recognition. Their job was not easy. There were money claims against the Chinese government requiring negotiation; there was the problem of what to do about Taiwan politically. Brzezinski simply put all of these problems on a back burner until the diplomatic recognition problem was resolved.

Over at the State Department, (more than 10,000 strong) many career employees, as well as political appointees, established, and operated U.S. foreign policy. There were groups assigned to the Republic of China (on Taiwan). There was a welter of bureau chiefs, desk managers, Deputy Secretaries of State and, of course, the Secretary of State himself or herself. There were three Deputy Secretaries, six under secretaries, eight Bureaus, an Assistant Secretary of State, a Deputy Assistant Secretary and a Principal Deputy Assistant Secretary before you get to the people who do the work. Definition and establishment of any policy or statement on China required many, many people up and down the chain. However, the Secretary of State and the State Department were NOT involved in this foreign policy initiative; to the contrary, Prof Brzezinski deliberately excluded them.

The IBM bureaucracy was no better. In 1975, IBM employed over 365,000 people in 146 countries. There were over 20 manufacturing plants worldwide building computers and computer technology; there were more than 10 development laboratories working on computers for the future; there were three research laboratories seeking new computing techniques. To administer this vast enterprise the company divided into 3 major subsidiaries containing more than 8 divisions and innumerable departments providing functional support for all activities. The company had more than 150 corporate type officers, group executives, and general managers to operate the bureaucracy. Marketing operations were the responsibility of three separate marketing divisions depending upon the product or the geography involved.

To illustrate this immense bureaucracy, picture a sales transaction. A sales representative deals with the customer; his local manager approves or disapproves; this manager has a geographical manager above him to make another decision. Above him is another geographical area manager to approve or disapprove. On top of these decision-makers, a division director or general manager (with a staff) has made some of the rules under which his subordinates will treat this sales transaction. Above him, a senior executive (with a staff of experts) made more of the decisions affecting this potential transaction. Our little sales representative in this illustration for IBM (at that time) has at least five levels of authority affecting his actions.

If this were not bad enough, there were legions of others (so called "staff") at various levels that had pieces of the action. You had accountants and pricing experts engaged in making sure the price was set right and rigidly adhered to; you had lawyers engaged in writing and enforcing the rules of engagement; human resource experts made sure employees were fairly treated. There were reams and reams of regulations and manuals to guide each employee and manager or director along the path of corporate righteousness.

At the top of the management triangle, the Chairman and President "ran" the company!

A substantial change in government or business direction raises major questions. In Communist China, a group of senior officials discusses and make the decision. It is well to remember the Chinese bureaucracy, designed by the Russians, operated from top to bottom, not the other way around. It was nothing new to make decisions at the top and have them implemented from the bottom. Chairman Mao did that for almost thirty years. The purchase of an embargoed computer simply created the question of a cover plan required by that embargo.

In the American government, we have a vastly different method called "elections". In this system, the voting population decides who shall run our government for a while. These elected officials, in turn, make decisions supposedly in tune with the promises they made to the voters electing them. The system becomes a little complicated when a three part Federal government is involved; the elected legislative branch must pass laws, the elected executive branch must implement them and the appointed judicial branch must make sure the laws are obeyed. However, foreign affairs are exempt from this tri-parte arrangement, at least in part. The executive branch controls foreign policy sometimes. Nevertheless, even in the executive branch, the bureaucracy is involved; each department has its turf and its operating rules and responsibilities. President Carter and Security Advisor Zbigniew Brzezinski simply ignored them!

On the commercial side of this bureaucratic triangle, the situation in IBM looked much the same. When the Chairman of the Board decided it was time for IBM to make plans involving the Peoples Republic of China, he ignored his own marketing staff bureaucracy (where primary responsibility for such actions lay). He called the executive responsible for that part of the world to ask him for a marketing strategy; he, in turn, ignored his own marketing staff bureaucracy (where primary responsibility for such actions lay) to ask the senior executive most knowledgeable of Asia for a marketing strategy definition to present to the Chairman. Both Chairmen simply ignored all the "experts" they had at their disposal!

The only open issue on the business side required an excruciating description of the civilian use of this computer on the application for an export license. The American embargo required IBM to find an exception to the prohibition of exporting computers to China!

In the US government, much the same thing happened, although on a much different time scale. National elections and their aftermath slowed actions down. Within a short period, the National Security Advisor (on the President's staff) ignored the entire State Department (where primary bureaucratic responsibility for such actions lay) to change the US policy. The President formally recognized the Peoples Republic of China on January 1, 1979 as a sovereign nation after almost thirty years as an outcast. Concurrently, the President de-recognized the Republic of China on Taiwan and explicitly declared there is only one China.

We join this environment somewhere after China's decisions but before the United States decision.

The scenario we envisaged included other influential people not mentioned before. David Rockefeller, an avowed internationalist and China proponent, was the Chair of the Chase Manhattan Bank. The bank, and Mr Rockefeller, was interested in accelerating direct connections between American commercial interests and mainland China; he was interested in direct diplomatic connections between the Peoples Republic and the U.S. government. In one sense, he was the complete philanthropist. His family built the first Western Hospital in Peking in the 1920's. His family (Standard Oil of New Jersey) brought light through distribution of kerosene lamps to the Chinese countryside for decades before World War II. In another sense, he was the complete commercial traveler. Mr. Rockefeller had personal connections to China; his bank had commercial ties with the State Bank of the PRC. Those connections would prove valuable when a free flow of credits and payments were established. His visits to China in 1973 (directly after the Nixon visit) and 1977 were precursors of the United States movement towards diplomatic recognition of China which would automatically cancel any embargos.

I understand Mr. Rockefeller organized the Chase Pacific Trade Advisors in 1975. Chase Pacific was a consultant group, closely allied, if not owned by the bank. He hired Ken Morse to run it. He was an international entrepreneur. While attending a UN sponsored meeting, he had met Bruce Langton, a IBM Vice President for Finance in the IBM Asian unit. Bruce Langton introduced Morse to the President of his unit, Bill Eggleston. IBM Americans/Far East Corp (the Asian unit) hired Chase Pacific as their consultant for PRC marketing. These events took place in the winter of 1975.

Moreover, there were others interested and influential. A group of academic scientists called the Committee on Scholarly Communication with the Peoples Republic of China. (CSCPRC) arranged for scientific interchanges from 1974. Although these exchanges were one way at the beginning (to China), the interplay between very influential and well placed people on both sides of the Pacific fostered subtle political activity. In 1974, for example, a group of US solid-state physics experts from academia and business (including one from the IBM Research Laboratory in Yorktown Heights, NY) visited Chinese universities. Many of the Chinese scientists had degrees from American colleges and universities; some had worked for the United States government on wartime projects. Many had returned to China when the Communist government indicated better treatment for returning intellectuals

When the President of Beijing University, (Mr. Cho Peyuan) a physicist of world renown, reports to a Vice Premier of the Peoples Republic (Mr. Deng Tsao Peng) a visit by influential colleagues from the United States, I should imagine he listens. When the President of the American National Academy of Science (Mr Philip Handler) speaks of the Peoples Republic of China to the American Secretary of State, (Mr. Cyrus Vance) or to the National Security Advisor (Prof Brzezinski) I should imagine they listen.

There were many such groups welcomed by the Chinese before Mao's death, before Deng's ascension and before diplomatic recognition of the PRC by the United States.

The commercial world, hypnotized by the sheer size of this very new, unexplored market, forged ahead! The scene was set for IBM's entry into the vast, mysterious, and unknown Chinese Communist market!

Chapter 3 – Contact!

New York Times, Feb. 12, 1977

"CHINA INDICATES CONCERN OVER U.S. DÉTENTE POLICY"

While the new Chinese industrial revolution was slowly getting started in China, we were having a slightly more democratic internal debate about the contents of this first computer seminar. There were those on the technical side who felt that describing the most advanced technologies was the way to go. They could put on an impressive show. There were others on the sales side who felt that we should tell them that we had software and management answers to every conceivable problem, even problems they might not have. The sales people felt that a shotgun approach was sure to hit a responsive note somewhere. And, of course, there were those who felt we should only talk about the products that were not embargoed. Last, but not least, there were those who felt we shouldn't go there for any reason! Since we were in a headquarters location in the U.S., most of the people involved in the discussions had little or no experience with embargos or trade restrictions of any kind; nor did they have experience dealing with a Communist country.

It's one thing to repeat sales messages that we have the best, the fastest, and the most advanced computers. If the listener believes you and has the money, you take the order, the computer is delivered and the cycle is complete. It's quite another to persuade the listener that even though we have all this wonderful equipment, we cannot deliver any of it to you. Alternatively, if we can deliver a computer, you Mr. Customer will have to install it, you Mr. Customer will have to maintain it. Our country is a member (and founder!) of COCOM; COCOM has an embargo on computers for China. We could be selling a computer big enough to be an embargoed computer to an embargoed country! What a dilemma we faced!

Before selecting members of the IBM delegation, decisions regarding the subjects to be discussed had to be made. Most IBM computers were embargoed "high technology" exports no matter which way you looked at it. Current computer products were forbidden because they were "current". By definition, they were really high technology. Even I could understand that computers using the same solid state technology as nuclear submarines were "verboten." Our Chinese audience would laugh at computers that used technology based on 1930's radio tubes (which they had in China) and would certainly note the absence of anything not up-to-date.

On the one hand, IBM publicly touted all its computers to be the most advanced of them all. On the other hand, to our government, we had to claim that some of these very same machines are really older technology not covered by the embargo. It was difficult to claim that the IBM computers actually in use by the U.S. Government at that time were so technologically deficient that they presented no threat to the COCOM embargo. Some compromise was necessary.

John, on my advice, decided to make no mention, unless asked, about equipment models we couldn't export to the Chinese. We did not want to underestimate the Chinese level of understanding, but we also did not want to spend a lot of time describing something we couldn't sell and export to China. That would be the greater evil. So, he instructed the technical people to concentrate on the smaller end of the product line. We had several models of small and intermediate sized computers available that had been previous exceptions from the embargo. "Be prepared to answer anything about larger models, but don't offer that information gratuitously." If questioned about larger models, be open and educational, but finish every answer with the words, "We probably can't deliver this anyway." The technical group even planned to bring a "computer terminal" a typewriter-like device with them to demonstrate the power of the smaller computers.

This entire discussion could be irrelevant if we knew the full intention of our new Chinese customers. Had there been full and open discussion, any computer would have fit the bill. Had we known this computer, when installed, was going to be the demonstration machine, a machine for education we would have stepped back. The whole embargo usage factor would make our job almost impossible. We all knew our computer, if ever installed, would be a first. We were so enamored of our products we couldn't conceive a computer purchased just for demonstration; the machine had to perform some business purpose, but what? After all, if we made a deal with the Chinese, we would have to prepare an application for an export license detailing how it would be used. Had we but known!

The first layer of deception was laid down. Did our counterparts in China know of the deception? I don't know. However, it is safe to assume some did, some did not.

The business model the Chinese were pursuing was simply "get modern computers". Not once in all the time we spent with them was there any indication of a specific use of the computer other than to run some FORTRAN mathematical design programs. Those programs, by contrast, could have been run on a calculator. That's an exaggeration, but to the point. The centrally planned purchase merely was a continuation of the state-owned and run manufacturing system in place at the time. We invented uses, we spent time explaining how a computer is used in the U.S. The

Chinese agreed to everything we said. The one thing neither we nor they considered was the immutable laws of unintended consequences. On a grand scale, our sale pitches taught them the most important aspect of modernization; thinking outside the box of Communist central control.

Mr. Wu did not describe the audience he was assembling. The telexes speeding back and forth contained no information about who we were going to be talking to. Mr Wu offered no information about his client or what they wanted to do with this computer. Although it did not make much difference for the hardware engineers, it made a lot of difference for the software people. Were they going to talk to bankers, accountants or engineers? The only thing we were able to find out was that the First Ministry of Machine Building was involved. We thought they controlled factories that manufactured many different things, from heavy machinery to telephone wires.

The people in Beijing and Shenyang did not have similar problems deciding who should attend this free school on computers that IBM was preparing. Mr. Shu and Mr. Mu were available and planned to attend. The seven new men that had just been moved to the factory from the boat yard were available. Big Mu had not yet appeared on the scene. He was not only just finishing his computer studies getting married as well. So, he couldn't attend the seminar. Someone from the Beijing Ministry had to attend. But it had to appear this program was not for the Ministry in Beijing. To this day, I do not know who the Ministry person(s) attending that seminar was. The seminar schedule was fixed; it had been changed once already. The Americans did not want the Chinese schedule to affect their November holiday season. Nor did they want the schedule to interfere with their vacation-touring in the Far East pre or post seminar. Such thoughts were purely American; it was axiomatic the Chinese did not think like that.

Making an educated guess, we chose assembly factory management software using computer-generated data. IBM had a lot of experience with this subject. Unfortunately, there are many kinds of factories. There are continuous assembly plants and job-lot process plants; very different from each other. There are one-unit factories that build space shuttles; one at a time. We did not know which one to address. We didn't want to explain any software products that have the words "total" or "total management" somewhere in their title. Naively, we thought that since Communism was a "total" solution to something, we shouldn't look like we were competing with it. Independently, we had sometimes wondered about those kinds of titles. All IBM computer solutions were routinely touted as "total" solutions. How could you have a new "total" solution every couple of years? Wasn't one enough?

We thought that job-shop factory control and management was particularly appropriate for the Chinese. The Chinese had imported the Russian central planning system. I had experience with Russian central planning during the time I had spent there. Factories and production were run on plans made in some far distant city by some nameless clerk manipulating numbers. The work plan generated for each worker was prepared the same way, i.e., prepared by someone far away. The worker's plan determined his pay and production. Everybody had a work plan. Both the factory plan and the worker's plan were prepared without any local feedback. Over time, the plans became a total fiction. Sometimes the "actual" numbers were just as fictional as the planned numbers. Reality was ignored.

I worked with an IBM'er from our subsidiary in Germany while I was in Russia. I don't remember his name. He had been a prisoner of war in a Siberian gold mine labor camp for ten years after the war. That's another story that needs to be told. He described the operation of the mine plan to me. Each worker on each shift had to fill a fixed number of steel buckets with material from which the gold was extracted. It took so many buckets to fill a car on the ore train that collected the material. The total number of filled ore cars for that shift was the mine's production.

There were three shifts operating each day. The production quota consisted of so many cars per day. The "plan" set by Moscow, called for so many ounces of gold smelted each day, etc up the line. That way, the Moscow plan of selling so much gold on the international market would bring in the requisite amount of money the central plan called for.

That was the "plan". The reality was that the workers reported the correct "plan" number of buckets filled; the management reported the correct "plan" number of ore cars filled; the smelter reported the correct "plan" amount of gold delivered to Moscow. When Moscow sold the entire "plan" production, there was a shortfall of about 40% in the amount of money realized. After voluminous checking of their production records, the leaders decided that someone or some foreign country had somehow stolen the missing 40%. Theft had not been factored into the plan; theft was not a socialist activity. The plan was met; the missing 40% was stolen.

As in Russian, no one ever wanted to be responsible for missing his personal plan or the collective plan sent down from Beijing. Remember, the only plans the Chinese have are successful plans. A worker might be responsible for completing five tasks each day; the factory might be responsible for completing fifty products each day. No matter how many tasks the worker actually completed, he would report five completed tasks. He was paid for five tasks. Theoretically, if he didn't complete them, his pay would be reduced; if his pay was docked, he might go on strike or join a mob. So, his boss said nothing. The factory always reported an acceptable number sometimes unrelated to reality. And so on up the line. Of course there were some realities that equaled the plan. In fact, I read that a factory official in some western province was executed for falsifying his factory's results to achieve the plan. I thought that any Western system and, certainly any computer-based system, should be a welcome change. How naive I was!

When I worked in Moscow, I become friendly with my Russian translator. His name was Igor. He was absolutely fluent and colloquial in English and German. We paid him $25.00 US dollars an hour for his work. In four days he would make as much with us as he made in his regular job in a month. His regular job (remember, everyone had to have one!) was as a translator with something called the Institute of Railroad Construction. His work plan consisted of translating three articles (of undefined length) from German publications into Russian. He told me that he was able to complete the three articles by 8:00AM each workday. He would spend the rest of the day free-lancing with IBM. And, the odd part of this story, if what I just told you isn't odd, is that everyone knew it. That was the system!

As John was completing the arrangement for taking his troop to China, he and Charlie Swift had several sessions with IBM executives in September 1976. They were nervous and concerned. The first one was with the President of his division, Bill Eggleston. Bill informed them that although John was in charge of the IBM delegation, our advisor from Chase Consulting, Ken Morse, would be in overall command of the mission. Whether that was his original thought, or whether that idea came from corporate headquarters in Armonk, New York, it was impossible to tell. John didn't take kindly to the idea that IBM was taking a back seat to an outsider on a sales mission to promote IBM business.

He made his feeling known to Bill. There was some discussion, but John's position was logical and clear. The arrangement with the consultant was backwards. John asked, "What happens when Ken makes a commitment on our behalf that we don't agree with?"

"What do you mean?"

"Suppose the consultant agrees to a discount during some informal talking. Will you or I be held accountable for that?"

John continued. "I don't have any objection with a consultant advising me on Chinese manners and culture, but I simply don't buy a consultant leading an IBM sales mission."

Bill agreed reluctantly that John should lead the delegation.

The next briefing was with Ralph Pfeiffer the CEO of our division. His edicts were simple and clear; it was a real short meeting. First, there was to be no repetition of the IBM organizational fiasco in the Soviet Union. There, based on nothing but the U.S.S.R's size and perceived potential (sounds familiar, doesn't it?), the managers built up an organization of 75 people; there were two signed contracts; that was it. Nothing of any consequence, other than net losses, ever came of that operation. No one could be sure it was because of the embargo, or because of the Russians. Everyone was betting on the future, which unfortunately, never arrived. Ralph did not want that repeated in China.

The second edict given to John was that if there were ever any mention of China and IBM or of China and Ralph Pfeiffer in the business or public press John would be looking for another job the next day. Although not expressed quite that way, the impression John carried out of that meeting was that and more. There was no misunderstanding. There was to be no publicity, accidental or otherwise, either inside or outside of the company!

The briefings were complete. The speakers and the curriculum were complete. Brad Foss and Bob Creasy handled the hardware, Steve Holton handled the control system software and John Makaapi handled the factory applications software. They, along with Ken Morse and Mary Wadsworth from Chase Pacific, made up the delegation. They would be talking about smaller systems, software and manufacturing applications. Since we still didn't know who would be the audience and what their interests might be, it was the best shot we had.

In late September, 1976, John took his "dog and pony" show to Beijing. Not once during the entire week of presentations was the identity of the factory revealed. Not that it was concealed, just that no one popped up and said, "I'm from the Shenyang Blower Works in Shenyang and we have to run programs from Italy," or something like that. Mr. Wu introduced himself as Wu Xiao Xian from Techimport. Mr. Mu, and Mr. Shu and Chen were introduced by name and that's all. Other than Mr. Wu from Beijing, no one else was identified by Ministry or bureau or factory. There were others in the audience who remain unidentified to this day. We now know that some of them were security guards set out for our safety; that was never explained. Others were from the Ministry in Beijing. Such explanations would do nothing but create worry, so why bother. Except for the blue Mao suits, all these men could have been from San Francisco or New York.

Mr. Shu's interest in engineering and design programs was totally unknown to the speakers. Had we known, IBM had other people who were living encyclopedias on the subject. Mr. Mu's interest in machine tool computing and numerical control applications was never revealed. Had we known, IBM had other people who literally invented the subject. The fact that neither of them was interested in factory management software ever came out. John Makaapi was going to tell them anyway. The fact that they both worked for the Shenyang Blower Works was unknown. They both sat through four or five days of intense computer descriptions, then equally intense application programming explanations. It was the polite thing to do. The other men in the audience followed their leaders' examples; they sat and listened intently. The important fact that the installation was going to be used to educate wasn't even hinted at.

If silence is deception, then we were deceived by the Chinese silence. In turn, we later deceived ourselves by assuming, and later believing, our sales pitches about the use of the computer. After all, it worked in the United States, why could it not work in China?

The one person on their side who might have had some knowledge of computers and programming, Big Mu, had not yet been assigned to the Blower Works. He was finishing his advanced college courses. He didn't join the Chinese team; excuse me, "delegation", until late November 1976. The IBM delegation was already home. Moreover, nobody was told that he even existed.

The first cultural gaffe occurred even before the seminar got started. As the speakers were unpacking the cases of materials they were using in their presentations, John came across a cardboard box that he did not recognize. He opened it and found a couple of hundred rhinestone tiaras, things that Queens and Princesses wear on their heads. Mr Wu had been responsible for getting all their boxes from the airport to the hotel to the hall. John called over to him. When Mr Wu arrived, with translator in tow, he showed him the tiaras and asked what he should do with them. Mr. Wu was completely flustered by the sight. The translator looked at Mr. Wu then looked back at John as if maybe this was one of those American jokes, or maybe it wasn't an American joke. John put one of the tiaras on his head to illustrate the joke. Mr. Wu did not crack a smile; he just looked at the tiaras, then at John, then at the tiaras again. Maybe he was thinking that this was one of those jibes at the Chinese, or at the Communists since they don't have princesses; there was no way to tell. One of the other speakers came over and noticed that the carton with the tiaras in it wasn't IBM's; it had another name on it. Everyone smiled and laughed; Mr. Wu laughed harder than anyone else. He was off the hook. The real question was what in the world was a case of rhinestone tiaras doing in Beijing, China?

As the speakers were driven to and from the building where the seminar was held, they noticed a lot of activity on the streets. There were groups, particularly around Tienamin Square, carrying placards which Mary translated for them. "Execute the Gang of Four"; "Jiang Qing (Mao's widow) forged Chairman Mao's will", etc, etc. Mary translated another one as "Our Leader Hua Go Feng is great" or something like that. No one knew that the "Gang of Four" was under house arrest; no one knew that President Ford stated that China-U.S. relations couldn't be rushed during a campaign debate with Jimmy Carter. The streets were a little scary but the taxi drivers seemed to avoid the worst of the crowds. The drivers had to work hard enough to avoid hitting the bicyclists who were as numerous as fleas. As soon as the Americans arrived at the seminar, it seemed they left one world and entered another.

The presentations went well. The translator, a Madame Liu was as technically competent as could be expected. Remember, there had been no technical contact between any user group and any computer group for forty years; political contact was only about a couple of years old and sporadic at best. Speaking English was a learned skill; there were no native-American teachers for these people.

A side note here. Actually, there were a few native-American translators (nine, as I recall) left in country when Chairman Mao conquered Beijing in 1949. They were Communist, of course, and remained in China by special dispensation from Mao. All were repatriated later along with their Chinese wives; also by special dispensation.

There were the abnormal translation problems when speakers insisted on using acronyms. Words like CAD/CAM and CADAM, which stood for Computer Aided Design and Manufacturing, (standard "in" computer acronyms in Western factories) really threw the translator into a tizzy. She would scream "WHAT?" whenever the speaker used one of those words on the fly. At first, the Americans thought that someone had said something terribly impolite or unknowingly insulted someone. In contrast, when Madame Liu was translating during a non-technical event, she was a lovable, smiling and jocular woman. In fact, of all those people early on in our relationship, she was the only Chinese who wore something of color along with the battleship grey or blue Mao tunic.

At other times, when she thought that someone had said something terribly unfair or demeaning to the Chinese, she would shriek "WHY". Those shrieks were disconcerting to say the least. Between the "What's" and the "Why's", you couldn't anticipate what she would do. Her shrieks would cause the speaker to stop short to explain that CAD/CAM meant "Computer Aided Design/Computer Aided Manufacturing" or what CADAM meant. He would lose the rhythm of his presentation and literally have to try to remember where he was interrupted. That's the price paid when you are not used to speaking through a translator. They never have a problem at the UN because they use simultaneous translation, not serial translation as we did. Simultaneous translation puts the burden solely on the translator; serial translation puts the burden on the speaker as well as the translator.

During one session, John Makaapi, the manufacturing application expert, was deeply into his explanation of BOMP an acronym for Bill of Material Processor. It also sounds a lot like "bomb." A bill of materials is a very detailed list of every single part of a product or assembly. It's a very important piece of any computer application in a factory. Because of that, John used the words "bill of materials" and "BOMP" in his talk many times.

Each time, the Madame Liu used the Chinese word that meant "that thing" whenever John said bill of materials. I guess she preferred "that thing" to a "bomb". Mary, our consultant translator, was listening to the Chinese and caught the repetition. In Chinese, John's explanation came out as "That thing" does that, or "That thing" is exploded, or "That thing" must be divided up etc. Unfortunately, there was several "that things". Which one was he referencing? His explanation became meaningless. The Chinese audience would never stop him to ask, it was too impolite. At a break, Mary told him what was going on and suggested that he define a bill of material using some other words. He became incensed and stalked away. After all, no one in the audience had asked a question.

After the break, John started out by asking his audience if they understood his explanations. His question to the audience put them in a bind. If they said they understood then John would be happy but they really didn't know what a bill of materials was. If they responded negatively, everyone would lose some face. The audience lost face because they didn't ask any questions.. John lost face because he lost his audience. Therefore, they all said that they understood. Who really knows?

That evening, Mr Wu invited all the speakers to a banquet. At about 6 in the evening, he appeared in the lobby of the hotel with two of the translators who had worked the seminar that day. Mr Wu put all the IBM people in a succession of little taxis, where they were carted off to a restaurant about 10 minutes away. Upstairs from a very nondescript entrance was a succession of rooms of varying sizes, each with a table or tables set for dinner.

Mr Wu led everyone to a room where there were three round tables, each seating ten people. The seminar audience was already there. Mr. Shu and Mr. Mu were there, along with the others (as-yet-to-be-identified-people) from the seminar. He split up the IBM people among the three tables, holding John Ryan and Ken Morse aside.

"Mr. Ryan, please wait. There are other gentlemen coming." Mr Wu told John through the translator. Wu appeared to be slightly nervous. The translator was even more nervous.

"Oh, who's coming?" John couldn't wait. Although John was not impatient, everyone he knew was already seated.

"Please, wait, please" The translator repeated. Now the translator, without any word from Mr. Wu, held John's sleeve.

As he was doing this, two other Chinese gentlemen arrived, one younger than the other. The younger one had a smile on his face; in fact he never stopped smiling. As he stepped up to Mr. Wu, John noticed that his Mao jacket was not made of the same wrinkled material like everyone else; his tailored Mao jacket fit him perfectly. His pants even had a crease. He was a small man, shorter than Mr. Wu. Mr Wu seemed to be condensing himself in front of these gentlemen, as if he did not want to be taller than they. Rangy John, however, towered over everyone. Even before anyone said anything, John realized that these new people were higher up in the pecking order than Mr. Wu.

Mr. Wu introduced the younger one to John. "Mr. Ryan, I would like you to meet Mr. Ma, the manager of my bureau." At least, that is what the lady translator said. The Chinese language introduction took much longer than the English one. John suspected that his title was something else, he never heard the title "manager" in China before this. I don't think Communists have managers, they have directors.

Mr. Ma stepped right up to John with his hand outstretched and in English said, "Mr. Ryan, Mr. Wu has been telling me what a wonderful seminar you have put on for us. We thank you." John was stunned. This was all in English, and unaccented English at that. Except for the translators, John had not met any Chinese who spoke or admitted to speaking English. The translators were speaking for someone else; this gentleman was speaking for himself. Maybe Mr. Ma was trying to impress John, or Mr. Wu, or somebody else. Our experience later on with English-speaking Chinese in the PRC was that they tended to use English only when they were one-on-one, never in a group. After all, they probably did not want to be accused of giving secrets away. This was another Communist phobia.

"Mr. Ma, I am pleased to meet you." John said. He was flustered by the sudden English.

"I would like you to meet our Director." He turned to the older man. But this time he didn't stick to English. The English was immediately followed by a spate of Chinese apparently to get the older man into the conversation.

"Mr Something-or-other (Ma was speaking so fast that John didn't or couldn't catch the man's name.) I would like you to meet Mr. Ryan." At that, the older man's hand shot out and his lips turned into a smile. It was as if a switch had been thrown. He mumbled something that neither Mr. Ma nor the lady translators choose to repeat in English. Mr. Ma's English was meant to impress this gentleman John guessed. Mr. Something or other was Ma's boss.

"It's a real pleasure to meet you, sir," John mumbled back. This was immediately translated by Mr. Ma. John was looking down onto this gentleman's head. Unlike the others in the room, the old gentlemen's hair was gray, not black. He was wearing glasses and looked well fed, but he had tired eyes. His Mao suit was a well tailored grey, not blue like the others. All the others in the room had stopped talking when he appeared. He had to be somebody important.

Mr. Something-or-other shook hands with John and Ken (who up to this moment had been ignored) and without saying another word sat down. Mr Wu quickly placed John on one side of Mr. Something-or-other and Ken on the other. Then he sat down in the next place and Mr. Shu and Mr. Mu slid in next. It became quite obvious that there was a pecking order here. The position at the table opposite to Mr. Something-or-other (furthest away) would have to be the low man on the totem pole. And so it was. One of the nameless attendees took that place.

Everyone was delighted with the food. I won't go into detail here about the food, but it was unlike any Chinese food these Westerners had tasted before. But even the food paled into insignificance when the toasts began. Mr. Something-or-other started it off. Funny thing, though. He stood up, raised his glass, and Mr. Ma announced his toast. John noticed that the older Chinese man did not drink. He merely lifted the glass and held it to his lips, but did not drink. Apparently drinking was for the young, even in China. Every Chinese toast had to be responded to. Every American toast had to be replied to. Friendship toasts were the most common, followed in frequency by good-health and long-life. We soon figured out the drinking part of the toast was the most important; the words less so. The banquet ended on a boisterous note; every one slept well that night.

The next day, several speakers had another problem that had nothing to do with translation. Apparently, this problem is endemic among American technicians and engineers, particularly IBM engineers. Even though they make speeches or presentations on technical subjects all the time, many of them cannot answer a question in a straightforward manner. Short answers are impossible. Words like "Yes", or "No" or best of all, "I don't know" are simply not in their vocabulary.

Many questions are answered with a discourse of the total knowledge of the speaker on the subject or any related subject that comes to mind. Invariably the speaker covers so much ground in his answer he not only loses sight of the question, but many times loses his audience as well. If you add translation to the mix, credibility becomes a real issue. John had to constantly remind the speakers to "Keep it Short and Keep it Simple!"

One incident deserves mention. There was a lot of concern about explanations and descriptions of computers that were embargoed. The embargo covered not only the physical hardware, but also covered the technical information surrounding the hardware. It seemed logical that the best course was not to mention any of them. Then we wouldn't be forced to tell the audience that we couldn't deliver them. That would be like rubbing salt in an open wound. We knew that the Peoples Republic of China could not and did not recognize the existence of COCOM. So mention of CCOM was a political minefield of technology exports to places like China. Our judgment was that it was best to avoid the whole thing if we could.

That decision didn't sit well with Brad Foss, one of our technical experts or with Ken Morse, our Chase China consultant. After completing his presentation on intermediate computers (export exception on a case-by-case basis) Brad came up to John in the back of the room and quietly said,

"We have to tell them about the large scale computers (export not permitted)! In the interest of exchanging scientific information, we should tell them about advanced computers." He was very earnest; his voice rang with self satisfaction.

Looking up at him John said "I haven't heard anyone ask a question about large scale computers." John was annoyed, why was this question coming up now? Didn't this man understand the situation?

"I know. But we are all engineers here (how in the world did he know that?). We shouldn't put up any barriers to information. We should tell them what we know." (Notice the "tell-all" syndrome.) He raised his voice one notch; he was even more earnest.

John answered quickly "No way!" He began to get up out of his seat. He couldn't answer this guy while looking up at him.

"I'm going to bring it up when I review my presentation with them."

This exchange took place within Ken's hearing. He joined in.

"John, you really should have Brad tell them about the advanced computing equipment. They will really appreciate it. It's the friendly thing to do." He was using his authoritative consulting voice that brooked no disagreement.

Now things were beginning to get out of hand. There was another speaker on the stage. Two men were standing with John mumbling in the back of the room. If they continued, everyone in the room would realize that something was going on.

John glared at Ken, and said to Brad, "Let's you and me step outside so we can talk." mumbling going on in the back of the room

They went out into the hall and into another room.

Brad said, "I really don't agree with not telling them everything. If they find out we didn't explain all our big computers, we look like jerks" This was a religious experience for Brad; his eyes were shinning, he was using his hands for emphasis. He couldn't stand still; the scientist in him was rebelling. John was preventing his sharing everything he knew with fellow scientists.

"Brad, if you even begin to bring the subject up, I'll interrupt your pitch and ask you to leave. Then I will personally put you on the next plane to Tokyo." John was adamant. His eyes were glinting; he stared right into Brad's soul. He had to get through to this guy or be forced to do something publicly. That wasn't good.

"John, I think you're wrong. There should be a free exchange of technical data." Brad's expression now became plaintive; John's resistance to scientific purity was unnerving him. And, where did this "exchange" thing come from? This was a one-way seminar, us to them!

"Brad, remember what I just told you."

Brad, his face getting redder and redder by the second retorted, "I'm going to call Bill Eggleston (their IBM boss) and tell him what you are doing". In a democratic society you can threaten to do this. Actually doing it was another thing altogether.

John trumped him. "Great. Be my guest." John picked up a telephone and handed it to Brad. "And, when you've finished with the call, I'll take you to the airport."

That trumped the situation. There was no way you could pick up a telephone in Beijing and talk to someone 8,000 miles away just like that. You couldn't talk to someone across the street! The telephones didn't work like that. Direct Dialing didn't become real for another 25 years!

Brad stalked out of the room.

The subject of very large computers never came up. Maybe the Chinese realized that but remained polite to the end. I think that's true for the Beijing Ministry people. I think the real reason for the Shenyang people was that they really didn't' care. Now we know that they only wanted a computer to run the Italian programs. The central planners just wanted any modern computer, large or small for their education project; the revolution demanded it.

The seminar ended on a high note. Mr. Wu thanked John profusely and everyone went sightseeing. Nobody knew that the audience came from Shenyang. Nobody knew that they needed an IBM computer for the Nuovo Pignone programs and nobody knew of the "NEW" grand plan for China.

After the close of the sessions, everyone went back to the Beijing Hotel. Everyone was whispering about John's tête-à-tête with Brad. At dinner that evening, they saw John Glenn, the U.S. astronaught enter the dining room. Everyone started talking about him, but nobody went over to greet him. A little later, they saw McChesney Martin, the Chairman of the U.S. Federal Reserve Bank come into the dining room. A game began to decide who recognized these big wigs soonest. We were so naïve we never realized that we were part of a blizzard of modernity sent to China from the U.S. of A. With such distinguished company to gossip about, the business between John and Brad was forgotten.

At breakfast in the hotel the next morning, everything was back to normal. By this time, the troop had been in Beijing for a couple of weeks. Mary, our consultant translator, was at breakfast with all the men in the dining room. Mary was a small lady. She was a very charming, single at the time, young woman thoroughly enjoying being the only female (and a necessary one!) in this group of displaced Americans. That morning, she came to the group's table wearing a dress that showed a great deal of cleavage. At home this wouldn't have caused a ripple. But in Beijing, with these men, it was a little different. John M. looked across the table at Mary and said with a completely straight face, "Mary, I've been away from home for a long time and I really don't need any reminders of what I got married for. Could you please button your dress up?"

Mary, completely nonplussed answered, "Why sure John, but I'm happy that I reminded you of your wife." Everyone laughed and went back to their fishy smelling eggs.

After breakfast, everyone trooped around the corner from the hotel to a carver's shop in an arcade just off Wang Fu Gin Street. Each man had a hand carved soapstone seal made with his name in Chinese characters. The little seals cost $ 5 - $7 U.S. Dollars, a real steal. If you couldn't sign your name you could use the little seal to stamp your identity. As soon as everyone got home, the little seals went into drawers never to be seen again.

Ken and Mary went off to read the posters stuck up on the walls of Bei Hei Park on the other side of Tienamin Square just down the street from the hotel. The subject of the "Gang of Four" the self-proclaimed successors to Chairman Mao, was particularly hot at the time. Although there were few "Gang of Four" supporters evident, it was apparent that the move to modernization was not shared by all.

Although the domestic political turmoil was intense, the IBM group was faintly aware of it. And, if the Chinese audience was aware of what was going on, they certainly kept it to themselves. Both the Americans and Chinese seemed to be in a computer education space suit totally isolated from the outside world. Once in the building, all the turmoil, wall posters and street demonstrations outside seemed on another planet. Since Mary could read and speak Chinese, she was more likely to see and hear the debates going on. Everybody else just did his job and acted as tourists when they could. At the end of the two weeks, everyone went home for the holidays

The Chinese were particularly happy to get all the printed manuals and documentation that the speakers had brought with them. Even though it was all in English, every copy of every manual was snapped up. The attendees even took the magazines that the Americans had purchased for reading on the airplane. At the close of the day's session, there was no cleanup; the place was picked clean.

Now What?

In a typical IBM marketing situation, the next thing that was supposed to happen was that the people in the audience contact IBM. They ask specific questions about specific computers and specific software unique to their specific organization and specific problems. From that question and answer period, a sales proposal is prepared. The sales proposal describes what we have to sell, how that product will help them specifically and how much all of this is going to cost. The whole process is tailored to the specific customer's situation.

In this case, none of this was true. Whether intentional or not, no specific questions about their problems, their usage or their intentions came up. It was all very, very secret. We now know that most of the audience didn't have a clue as to the purpose of purchasing a computer!

In the United States, we all waited. We thought our arch Japanese competitor Hitachi was making a bid. The presidential elections came and went; Jimmy Carter, an avowed proponent of better China-U.S. relations was elected.

Mr. Shu and Mr. Mu wanted an IBM computer because that's what the Italians had. All that computer application stuff was illuminating and very, very interesting, but it had almost nothing to do with the Italian programs. The Ministry wanted an IBM computer because IBM could get it past the embargo. Techimport (Mr. Wu and his bosses) controlled who would get the contract for the computer system. Mr. Wu thought that he would have to pay a premium for an IBM computer compared to any others of the same power.

Mr. Shu and Mr. Mu, now accompanied by Big Mu, travelled to Beijing several times in December trying to convince Mr. Wu that IBM was the vendor that they wanted. It wasn't easy. In their system, the importing company, in this case Techimport had the dominant voice. It wasn't as if Mr Wu had any personal preference; his view of his job was to purchase the best product for the best price for his client Big Mu sat through these meetings absolutely mesmerized by these contacts with high and mighty people. After all, he had only just finished graduate school.

The final scene played out when the Vice-Minister for Science and Technology in the Ministry in Beijing, Mr Suen You Yu, asked to see Mr. Shu and his boss, He Ju San, the Managing Director of the factory. Mr. Shu explained his reasons for the IBM choice.

"We think that the IBM product is the best in the world for us. We have looked at others in the literature, but it appears all agree that IBM's product is the best." His quiet voice dominated the room. He had all the literature in front of him.

"What about the Italians?" Mr. Yu was not totally impressed by his quiet dignity. He pushed the papers back towards Mr. Shu.

"The Italians do not make any computers, in fact, they use IBM's." He moved the papers back to the middle of the table.

"What about the cost?" This time he pushed the papers to the side. The information on the papers was not going to be part of this discussion.

"We don't have their offer yet; we believe it might be a little higher than their competition. We are willing to pay a little more, if it is a little, to get their products." Mr. Shu was not going to be intimidated by a Vice-Minister.

"What do you say, Mr He?" Mr. Yu switched gears; he was putting the Managing Director of the Factory on the spot. If he agreed with Yu, he was letting his men down; if he agreed with Mr. Shu, he was risking his job. His eyes went from one man to the other. He slowly moved the papers back to the center of the table.

The Managing Director concurred with Mr. Shu.

Mr Suen You Yu agreed.

Another shot in the new revolution had been fired!

Many years later, they told me that they believed that Mr Suen You Yu made a call to Mr. Jiang who was below him in the pecking order. Remember Mr. Jiang. He was the official who had a lot to do with the selection of Italian technology in the first place. He was the head of the Foreign Affairs Bureau and an electrical engineer to boot. Mr. Mu thinks that Mr Jiang made a call to the head of Techimport and the die was cast. As a matter of fact, years later I concluded that events were engineered by these officials in Beijing. I now believe that the party politicians in Beijing at that time, particularly Mr. Jiang, knew of embargoes, limitation on computer exports, and IBM. They outlined this plot, we merely played our parts. They wrote the music, we sang the lyrics. The People's Republic of China couldn't wait for political diplomacy, recognition by the U.S., relaxation of the embargo, or anything else to get these computers that were at the heart of their new revolution.

Of course, we knew absolutely nothing of these Chinese machinations. Back in the U.S.A., we thought that a Japanese computer manufacturer would be our chief and perhaps only competitor. Their hardware was a good match and their price was invariably lower. However, Japanese competition wasn't even on the horizon.

The Chinese, we learned later, would never buy from the Japanese unless theirs was the only product. The Chinese, including the people involved here, had extremely unpleasant memories of the Japanese occupation of their country. The Rape of Nanking, emasculation of their education system, and the brutal oppression by the Japanese ranked way up there in the memory of most Chinese. Besides, we had the factory management software; the Japanese did not. The fact that the Chinese didn't need factory management software at that moment was irrelevant. We had been asked to provide general information on our products; we had done that. The Chinese had thanked us and bid us farewell. No one knew what was supposed to happen next. The music was playing and no one gave us a cue. We waited and waited and waited.

Chapter 4– Setting the Stage

New York Times, January 17, 1977
"CLEAN UP OF POSTERS IN PEKING"

Mr. Wu sent us a telex very early in January 1977.

> "My client desires a proposal discussion in Beijing
> at your earliest convenience. Please send names
> and proposed dates. Thank you"
> > China National Technical Import Corp.

We were totally mystified.

Propose what?

Propose to whom?

But, true IBM'ers that we were, we could and did put together a lot of boiler plate proposal stuff right out of our sales manual and had it typed up. We chose the smallest computer that we thought we could get away with (an exception to the embargo), along with some standard factory application programs. The pricing people took the proposal and calculated the U.S. prices plus 20% to cover any complications that might arise. We did not know their pricing methodology but after we received their numbers it was easy enough to figure it out. In IBM at that time, pricing people and marketing people only met in the chief executive's office; the sales staff was not aware of how IBM priced their products. The pricing people had their own, almost independent, bureaucracy. Since we were doing this in such a hurry, we had to accept whatever the pricing people would give us. We had no opportunity to review it. In special and unique circumstances like this, marketing people could question the pricing. Not this time! It was our intention to bring something credible to Beijing so that we wouldn't be laughed out of the room. It was all very, very exciting.

We were finally going to see our customer!

John Ryan was phlegmatic about the whole thing. Since he was familiar to most of the executives concerned with a China proposal, he could get accelerated action.

"John, there is no way we can ok this proposal without our guys studying it in detail" Bill Lynn, the pricing executives told him. "After all, we've never done a proposal for the Peoples Republic. We'll have to have Corporate look it over as well." John was astounded by this bureaucratic response. The company was supposed to be de-centralized; these activities were supposed to be local.

"Bill, you do whatever you want to. We are leaving in three weeks for China and that proposal is coming with us." John's voice was calm, dangerously calm. He stood up to leave.

Bill answered, still not getting the point, "Three weeks, hell, it will take that long to find the right guys to do the work." Bill was an established bureaucrat in the IBM system of management. His job, and those who worked for him, was to get it priced right. If he didn't agree with you, the only next step was a meeting in the President Bill Eggleston's office to resolve the issue. Most did not want to risk the President's office; it could go either way in there.

John's voice got hard. "Bill, let me use your phone for a minute. I want to call Ralph Pfeiffer to tell him that we have to put off the China proposal trip because we can't get a price." Bill was reaching for his phone to push it over to John when these words finally got past his ears into his brain. He stopped short.

"Wait a goddamn minute John. Don't get so tough. We'll get it done!"

John and I got our invitations from China, and our China visas and tickets; we headed out to Tokyo on February 4, 1977.

The following afternoon, accompanied by Ken Morse and Mary Wadsworth our consultants, we boarded our flight for Beijing. Ken's attitude during the seminar situation with "total disclosure" really caused John to review the necessity for a consultancy at all. Even after John had voiced his objections to Charlie, we were forced to take them with us. We needed a translator. We couldn't get Mary without Ken.

At that time, flying to Beijing was no small task. Non-stop flights were not available. We had to fly to Tokyo first to overnight there. The New York to Tokyo flight took about fourteen hours. It must have been the furthest that airplanes could go without refueling. However, it was not always like that. Ten years before, my family and I took that same trip. It took some twenty-four hours and you always had to stop in Hawaii. Boredom sets in about halfway across the Pacific. I began to think about the first time that I made that trip. It was the time when my family and I moved to Japan. Isn't it crazy what you think about while waiting for sleep 40,000 feet over the Pacific?

At that time the only west-bound airline service from Japan to China was Pakistan Air Lines. I have never figured out why

Pakistan was allowed to fly into and out of China. Other than Iran Air Lines, no other non-Communist airline was allowed. Air France had some flights early on, but no one wanted to go to Paris first. Maybe it was because the Chinese felt that Pakistan had enough of their own troubles at that time and therefore posed no threat. Who knows?

Our Pakistan flight arrived in Beijing a little behind schedule; we were about an hour and half late. The plane left Tokyo on time, about 5 PM. The flight was supposed to take about four hours to Beijing. Nobody had mentioned that the airplane was going to stop along the way. It just did. The unscheduled, but apparently, normal, stop in Shanghai had added quite a bit of time to the flight time between Tokyo and Beijing. Everyone else on the plane, all four of them, must have known of the stop. Maybe John, Ken or Mary was aware of it, but no one told me.

There were two men who looked like they were from Pakistan (naturally, since we were on Pakistan Air Lines!) and two Japanese. The Pakistanis were both swarthy with immense mustaches, one older than the other. You can always tell Pakistanis, the men don't wear underwear under their western style shirts. The material of the shirts is always thin looking. I guess because it's so hot where they come from. Since the shirt is so thin, you can tell if there is an undershirt underneath. The Japanese were two middle aged businessmen. You can see thousands of these businessmen on the subways in Tokyo. Dark grey suits, white shirts, straight collars, bizarre neckties and hair slicked back. The colleges in Japan must teach a course in "Basic Business Suits" to all their male students; every one of them is a duplicate of the others. They were conversing with each other in thick, guttural Japanese, which sounds like two Sumo wrestlers trying to scare one another.

The airlines did not want to fly near the Korean Peninsula since a commercial airliner had been shot down there. I imagine that the Chinese authorities did not want airplanes from the

West to fly over some parts of China. The direct flight path from Tokyo to Beijing was forbidden, partially because it would over fly a part of Korea. There must be things under that flight path they did not want us to see from 30,000 feet up in pitch darkness. We crossed the coast just before the landing at Shanghai, passing from the blackness of the South China Sea to an even blacker landscape. John and I expected to see a burst of light from the city. After all, Shanghai is one of the largest cities in the world. We saw nothing. Then we saw a sprinkling of lights here and there. Finally the airport runway (outlined in tiny lights) came into view and we were on the ground. Some guy came on the speaker and told us that we had to get off the airplane, "Take all your bags with you."

Since we hadn't been warned of this stop, I thought we were all to be arrested for something. No one said we were in Shanghai. We knew this was not Beijing; the flight time was too short. We all got our stuff out of the overhead racks. The racks were just that, racks. The doors didn't work and there were some missing. The cabin door had been opened. The winds, the cold Chinese winds, whistled down the aisles. We walked to the front of the plane. The Pakistanis thought this was great fun; the Japanese gentlemen just kept right on talking.

Through the open cabin door, I thought I was to get my first glimpse of China. Only, I didn't get a glimpse. I got a big view of a black nothing. All the lights on the runways that we had seen from the air had been turned off. It seemed all the lights had been turned off everywhere. Maybe the Chinese were expecting an attack right after we landed. I finally realized that the cabin door faced away from the terminal building. My view was toward the total blackness of empty runways and airport fields. It was unnerving, to say the least..

We walked down the steps and around the end of the plane. We were all bunched together in-between some forms walking alongside. The Pakistanis were chattering away as if it was a big joke; the Japanese guys had finally turned silent. Maybe they were as scared as I was. I think a couple of the escorts, who were just dark shadows, had guns. I thought I saw the silhouette of some rifle barrels against the sky, but I couldn't be sure. In the cold and the darkness, it was difficult to separate imagination from reality. I was scared silly!

The big dark shadow of the terminal building with grey windows, just like a penitentiary, loomed in front of us. The grey lights inside the building did nothing but outline the huge windows and height of the building. We were marched into the building through a small door at ground level. There were some noises from our escorts; they seemed to point to a flight of stairs. They prodded us up the stairs into a huge room. Our Pakistani companions finally turned as silent as the Japanese. I think everyone was scared at this point.

Inside the terminal, the dim lights magnified the size of the waiting room which looked like a football field. Beyond the windows nothing existed. The waiting room was totally empty. A long, low, bookrack was in the center of the room. The bookrack, from a distance, was covered in red paint. Closer, we saw that it was filled with rows and rows of little red books. Closer still, we could see that each red book was entitled, if the English one was a guide, "Chairman Mao's Sayings." in various languages. My guess is that there were more than 120 languages there. I took a couple as a souvenir. Twenty feet of Chairman Mao's Sayings, WOW!

No one could leave the waiting room. There were guards with guns at each of the doors. I didn't have any doubts this time. I know a rifle when I see it. The guards looked like they had slept in their uniforms and just got out of bed. The guns made the difference. I really hadn't wanted to leave the room anyway. Even though there were a couple of moments when I thought I had to use a bathroom, possibly out of stress, my mind rejected those thoughts instantly. We just sat there and froze. No one asked us any questions; no one asked for our passports, no one said one word to us. A PA system sprang to life and broken

English suggested (?) that we go to Gate A to get on the plane to Beijing. To my ear it sounded more like a command than a suggestion. We re-boarded the plane. To this day, no one has given me any idea of the reason for stopping in what we thought was Shanghai.

The landing at Beijing was just like the one in Shanghai. A sprinkling of lights, coupled with the outlined runway was a duplicate of the Shanghai arrival. Then, as in Shanghai, we walked in total darkness down the boarding ramp from the plane. The wind ripped around us as we walked to the terminal building. It was cold, the kind of cold that goes right through you.

When we got to the door to the terminal, there was a Chinese man along with a little rotund Chinese woman waiting for us. Mr. Wu, whom John had met several months ago, was dressed in a very long blue overcoat. The thick coat looked like it could also keep a horse warm. The same color hat was pulled down close to his ears but it was still recognizable as a Mao hat. Ms. Ma, as she introduced herself, was his translator. She was dressed in the same way, but she had a scarf wrapped around her head and ears. John and I, being macho Americans, were dressed for the southern latitudes. Ken and Mary had a little more sense, they had on overcoats.

Through the translator, Mr. Wu welcomed us to China and asked us how our journey had been. He spoke through clenched teeth, perhaps to keep out the cold.

John replied, "Fine. How have you been, Mr. Wu?"

Ms. Ma translated that, but it seems to take a lot longer than John's remark. I think her words were stuck together by the cold.

Mr. Wu asked, "Do you have a lot of luggage?"

"Quite a bit."

"Oh"

After that, silence descended. Mary kept her Chinese up to date by trying to carry on a conversation with them, but it didn't seem to be very deep. We couldn't get into the normal chitchat of an arrival. I think that the intense cold froze up everyone's vocal chords. We all waited for the baggage to be unloaded from the airplane, hopping from one foot to the other. No one wanted to take his hands out of his pockets, or waste any heated air on conversation. They pulled the baggage cart right into the room where we were waiting. Everything was placed in a pile in the center of the room. Even though there were only eight passengers on the flight from Tokyo, the amount of luggage on those carts suggested that all passengers were moving their homes to Beijing. We had to drag many suitcases from the pile to find ours.

We had brought many cases of books and manuals supporting our proposal. That made for lots of baggage. Mr. Wu said something in Chinese to any who could understand. Later, Mary told us he said "They must be staying here for a year". Only she could understand. We finally located all of ours. Then we tried to find something to load it all onto. Even after Mr. Wu went looking for a baggage wagon, we could find nothing. So, we had to lug it all out to the street. Although it was a big pain, it was better than standing still trying to make conversation while we were freezing. The questions going through my head as we waited and froze remained unanswered. Why would the Chinese build a big terminal like this? Why don't they heat it a little? Why don't they provide any baggage carts or something for the passengers?

We followed Mr. Wu through a little passageway between some high desks. A little man looked at our passports and then stamped them. Mr. Wu said something to him that sounded curt and commanding, but who knows? My impression was that the little man was there to do as he was told. I have been though many Immigration Counters around the world. Everywhere else the immigration guards are intent on keeping unwanted visitors out of their country. They compare the passport picture with the face in front of them even though all westerners look alike, just like all Chinese look alike to the westerners. They check the date on their stamp. This guard didn't seem to care if we came or went, just do it quickly. He had his hands in his pockets as we came up to him and quickly put them back when he was done. Maybe he couldn't read English, but he could look for the requisite Chinese visa and whack it a couple of times. That was another thing. Anywhere else, one whack should have done it. The passport had arrived in China, "Whack". Nevertheless, here it was two whacks, two stamps. I never did figure that one out, not that it made any difference in the general scheme of things.

Outside on the street, Mr. Wu helped us load all our stuff into two cars. It took a couple of trips to get it all. Of course, our bags and boxes didn't fit into the trunks, so the front seat next to the driver had to be utilized. There was luggage left over. As a last resort, the entire luggage pile was put into one of the cars while we had to get into the other one. Even at that, it was a squeeze with three of us and two of them. This gave Mary some more opportunities to practice her Chinese close up. We started off.

We saw nothing. We traveled down a street that was not a highway, but rather a country road. I think it was lined on each side by a row of tall trees. In the darkness it was hard to make out anything alongside the street. When the driver came to an intersection, he slowed a little, but kept right on through. I didn't think that he expected any cross traffic. After a while we came to a lighted portion of the street. We really slowed down. People were sitting on the ground on either side of the road reading newspapers under the streetlights. If it was a particularly big streetlight, there were a lot of people; smaller lights meant fewer people. Behind the people was total darkness. Then we came to a very wide street with many streetlights, but no people.

I asked Mr. Wu, "Where were all the people? Actually, I turned to Ms. Ma and asked her to ask him. With all the people stuffed into the car, it was actually warm.

Ms. Ma translated, "We are in the city now. This is Beijing."

"But there were many people under the street lights a little while back and there are none here." I was really curious.

Ms. Ma translated that under a cloudy breath of air.

"Back there we were in the country. The people are permitted to do that in the country. Here in the city, it is not permitted because of the traffic."

"City? It all looks the same to me."

Mr. Wu grunted to signify the end of the conversation.

I would have thought that a more accurate answer might have been that the people reading under those lights probably didn't have electricity or lights in their homes or apartments. However, an admission of a deficiency in the system was unacceptable. I learned that in Russia. I guess it was better to say the authorities allowed or not allowed the practice as the case might be.

We arrived at the Beijing Hotel. The car drove right up the ramp to the front door. There was an impressive young man in a uniform waiting for us. He didn't move a muscle. He just looked through us and waved us past into the lobby. And what a lobby it was. Marble floors and walls made it appear very cold and very, very large. In fact, it was very cold. Everyone was dressed like Mr. Wu and Ms. Ma even though we were indoors. Between the cold terminal at the airport and the cold lobby of the hotel, I was convinced that the Chinese had not yet adopted central heating, or any heating for that matter. Our footsteps echoed on the marble floor as we walked over to the registration desk

Registration was really simple. At the desk we showed our passports to a pleasant young lady in many layers of clothing. Mr. Wu said something to her and it was all over. The young lady gave Mr. Wu four room keys. Mr. Wu said something to Mary in Chinese then gave her a key and then gave each of us our keys. The whole process took about 30 seconds, or so it seemed.

There was a large map of the world facing the front entrance with a couple of potted plants on either side. The legend on the map was in Chinese characters, as were the names of the various countries. However, there was something very strange about that map. It was cockeyed. The United States, recognizable by its shape, was off on the right. It was almost off the map it was so far to the right. I thought, "Shouldn't the U.S. be in the center like it is at home?" All of China was dead center on the map! "They got it wrong." The reality was that they had it right, I had it wrong. I was in Beijing, China, not New York City. I resolved right then and there to keep my thinking a lot more flexible and a lot less judgmental... To reinforce the idea that their map was correct, I learned later that the two Chinese ideograph characters that make up the word for China literally translate into "Central Kingdom"

Finally, after a lot of goodnights and arrangements for the following morning, we went to our rooms. When we got off the elevator on the 9th floor, Ken and Mary went in one direction while John and I went in the other. I paid no attention at the time, but later who went where made a difference. I don't know what John or the others did (John probably took a bath, that was his thing) but I just fell into bed.

It wasn't daylight when I awoke. It was more like four in the morning. Jet lag had arrived! I got up out of bed, turned the light on and tried to read mind-numbing detective stories until daylight. I couldn't concentrate. I kept thinking about the trip from Tokyo, being in China and wondering what the next day would bring. Even though I had a lot of experience dealing with Socialist bureaucracies in Europe, and government bureaucracies in Japan, I had no inkling of what the Chinese bureaucracy would be like.

When I looked out of my window in the daylight, I could see the corner of the building across the street. The two sides of the building, at ground level, were covered with enclosed glass cases in which what looked to be pages of a newspaper were displayed. They had big print across the top and columns underneath. The cases ran about twenty feet along each side of the building. I saw people crowded in front of the cases reading what was inside. I figured that it must be a newspaper or something like that.

What was strange was that I never saw anyone appear to follow information from one page to the next. The people just stood in one place and never moved. Sometimes the crowd was several people deep. Maybe that meant that something important had happened. I never did find out. Another thing, I never saw anyone carrying a newspaper under his arm either.

There were monumental things going on. Of course, I didn't know it! One of the few ways that the people received any authentic information (if there was such a thing there!) was from those signboards and from the posters that popped up each day on the walls. We watched, but did not see, a government in turmoil as Chairman Mao's widow and several of her followers were making immense political waves. I learned later that one poster accused her of nagging Chairman Mao to death! She wanted to succeed to her husband's role; the more moderate party leaders wanted her dead. Apparently the newspapers told the government's story; the posters told the people's story. . Or, maybe it was the other way around!

John had told me the night before that he was going to go for a run in the morning so I had to wait until 8:30 to meet everyone for breakfast. John was a big runner in those days. The one time that I went with him he wore a bright red running suit. I suppose he wore his bright red running suit that morning as well. By the time he had covered the distance to Tienamin Square, he had developed quite a large entourage. He never figured out whether it was the running white foreigner, or the bright red costume, but he never failed to gather a group of kids running with him for a little while every morning. Since he started early in the morning, his running never interfered with our breakfast schedule. It didn't interfere that morning either. I was looking forward to my first breakfast in China. We all met in the lobby. Mary arrived first, Ken a little later and finally John came in so we could sit down. We all filed into the dining room.

And what a dining room! It was the size of a couple of gymnasiums at home and just as high. The room was filled with tables for four; all covered in white tablecloths, with impeccable place settings. If the china and the tableware had glittered, it would have looked like a royal dining room. But there was no glitter; it was all dull looking. If you remember pictures of parades for Communist holidays, they all showed thousands of soldiers lined up and marching as if they were one. The lines were straight; every motion was duplicated as far as you could see. The dining room looked like that. The tables, the silverware, the glasses were all lined up like the soldiers in the pictures. The inference was that everybody and everything marched straight and true to the Communist line! The windows in the room were sky high and ran down the length of the room. Each window had long white curtains drawn back to the sides. They had been white at one time. That morning they appeared a little gray, in fact, every morning thereafter they appeared a little gray.

A couple of tables were occupied. The room was so large that the people at a table at the far end appeared to be smaller than the ones close up. There was no one at the door to tell us where to sit. We moved to a table almost in the center of the room. As soon as we sat down a waiter in a white jacket came over to give us the menu. The menu covers were only slightly soiled, but in the excitement of the moment, it didn't matter. Mary said something to the waiter that sounded like "Wu Ping Lao Shan". He left instantly. I asked her what she had said. She told me that she had ordered some water.

"Ordered Water?" Why would you have to "order" water? Since I was an experienced foreign traveler, I only thought that; I didn't say a word. You have to go with the flow. "Don't act like an American" I said to myself. Take things as they come. Don't demand an explanation for every little thing. So what if you have to order water? What difference could it make? Go ahead and order water! I went back to my menu.

As expected, everything was written in Chinese. Why should I expect anything else? After all, we were in the premier international hotel in the capital city in the Chinese Communist world. So I asked Mary where the eggs and coffee were on the menu. She said there weren't any; we had the Chinese menu, not the Western menu. Of course, she was right; any dope could have figured that one out. She said that she would get the Western menu for me as soon as the waiter returned with the water. He did and she did. The waiter placed five little green bottles on the table and removed their caps. The water had arrived.

I found the scrambled eggs and coffee on the Western menu. This menu had the English language description followed by the Chinese characters. I told the waiter what I wanted. He just stood there and looked at me. He had a pad and pencil in his hand, but they didn't move. I repeated my order. He still didn't move. Mary put her hand on my arm and said something to the waiter in Chinese. As she spoke, his hand with the pencil moved. She turned back to me and told me that she ordered the eggs and coffee. Then she ordered John's breakfast as well.

"Am I going to have you do that at every meal? I asked her.

"No. You could have pointed to the line on the menu and he would have read the Chinese."

I had just received another lesson in foreign diplomacy. Never assume that someone speaks or understands English simply because he is trying to serve you! A subsidiary lesson was to be patient and think of several ways to convey your message.

We spoke of the impending meeting with the Chinese. John was going to lead the way in the meeting since he had been with Mr. Wu the previous November. Meanwhile, our breakfast arrived. The conversation petered out while we ate.

The meal was ok. The eggs smelled of the fish meal that they fed the chickens. That was fine; I was hungry after the long flight. The coffee was quite another thing. It was served black. I had to ask Mary to see if they had some milk or cream for the coffee. She looked at me like I was nuts. After a while the waiter brought a glass of white fluid. It was reconstituted milk, that thin stuff. I put some in the coffee until the color appeared right and added some sugar. I tasted it. I added some more sugar and milk. I had to give up after a couple more tastes and adjustments. I asked Mary if it was real coffee. She said she didn't know. I knew. It wasn't coffee. It was something else masquerading as coffee. I vowed then and there that I would bring for-real coffee with me the next time I came to China.

We finished our breakfast. Everyone went back to his/her room to clean up and get ready for our first session with the Chinese. We met back down in the lobby and went out front to get a taxi. Ken and Mary knew where we had to go. We had to use two taxis because we all couldn't fit into one with all the stuff we had brought with us. The taxis all looked alike. They were little things, Japanese made, I think. All had brown slip covered seats with room for two in the back. Mary told our driver where to go. We drove down the main street, past Tienamin Square and then turned off into smaller streets.

It was a brisk, bright day. We drove down crowded streets, but they weren't crowed with automobiles. The streets, from the buildings on one side to the buildings on the other, were crowded with people. People were walking; people were bicycling. It was just one big mass of people. Our driver seemed to keep his hand on the horn to make sure that he didn't hit anyone, particularly those on bicycles. On the other hand, maybe he was honking just to tell everyone that he was there and driving these foreigners, the only ones who could afford a taxi. But the noise from all the honking taxis was deafening!

On many street corners, I saw pallets loaded with Chinese cabbage, many 8' tall it seemed. At first I didn't recognize the cabbage, but after two or three corners I could clearly see the cabbages like the ones in our supermarkets, the tall straight ones not the round squat ones. Right next to the pallets of cabbage were sprawls of coal. These piles were unkempt compared to the neatness of the stacks of cabbage. At one pile I saw a woman fill a little pail with lumps of coal and carry it away.

I asked Mary what all of that was. She told me that she understood that the winter had been very bad and these stacks and piles were the government's way of distributing food and coal for heating and cooking. Each of the piles represented the surrounding communal or political unit; its members could take what they needed from the stacks and piles. I asked what would happen if someone who was not a member of that unit took something. Mary didn't know.

We turned a corner onto a street that had neither people nor bicycles. Apparently we had arrived at some sort of government district where people did not live. Identical looking buildings were lined up on both sides of the street. Our meeting was held in one of those buildings. Mary called the building "Er Li Go" whatever that means. It might have been the name of the building, or it might have been the name of the street. The building had no name on it, nor were there any street signs. I guess one just knew where it was.

The building was your standard Russian concrete style nondescript building made with government issued cookie cutters. They were just like the apartment blocks the Russians like to build. If I hadn't been taken there, I wouldn't have found it. Nor would I have ever been able to get back to it by myself. Thank God for Mary! Later on, once we were able to mimic the words "Er Li Go", we were always able to get there okay. Unfortunately, "Er Li Go" was the only Chinese words I knew, so it was the only place I could go! It was much easier if we had a translator with us. We would be in big trouble if our meetings were ever held somewhere else.

On to our first big meeting; not one of us understood that we were playing roles in the big, new Chinese industrial revolution that Deng Tsao Ping had designed. We were the pawns in a monstrous chess game that he invented.

Chapter 5 - First Meeting with the Chinese

London Times Mar 28, 1977
"BAN ON BEETHOVEN LIFTED"

The other players in Mr. Deng's industrial revolution were already on stage. Mr. Wu and Ms Ma were waiting for us in the lobby of the former apartment house (early Russian concrete ugly style). They were stage right. We walked in from the street. We were stage left.

In America, the lobby of a building or a company is meant to impress the visitor. It's your first view of a new place, a new company. It's grand; it's big, it's sumptuous! As they say, "First impressions last the longest." It was certainly true in this instance.

This lobby wasn't too big, just big enough to hold a little desk and chair. The chair was empty. This lobby was cold grey concrete that had been painted at one time or another. This lobby wasn't a lobby; it was just a place where the stairs started or the halls came together. I thought this was another Communist precept borrowed from capitalism; form follows function. Here it's been expanded into "Who needs form if you already have function?"

The meeting room was on the second floor. We walked up a set of concrete stairs in a dark hallway. I thought to myself that they must have just taken the steels bars out of the windows

85

and doors, leaving the concrete. This building had to have been built to Russian, i.e., Communist proletarian, standards. I would have thought that traditional Chinese would have been a lot more ornate with a lot of curlicues all over the place. Even if it was grey concrete, it would be decorated with curlicues. Concrete wasn't a Chinese building material anyway. The Summer Palace, outside of Beijing, had buildings made with wood, and even a marble boat, but never concrete. This building reminded me of the apartment blocks in Moscow, made by the same massive cookie cutter using concrete instead of baking dough. The sameness, the dullness, of everything was depressing.

At the top, we turned right and walked down a half-lit hallway parallel to the front of the building. Our room was just down the hall. The room was long and narrow, just big enough for an oblong table with chairs down each side. The room was about 15 feet by 25 feet; there was a window at the end. The table was covered with a green felt cloth, a very large thermos and some cups were on a side table. It was all very austere and coldly egalitarian. Even these furnishings felt Russian Communist. If they were real Chinese wouldn't they have a big round table with a beautiful big tea pot in the middle and gorgeous little matching Chinese tea cups in front of each place? In a crazy way, I felt at home. I had spent years in Moscow at just such a table!

As the four of us entered our meeting room, four men rose to greet us. They were dressed alike except for the scarves around their necks. Each wore a sweater under his Mao jacket. We could see it peeking out of the collars of each jacket. All of their jackets, except one, looked like they had been washed many, many times. The other one looked brand new. Later on, I learned that the gentleman with the new jacket was Big Mu, the newest member of their team. The sameness of the clothing (I often wondered, but never found out, whether their underwear was the same, too) kind of matched the sameness of the room, the building and, in fact, of all Communism.

Many months later I discovered that these jackets were mass produced in what I called the "Peoples Clothing Factory Number 44" which must have meant that there were 43 others just like it. Much, much later, I also discovered that there were other Mao jackets that were hand tailored in a variety of hand woven cloths. Although they looked the same from a distance, that's where the similarity ended. "Ah Ha", I thought, there are degrees of sameness. Dress followed position. Or, perhaps position followed dress. I knew enough about Communist etiquette to avoid commenting. So much for sameness!

All the Americans, Ken, Mary, John and I had on our negotiating costumes. Ken was dressed in his Wall Street best, complete with beautiful overcoat and scarf. Mary was bundled up in a stylish coat with fur trimmings that outlined her face. John was in period L.L.Bean, complete with lumberman's shoes just like Paul Bunyan. He looked like he belonged on the cover of their catalogue. I came right off the cover of Abercrombie and Fitch (the old one!). I had on my beige safari jacket with twenty two pockets, each big enough to hold a clip of very large bore rifle ammunition used to shoot elephants. Underneath I had a couple of sweaters. I always wore that jacket when I went to meetings in Communist Soviet Union. For tradition's sake I continued wearing it in Communist China. To top it off, I had my Nordic fur hat on; it was made of real silver fox fur. The impact of the difference in clothing was readily apparent. Affluence oozed from every stitch we wore; their austerity leaped from the faded Mao jackets they wore. We were all ready to go!

It was very cold in the room. February in Beijing is just like in Alaska. There was no heat. There were no radiators. There was no brazier with hot coals in it. There was no pottery stove under the table like in Japan. Where was all that coal we saw piled up on the street corners on our way here? Maybe the coal was just for the Chinese, they didn't want to waste any of it on foreign barbarians. On the other hand, since it was soft coal, burning it in here would eventually kill us. That's it! They were doing us a favor by not burning soft coal in the meeting room "Comrades, Comes the Revolution, We will all freeze together!" kept running through my mind. We kept our coats and hats on. My big fur hat from Russia (via Harrods in London) dominated our side of the room. Everyone sat down. Ms Ma and the man at the end of the table filled the cups with steaming tea. The heat looked wonderful to me. Everyone got a cup of hot tea. The six Chinese were on one side of the table, the four of us on the other.

Mr. Wu was seated dead center. He began speaking, with Ms Ma translating. He opened the meeting by extending his greetings to all of us. Although it sounded like a script, I admit his tone and body language conveyed his sincerity, at least to me. My years in meetings with people speaking in another language taught me to watch eye balls, facial expressions and body movements. They all told me Wu was sincere in his greetings. I felt they were not pro forma greetings; he was really glad we were starting. He then introduced Mr. Xu Bing Xian (Mr. Shu), Mu Rei Lin (Mr. Mu), Mr. Mu Chen Zeng (Big Mu) and Mr. Chen So Min (Chen) to us. That's all, just their names. John recognized Mr. Shu, Mr. Mu and Chen from the November seminar. His recognition disproved the Western notion all Chinese looked alike. Big Mu was much younger than the others and he wore the newest Mao jacket. We were told Chen was a translator; he was there to help Ms Ma with the technical material.

John responded by introducing me since this was my first visit. For some unknown reason, John mentioned that Ken and Mary were from our Chase bank advisors (Chase Pacific Trade Advisors) and were there to help us. Mr. Wu knew them; they had been with John the previous November. John told them that we were happy to be in China. Sure enough, during a break later that day, Mr Wu, with Ms Ma at his side, sidled up to John and asked him if Chase owned IBM. John said, "No, but why do you ask?"

In the beginning we were never sure questions were really questions; sometimes, at least in the West, questions are meant to humiliate the recipient; sometimes to make a little joke. In Wu's case, we became sure very quickly. His questions were intended to elicit information and nothing more.

"We try to understand all of our suppliers as best we can. We have never had a bank along with a supplier." He had a little smile on his lips; maybe he was zinging us.

John went into a long explanation of what a consultant is and does. Mr. Wu said "OH" a couple of times, but John was certain that he still thought that Chase owned IBM and that was the reason they were there. We just had our first lesson in making gratuitous remarks that you pay for later on! Had he not mentioned they were with Chase bank, this whole thing wouldn't have come up. Or, Mr Wu was zinging us in his Chinese way.

"We have a proposal for the purchase of an IBM computer system. This document is not meant to be the final proposal. It is a starting point for our technical discussions."

Mr Wu beamed. Either he understood what John was saying or John was saying something that he agreed with. That was odd. How could he agree with something he had no idea about? Insofar as we knew, he had never seen a computer proposal until this day!

On the other hand, a computer was a machine to him. All machines were treated equally; they had size and specification; they did something. Keeping things simple became a hallmark of our discussions.

"When we complete these discussions we will have a better idea of what type and size of computer would be required for your work. Then we will prepare our final contract proposal for your consideration."

John turned to me and I pulled out the proposal that we had prepared and gave it to him.

He handed it to Mr Wu.

Wu, without looking at it, handed it to Chen.

"Thank you for your efforts. Mr Chen will translate it into Chinese for us. Then our side will study it." While he was talking, I thought "that proposal was over 60 single spaced pages, how long it will take to translate it?"

Then he said, "Of course you realize that the People's Republic of China must use a Chinese language contract. For the purpose of <u>these</u> discussions, we will translate your document, but in the future the documents have to be in Chinese."

I recognized that remark from my Russian days. I had learned the hard way that these demands were always made; even though the demander knew there was no way we would accept. All international documents are in an internationally accepted language, Chinese was not one of them. I spoke up.

"Mr. Wu, we appreciate your requirements. We thank you for telling us at the beginning of our discussions. However, I am sure that you realize that it will be impossible for us to continue these talks on that basis. We are simply not equipped to conduct our business in Chinese. Apparently you understood that since you have brought several translators to the table."

As the translation proceeded through my response, the other people looked at one another. Apparently, some thought I had committed the insult of the century; I had objected to a routine statement of fact from one of the participants. After all, we were the guests in a Chinese country and should abide by their requirements. The Chinese entourage thought I was a crazy foreigner raising such an objection; the Americans thought I was crazy for calling a halt to a meeting just begun.

Then, as a group, their heads swiveled around to Mr. Wu. Mr Wu broke out into a big smile.

"No, no, he said. We can continue these meetings as we planned."

The Chinese group visibly relaxed in their chairs. We hadn't learned yet to watch Mr. Mu or Big Mu carefully when contentious statements were expressed. Mr. Mu's smile disappeared, he blinked and when Mr. Wu made his statement, the smile re-appeared and the eyes glistened. Big Mu's body stiffened visibly at my words, and then slumped when Mr. Wu responded. Physically, he was almost a rag doll with puppet strings attached. What was going on in his mind was mirrored in his body attitude.

"What about the Chinese documents?" I wasn't going to let him off the hook so easily. He brought the subject up, he had to bury it. I looked right into his eyeballs.

"I understand your position. We'll come back to this subject later." He looked right back. He was not cowed.

Ken was apoplectic. He started to say something, but the repartee with Mr Wu was so rapid he didn't get a chance. He began to get up, but John motioned him down. I must have done something consultants don't do. Apparently the consultant textbook for Chinese-Western behavior did not permit disagreement and calling a bluff this early in the game. Maybe he thought that every Chinese request should receive a positive response. Maybe he thought it impolite to refuse. I don't know.

Score one for the visitors. Later on, after several more instances of this scenario, we realized that "coming back to this subject later" were code words that meant, "Forget it". We never came back to a subject that had ended this way. It was Mr Wu''s way of closing a subject while retaining his theoretical right to return to it. We were reminded of this whole series of "gives and takes" a couple of months later when someone else told us that we had to give in on a particular argument because "we have agreed with you 32 times already and you only have agreed with us 12 times." Someone was keeping score each time the parties backed off from a position. The Chinese must believe that a fair and equitable negotiation consisted of an equal number of gives and takes and never mind the substance. In order to stay ahead in that score keeping, they would throw up a whole lot of specious arguments that they would later back off from.

Consider another side issue here. Our consultant for these Chinese negotiations had a completely different take on the interplay between Mr. Wu and me. He understood the Chinese; he had dealt with the Chinese before, I had not. I had been in many sales negotiations with Socialist governments before, maybe this was his first shot at Socialist business practices. I looked at John and we both nodded to each other.

Mr Wu continued. "In my opinion, it would be best if we were to discuss the technical requirements first. This is the normal way business is conducted here. After we agree on those requirements, as your side just mentioned, we will discuss the commercial terms and conditions. When we reach agreement on those, we will discuss the price." He smiled again as he spoke of the price.

The other Chinese were beaming. Mr. Shu was enigmatic but there was a shadow of a smile in the corners of his mouth. I couldn't tell what he was thinking. Mr. Mu had the smile on his lips, his hands on the table didn't move. His eyes told it all; this was the moment he had been waiting for. Big Mu was ecstatic; his smile went from one ear to the other.

In practical terms, Mr Wu was telling us we would decide exactly and in great detail, what we were going to sell, what he was going to buy on what terms and conditions and then come back to argue over the specific price we would contract for. In other words, if we were to discount our offer we had no chance whatsoever to discount the contents of that offer. In the IBM world I was used to product meant price and price meant product; they moved in concert, not separately. Our position may be arrogant, but it was a core business practice. In Mr Wu's world, product content and price were separate, each moving in any direction desired.

Now it was my turn to speak.

"Mr Wu, generally, our side has no objection to that sequence of events. However, there is no way that we can agree on technical contents, or even terms and conditions until we agree on the price."

Again, Ken almost came out of his chair. This time he turned to John and, in English, said "Wait a minute, we don't mean that!" You could have heard him in the next room.

John said to him in an undertone, "Sit down Ken, you're interrupting"

The translator heard all and was busy translating. All the Chinese were looking at Ken. They were all waiting for the next salvo.

Ken sat down.

The Chinese looked at one another. It was a bit unusual to watch the people on the other side of the table so obviously arguing among themselves. The language spoken makes no difference. I think Mr. Shu was embarrassed for us, his eyes were downcast; he was looking at the table. Mr. Mu was enjoying the spectacle immensely. He was positively beaming. Big Mu just sat there with wide eyes and his bottom jaw drooping just a little.

I continued. "Any change in the technical content immediately changes the price; any modification of our standard international terms and conditions also modifies the price. So, we would be happy to sequence our discussions as you require with the understanding that even though we may agree to something today, it may be modified when we discuss price later as you suggest." For me, this was a statement of an IBM fact that I had repeated many times.

Mr Wu didn't like that one bit. As he listened to Ms Ma translating, he turned to the other people, then turned back to glare at me. Big Mu shriveled up in his chair. Mr. Mu's smile disappeared. Mr. Shu didn't even blink. For them, this was like being seated in the first row of the hospital operating theater watching their favorite relative being cut up.

With Ms Ma's translation trailing him by one second, he slowly explained.

"We want to fix the technical content and then open price discussions. The reason we want to do it in this way is because the people who were going to use the computer system must participate fully in those discussions. Then they would know exactly what equipment and services they were contracting for. When the users understand that we could move on to commercial subjects which only I would be directly involved in."

A little side note here. Under their system as I understood it, Mr. Wu's explanation was theoretically correct. Since Techimport's function and total responsibility was commercial negotiation and since the users were the only people who knew what they wanted, a nice clear, clean division of responsibility between THEM was required. However, in the real capitalistic world outside of Communism, the technical specifications had a direct and immediate effect on price, and in that sense were not as separate as the Chinese might like. Besides, we gave them a priced proposal at the beginning of this meeting. They were starting out ahead of the game.

John was busy writing down everything Wu was saying. When Ms Ma stopped for a moment to take a breath, John leaned over to me to whisper "Wu's making that speech to them, not us." When Mr. Wu stopped, I suggested we take a break.

"Shu she ba", I said in Chinese. That exhausted my vocabulary. I learned how to say "Let's Take a Break" in every language that I worked with. I can say it in Japanese, in Russian and I had recently learned how to say it in Chinese. My negotiation mentor once told me that when the going got tough and touchy, "Lets Take a Break!" was always a solution.

Back in the United States, John and I had agreed on a couple of rules of the road, so to speak. We had agreed that I would negotiate; he would be the record keeper. This was essential to avoid complete chaos with two voices claiming to speak for our side. Following other rules I had learned in Russia, the person who is the negotiator sits in the middle, the translator to his left, others to his right. This way, everyone in the room knows who's who. In one-on-one meetings it is a lot simpler; when there are groups on both sides of the table some sort of protocol must operate. We both understood that there could be only one voice on each side of the table.

The Chinese followed these same rules. The record keeper was also important. As discussions went on and on, it was impossible to keep track of who said what, or agreed with what. More than once, the Chinese recollection of what had been said differed sharply with what had been written! That's where the record keeper came in. John was ours, Ms Ma was theirs. John and I had established some other ground rules to preserve our sanity. Among those were, "never interrupt", "never contradict", "never lose your cool". Nevertheless, the most important point was that I was the negotiator and John was the boss. Ken had violated a bunch of these rules. However, I must admit that he was not aware of John's agreement with me.

John, Ken, and I walked down the hall together. Ken wanted to know why we just didn't agree to what Mr Wu wanted and move on. He said that's what he would do and that's what he would suggest. I tried to explain to him that if we agree up front to Wu's scheme we will have lots of trouble when he asks for a discount. By that time we would have already agreed to the product content under Wu's agenda. No matter what we said, he would constantly remind us that we had previously agreed to some product point before; there was no reason to repeat it.

We would have given up any chance to modify the product content so that we could re price our offer. In my opinion, Wu was making this long involved speech not so much for us, as for the other people at the table. I agreed with John on that issue. Wu knew that nothing is fixed until the price is fixed. Wu had negotiated with foreign companies before. His attempt to have us agree in advance to separate price from the whole package was untenable. Ken couldn't see it that way. He was waving his arms all over the place.

"We can change the price any time we want", he said. He counted off one finger.

"That's true, but you don't want to lose face in the process and prove to them our words are not credible. We should set the rules up front, not as we go." Ken was getting on my nerves and my tone showed it. I was having enough trouble staying focused <u>across</u> the table; I couldn't simultaneously focus <u>down my side</u> of the table..

"I don't agree. We shouldn't put stumbling blocks in place when we don't have to." He counted off a second finger. He raised his voice a notch. I don't think he liked being argued with.

"Yes, you do when you are establishing the negotiating rules."

"Two." Again, he was counting with his fingers. "These are just preliminary talks. We can change anything" He was getting more agitated.

"They're only preliminary by the clock. I don't want any of these "little" things to come up down the line." I thought to myself that perhaps Ken had never been a negotiator. It's one thing to negotiate face-to-face; and quite another to be an advisor to the negotiator. His line was diametrically opposed to ours; we had a significant difference of opinion on how to conduct our negotiations.

Again, the Ken's China consultant manual must preach "agree with everything the Chinese want". After all, there are a billion people here; a new unprecedented market. We must look at the bigger picture, etc., etc.

Mr. Wu could hear this exchange. Ken's finger counting and emphatic statements along with my equally emphatic responses must have impressed him. We probably convinced him that Chase Bank did indeed own IBM. I leaned over and whispered to John and Ken, "We gotta have some ground rules right up front. If we start being a patsy now, we will always be a patsy!" John agreed; I prevailed. We went back into the meeting.

Mr Wu began where he left off. After a few sentences, he said, "In the interest of getting our talks moving, we will put this issue aside for later discussion." He was looking directly at me when he said this. Even though he was speaking in Chinese, I felt we had a tiny victory as I stared right back at him. He knew that we understood he was going to ask for a discount in the price. He had accomplished his objective. We had accomplished ours. The other Chinese were happy that the talks would continue; Deng's revolution could continue. It was a win-win situation for all.

These two scenes were the first hints, even though we didn't recognize them, of what was to come. On this, and many later occasions, it would seem that we were negotiating a treaty between the governments of China and IBM rather than a simple contract to purchase a machine. You give us the money; we give you the machine! In retrospect, we had just agreed upon the agenda for our talks just like diplomats do for a treaty.

We adjourned for the day. We had to regroup after this first session and Mr Wu had to wait for our 60 page document to be translated. Chen told me later that he worked all night to translate it. A staff of women later duplicated it by hand for all the members of their delegation. We went back to the hotel.

John and I took a walk down to Tienamin Square to look around while Ken and Mary were off checking out the wall posters of that day. Wall posters were apparently torn off during the day but replaced every night. It was the battle of the wall posters in Beijing that month! At the time, wall posters were the accepted way of expressing agreement or disagreement with what was going on. One day, Madam Mao would be vilified; the next she was an angel. We got all the poster translations from Mary.

At that time, Chairman Mao he was still revered as the founder and designer of the Chinese State. Right smack in the middle of Tienamin Square the tomb for Chairman Mao was under construction and had a large fence around it. On later visits, we could measure that reverence by the amount of progress made in the construction of the tomb since our last visit. As the reverence waned, the construction slowed down. As it soared, the construction picked up. It took over two years to finish the Mausoleum and then it was only open for a little while afterwards. John and I were one of the few foreigners invited to visit with Chairman Mao in his new home when it finally opened. I told John that I thought that Lenin looked much better in his tomb than Mao did in his.

Other than that, the square was deserted except for some Chinese tourists having their picture taken against the backdrop of the Forbidden City entrance. During that year, we never saw Western tourists getting their pictures taken; there were none. Tienamin Square, like all the central show places in the Socialist world, was immense. It covered an area about the size of 12 football fields. Before construction on Chairman Mao's tomb began, if you tried to see someone from one end to the other, it was much too far. When it was filled with people, as it was on subsequent visits, it was awesome!

While we were walking around the streets that February, the political situation in Beijing was churning. Every morning our taxi would pass the walls where new posters appeared daily. Only Mary could read them, but the fact they were there and replaced daily hinted that things were happening all around us. Even though the local political scene was far from stable, the government was moving ahead with their opening moves. The China National Tourist Bureau, yet another "bureau", signed an agreement with a British tour organization to allow tour ships into Chinese territorial waters, the first in 50 years. Strange to say though, we never saw any Englishmen in the hotel dining room. I guess they must have stayed at their embassy or they ate at a different time. The British, as well as the Canadians, were far ahead of the U.S. in normalizing their relations with China. At that time, such politics was transparent to us. It is difficult now to understand how narrow and naïve our thinking was then. All we knew was selling the first computer to the

Peoples Republic of China! All the Chinese knew was getting their factory modernized and following Deng's modernization dictates! Neither of us realized that we were pawns in a much bigger game.

Ken and Mary were far more knowledgeable about international politics than we were but they had their foibles. Ken knew (how, we never found out) that the Chinese government had a large stock of antique foreign home furnishings in a warehouse somewhere in Beijing. All foreign embassies were shuttered in 1949. All the furnishings were confiscated when Chairman Mao slammed the doors of China shut in 1949.

He wanted to get his hands on some of it. He spoke to Mr Wu about gaining admission to the warehouse.

The local government in Beijing, where many of the foreigner's buildings were found, gathered up all the confiscated furnishings and put them in this warehouse for storage. Subsequently, they established a retail store just off the main street near the Beijing Hotel to sell them off. It was called the "Theater Store." The connection with the theater was simple. In addition to foreigner's buildings, the Communists had expropriated the Chinese Opera theaters running at that time. Entire stocks of costumes, and stage props were put into warehouses. If nothing else, the Communists were well organized and disciplined. There had been little looting in the foreign homes and the Chinese theaters; most everything went into the warehouses.

Back to the costumes. Taking a huge gamble, I decided to buy one of the costumes. I thought that it would look great on the wall of my living room, a beautiful conversation piece. In addition, I thought that my wife would like it. I selected one of the more garish ones, taking great care to haggle over the price with the clerk. I ended up paying $90.00 for the costume.

The clerk and I were in front of the costume rack near the back of the store. I told him, "I'll take that one" in English. I pointed to one of the costumes. He took it down and laid it on the counter. Had I not pointed, I would still be there; the clerk did not understand one word of English even though the only customers in the shop were foreigners.

I looked at my selection. I changed my mind. I pointed to the counter and shook my head back and forth. I pointed at another costume on the rack and shook my head up and down. He took it down and placed it on the counter. I examined it and decided I didn't want it. I shook my head left and right. He put the costume back on the rack. I pointed again. We did this routine a couple of more times until my neck began to hurt. The last costume got an up and down head movement. Each costume was as grand as any other. The sale was made.

The clerk stuffed it into a plastic sack as if it were a rag. I took it back to the hotel, hung it up properly in my closet. I often wondered what the room boy thought when he saw that costume in my closet. I carefully packed it into my suitcase when I left China to go home. At home, my wife agreed was very pleased. But, before we hung it on the wall, she took it to an antique show to price it. As it happened, someone at the show offered my wife more than ten times what I had paid. Profit triumphed over principles and wall hangings. Anyway, when I went back to China, I could get others.

By the way, Ken did get to the warehouse. I wasn't with him, but John told me that he bought up a storm. I wonder if he still has any of the antiques that he purchased that day.

The next morning, after a bout with breakfast, the meeting began right on time. Some of the Chinese looked like they hadn't had much sleep but they were all ready to go.

"I guess the first place to start is with the size of the computer. If someone could describe what the computer is going to be used for, we could match the size of the machine to those requirements".

Mr. Wu answered, "Mr. Mu will answer." I thought I detected the beginnings of a script here with Mr Wu the stage director. Mr. Mu quit smiling, he was going center stage.

Mr. Mu started to speak in Chinese. He had a little notebook open on the table in front of him. He glanced down at it before speaking. As he spoke, Mr. Chen moved over to translate for him. He had to be on Mr. Mu's left; protocol demanded it.

"We need a very large computer that can handle all our engineering work as well as manage our factory." Mu said. He said that quite proudly; I was sure he was reading it in that little book of his. The word "manage" got our attention. Neither John nor I had heard the word "manage" or any derivative thereof used by the Chinese. We heard "ordered", or "told me" or "commanded", but never "manage." "Manage" may have democratic overtones or something; we were sensitive to these little nuances.

"Could you tell us how much engineering work? Like how many engineering drawings, how many products, how many product parts, things like that?" We needed some specificity. I said it very pleasantly. John was waiting; pen poised to get the first real information we had.

"The computer should be able to handle ALL our engineering calculations." He countered. He began to smile; he looked at Mr. Wu to see if he was on the right track. Wu ignored him. He was on his own.

"Could you put a range on the number of engineers who would be using the system?" We still wanted some specificity; it was impossible to get the right shoe if you didn't know the size.

"All of the engineers would be using the system." Mr. Mu came right back at me. No smiles now; no sparkle in his eye. He glanced over to Mr. Shu but he got no help there.

He couldn't ask Big Mu because Big Mu had just joined the factory a few weeks before. He looked at Mr. Wu; nothing there either. His eyes returned to his little notebook. I began to wonder if there was anything at all in that notebook.

"And how many would that be?"

"All of them." It became very obvious that Mr. Mu was very adept at not answering specific questions. I wondered if somewhere in his background he had been forced to answer questions. He was literally answering every question without telling us anything.

We tried a different tack. "How many employees work at your plant?"

"Many."

"How many?'

"Enough to complete all our work." We were going in rapidly decreasing circles at ever increasing speeds. Mr. Mu was not going to give us any information of value. He knew what he was doing. He wasn't smiling; he was squeezing his little notebook so hard his fingers were white.

I turned to Mr. Wu. "It will be difficult to specify the size of the computer if we don't know the size of the work load. Is it possible to get some idea of that work load?"

Mr. Wu said, "Let's take a break." Wu knew what we were getting at. We hoped that he would read the riot act to Mr. Mu during the break so that we could get some definitive information. Maybe this predilection to secrecy could be sidetracked; we hoped so.

While they were out of the room, we commiserated with ourselves. If we didn't get something on which we could base the size of the system, we'll have to invent it. If we invent it, we have to defend it by ourselves in Washington when we try to get our export license. There was no way we could tell the Chinese that; Mr. Wu would erupt if we mentioned governments, licenses and the like. I told John that I felt like they thought we were from the CIA. Maybe we ought to tell them that. He didn't crack a smile. These questions from a vendor, although normal in the U.S., were verboten in this society.

Mr Wu led hi team back into the room. We began again. This time, all the Shenyang people were smiling, even Mr. Shu.

Apparently whatever worried them about specific answers had been allayed during the break.

Mu began. "There are approximately 3000 workers at our factory. We make heavy duty machinery. Each piece separately designed." I looked at John; he looked at me and winked. We had a breakthrough of some kind.

"How many different pieces are made in a year?" I asked.

"Right now, about 50." he answered. Now his eyes were twinkling again. He was enjoying this.

"Approximately how many parts are in one product?" I asked.

"We don't know exactly." This time, I believed him. But we still needed some specificity.

"Just a guess then."

Mu turned to his companions and consulted with them. The chief talker was Mr. Shu. He did some calculations in his little notebook and said something to Mu. Big Mu made some notes in his little notebook.

Mu turned back to us and said, "About fifteen hundred." His eyes were actually sparkling.

Now we had something to go on. Mentally, we went through the calculations. It was too much. Using our rule of thumb these numbers called for a large scale computer.

I turned to Mr. Wu, "Can we take a break now?" This morning, our first with real facts and numbers, was turning out to be a series of breaks with intervening questions. He agreed. John and I did some calculations. Our questions had been aimed at a determination of the size of the data file that would be required. If we could estimate the data file size, we could factor that information into the speed and size of the processor necessary to handle it.

During one of the breaks, Wu, with Ms Ma right behind, came up to John. After a little chitchat, he again asked John if Chase bank owned IBM. He said that from the conversations, he thought that Ken was telling John what to do. John assured Wu that was not true; Ken was an advisor. Whether Wu was truly confused, or whether he was pulling John's leg, who knows? I'd vote for leg pulling.

This conversation became the pattern for the next couple of weeks. Although we could have prepared a proposal for the largest exportable computer system and be done with it, it was not the IBM culture to be so didactic. We had to match the power and capacity of the computer system to some kind of job we could relate to. That way, later on if the computer was a bad fit, we could check on the data loads to see if they changed. And, they normally did change. Therefore, day after day, we would ask the kinds of questions the answers to which would help us size the computer.

"How many orders do you handle in a month?" I asked Mr. Mu.

"We don't have orders." He answered without a lot of enthusiasm. I made a questioning face. He knew I didn't believe his answer but that didn't prompt a correction. My head was whirring. How can a factory make things for customers and not have orders? I'd never heard of such a thing! Whoops, wait a minute., reality just snuck in. We were dealing with a Communist central planning organization. Orders, or their equivalent of orders, came down from the central planners, not from customers. Score one for Mr. Mu.

I kept right on. "How many people are on the payroll?" I thought for a moment that Chinese semantics was tripping me up. Should I have said, "How many 'workers' are in your factory?"

"We don't know." That answer was totally incredulous. I rolled my eyes up into my head and shrugged my shoulders. Maybe he didn't know the answer, but someone did. Again, a light bulb turned on in my head. Under Chinese Communism, entire families were supported by the factory. Housing, medical facilities and many other things were provided by the "employer", the work place to which the worker was assigned. So, in that sense, his answer was perfectly reasonable when given at that table. He couldn't know the extent of the paid work force as well as the non-work force.

The Chinese were unprepared for that kind of questioning. I believe that at least half of the answers were made up on the spot. Much, much later, Big Mu told me that he and his companions were amazed at all the questions we asked. He was coming from a Communist environment that emphasized secrecy and avoided people knows a lot about things that didn't concern them. He was coming from a centralized planning and control environment where the answers to many of my questions were really unknown to his group. We were coming from an environment that emphasized everyone's knowing everything even if it really was none of their business. To them, we were a big show, albeit a serious one, and a wonderful peek at Western business.

One very important fact came out during the questioning. Mr. Wu mentioned that they were buying something he called "technology" from an Italian firm called Nuovo Pignone. Even when I asked him, what "technology" meant, he did not answer. He was not evasive; he just didn't answer. I thought maybe he just didn't know.

By this time, we began to read the visual clues in the Chinese eyes, face, brow and physical movement. At least, we thought we could. Actually, we thought it was no different from an American customer interview; if you turned off the sounds coming from the customers and only dealt with their visual appearances you could get the idea. But the understanding took a long time to develop.

Of course, we did not know, nor were we told, that the computer applications the Chinese were planning, at least at the factory level. The Italian computer programs (the technology) from the factory in Milan were the computer applications, again assuming those applications were the ones Beijing was interested in.. The dictates from Beijing relative to modernization were the reason. If we had known that, we could have been out of there in a week! For reasons I still don't understand, the Shenyang people never brought the subject up. Then again, we never asked about those programs. It could be they were enjoying this new way of dealing with a vendor; it helped them think through their entire process. It could also be they wanted to learn about the Western way of business. It was part of their modernization process.

On and on we went! As we all became accustomed to dealing with each other and with dealing through translators, it got a little easier. During the third week, while we were discussing the need for computer terminals, we discovered that the Shenyang people had made the connection between our questions and resulting computer configuration. Their terminal requirements put a terminal on almost every engineer's desk. It was obviously too much. Later on, as they got into the swing of things, Big Mu came up with requirements that needed a space station level computer to satisfy. Mr. Mu needed a computer to be directly connected to all of his massive machine tools, while Mr. Shu needed a computer to be connected directly to all of his draftsmen.

No one even whispered that these computer applications were not the ones anticipated by Beijing; we were describing a fantasy!

Remote computing, the technical term describing their wishes, was a no-no in the world of embargoes; remote computing is the way rockets and ballistic missiles are controlled. We wouldn't even apply for an export license with remote computing in it; we would be laughed out of the Commerce Department in Washington.

It was a lot of fun, but we had to put a stop it.

After one of those days, I mentioned that the preparation of the final, priced proposal would take us a long time. We could only do that preparation in the United States. Since there was no way that IBM could maintain this computer in China (as we usually did everywhere else), we would have to propose training programs for their engineers to maintain it themselves. The training program would have to cover the computer hardware and the software as well. The program would have to cover each machine and each software package; hence, the importance of the configuration we were attempting to design. We couldn't do those calculations and scheduling here in China.

The grand ideas came to a halt. It was easy to see that the larger and more complex the computer and its programs, the more training and trained people would be required to maintain it. The larger and more complex the computer and its programs, more and more money and time would have to be spent on supplies, parts and training. They thought the budget they had received from Beijing was finite. Mr. Shu and company finally calculated that, even on a proportionate basis, there had to be some balance between computer size and the money they thought was available. .

Our workday was long and tiring. It was very tiring to speak through a translator all day long. It was very tiring to sit on the edge of our seats carefully watching Mr. Wu's eyes; or watching Mr. Shu's body language, or watching Mr. Mu's hands for a reaction to what you said a few minutes ago. Many statements had to be repeated, in some way, at least twice After the first couple of days, our speech patterns changed to allow the translator to work smoothly with us. The acclimation process was painful and slow. The concentration required was very taxing, not only for us, but for the Chinese as well.

We had Americans with us (our consultants) one of whom spoke Chinese. Mary listened to the English, and then listened to the Chinese translation. If we were tired at the end of the day, she was doubly so. She could compare the two language interpretations very quickly. Her core culture was the same as ours. If there was a significant gap between the English and the

Chinese, the statement would have to be repeated in a slightly different way so that the thought was translated, not just the words. Sometimes, because of the technical nature of these discussions, it took three or four repetitions to get the thought across. It was slow and tiring. The translation torture didn't let up when the sessions were over. It was repeated back at the hotel. There the subject matter was food or laundry.

On top of all that, either John or I had to report verbally to Charlie and other staff people a couple of times a week. The time difference was twelve hours; 7 o'clock in the evening Beijing time was 7 o'clock in the morning New York time. Each telephone call had to be scheduled with the telephone operators in Beijing. Sometimes they were late, very late. The result was that we were on the telephone either late at night or very early in the morning. Those days turned out to be 18 hour workdays for us and there were a lot of them.

By the time Sunday came around, we were exhausted. Although Sunday didn't mean anything to the Chinese, they let us take the day off from discussions. While I suspect the Chinese were working, we could relax. Since no one was working on Sunday back in New York, it was a quiet day for us as well. We slept until noon or beyond. After breakfast (lunch), we sometimes went back to bed. There was no other way to recharge our batteries. It was work before breakfast, off to discussions, then work after supper. Six days a week.

Sometimes, Mr. Wu felt sorry for us and arranged for some diversion. The first excursion that Mr Wu arranged was to the Great Wall of China and the Ming Tombs, both of which are about an hour and half north of Beijing. Ken and Mary were left to their own devices, which seemed to please them. Ms. Ma had picked up picnic lunches from the hotel dining room. Mr Wu, Ms. Ma, John, and I piled in the little beige upholstered car that Techimport had arranged and off we went!

The ride was interesting. Since our only sights of Beijing had been the discussion rooms, the hotel and various restaurants, everything was interesting. When we left the center part of the city, we passed through what appeared to be an apartment section. The apartment houses appeared to be empty. However, the sidewalks and the curbs were crowded with cardboard and wooden shacks, or so it seemed. Mr Wu noticed my interest in the shacks and people. This was a unique view of Chinese home life.

I asked, "Why all the shacks?" Before he answered I had to explain to Ms. Ma what "shacks" meant. He explained.

There had been a terrible earthquake centered in Tentsien some 8 or 9 months before. Tentsien was about 90 miles away. The shocks, Mr. Wu told me, had been felt in Beijing. At the time, all the apartment blocks that were taller than 2 stories were evacuated. The people erected these temporary dwellings so that they would have somewhere to sleep. The government had not been able to inspect the apartments so that the people could return. Therefore, they stayed in the street. He said that he and his family had spent about a month in the street like that. He said the government would soon have everyone back in their apartments. In the narrow confines of our business life, we had heard little about the Tentsien earthquake although there was a small mention of it in Western newspapers because of the large loss of life.

We left the city behind and passed through the countryside. It was the middle of the winter. We saw no one, just a lot of frozen ground all the way to the horizon. I drifted off to sleep. John poked me awake as we were entering a cleft between two hills He said, "We're here". I said, "Where?" He said, "The Great Wall". I didn't see a thing until we drove right up to the gate in the wall and then the walls were all around me. As I looked left and right, the wall undulated up and down the surrounding hills. The walls went as far as we could see.

Everyone got out of the car. We walked up the stairs inside the wall to the top of the battlements over the gate where the car had stopped. We were quite a ways up. From this vantage point, you could really see the Wall climbing up and down the hills far into the distance. The Wall appeared to crumble far in the distance. Mr. Wu explained that they had only reconstructed this part for the tourists. Much of the rest of the Wall had fallen down as we could see. It was most impressive! In addition, it was very cold! The wind chill on the top of that Wall had to be 40 below 0.

Mr. Wu turned to me and said, "Let's walk on the top of the wall to the next tower". His breath came out in icicles; I think the icicles tinkled when they hit the frozen ground. He wasn't smiling either. He pointed a gloved hand toward a tower that was a long way off. Ms Ma was translating into a thick scarf wrapped around her face.

I looked at John. He had on a pair of ear muffs that he brought with him from the States. He was bare headed. There were tears in his eyes; certainly not from sadness, but from the intense cold. He slowly shook his head left to right to stop me from calling Mr. Wu's bluff.

I politely refused Mr Wu's proposal. He laughed. I imagined Mr. Wu had used that line on every other foreign vendor he brought to the wall. Just so that he wouldn't get the best of me, I offered to race him back down the stairs. He demurred and we were even. We climbed down the stairs. Even though the temperature was below freezing, it felt warm inside the walls in comparison to outside on the top. We got into the car and were driven a short distance to a picnic house where we could enjoy the box lunch prepared by the hotel.

Inside the picnic house, there were long picnic tables and attached seats. We grabbed one, but there wasn't a soul there to compete with us for it. There was no heat inside this building. Our driver had thoughtfully brought one of the large ubiquitous thermos bottles, just like the ones at Er Li Go, filled with hot tea. He didn't know it, but he saved John and me from a frozen death, even though neither of us drank tea. We did that day and were very thankful for it. We eagerly opened our box lunches.

Surprise, Surprise. The cooked chicken inside was frozen, or at least very cold and very hard. The apple, somewhat hardier, had survived. In fact, it was the memory of that boxed lunch that kept me from going back to the Great Wall many times later in our visits. Then I made a blunder, a stupid Western blunder that, if I had given it one minute of thought, I wouldn't have made. I laughed and said to Mr Wu and Ms Ma, "Never mind, I'm on a diet anyway", joke, joke. Ms Ma began translating as soon as I began speaking, but stopped very quickly to ask me, "What's a diet?" I had to explain what a diet was in the West. That took a little bit. Then when she translated that for Mr. Wu, she asked me "Why do you have to be on a diet?" By the time I explained that I had tried to tell a joke, etc. I was so far out in the left field of conversation that I said, "It's nothing, forget it." They were completely baffled by all of this. I thought to myself, never again! But, of course, it happens all the time.

We left the chicken to get back into the car. After a short drive we arrived at the Ming Tombs. This was another awesome, inspiring sight. We walked down the entranceway into the first of the tombs. As we passed from the outside into the first room of the tombs, my attention was diverted to a very large sign in English and Chinese high up on the wall. I don't remember the exact words, but I remember the thought very well. The sign commemorated the 6 million peasants who had labored, and died here, to build this monstrosity of a tomb for a decadent Emperor! It went on to say that the government had left this tomb intact to show the world the inequities of the Imperial World that the Communists had to overcome.

The tomb itself is impressive; several stories high and filled with a monstrous sarcophagus. The tomb had been looted several centuries ago. There was nothing of value left. The enormity of it all left a lasting impression. As we were leaving the tomb, I pointed the sign out to Mr. Wu. Ms. Ma explained it for him even though there was Chinese text as well. When she finished, he grunted a couple of times, but she didn't convert the grunts into English. Since the sign was so obviously a piece of Communist propaganda, I was about to comment to him about it, but common sense took over. We walked over to our car and got in.

It was another short run to the Avenue of the Animals. The Emperors wanted everyone to know where their tombs were. A road was built to show the way. On both sides of the road, the Emperors had their sculptors create larger than life sized images of animals, pairs of them up and down the road. There were elephants twice life size, there were camels, as well as some animals I didn't recognize. We took some quick pictures and left for the warmth of the car. On the way back to the hotel, I asked Mr. Wu how many times he had been there with foreign visitors. He thought for a minute or two and said, "I think I have been here more than 50 times and each time is more interesting than the last."

His very diplomatic answer stumped me. I had to respond. I told him, "I promise that I will never ask you to take me here again, as long as I live!" We all laughed and went back to the hotel.

We were still frozen the next day. There was no heat in the room or building where we were meeting. The only warm thing in the room was the ever-present tea thermos kept full of steaming hot tea throughout the day. During the morning break, John asked Mr. Wu how he managed to look warm while the rest of us were frozen. John particularly pointed to Mr. Wu's shoes. They looked like they had very, very thin soles. John had monstrous L.L.Bean boots, but his feet were still cold. After the translation, Mr. Wu broke into a grand smile. He put his foot on the edge of the table and slipped one of his shoes off. He showed the inside of the shoe to John. It was filled with chicken or duck feathers!

We had some more sessions, but nothing new came out of them. We were not going to be told of the Italian computer programs. Based on the information we had squeezed out of them, we had to concoct a scenario that would pass muster, not only within IBM, but also with the US Government. Mr. Wu gave us a goodbye banquet at which the Shenyang people gamely tried to get us drunk. We were getting experienced at this sort of thing and after a month of meetings we were great friends.

The banquet started out slowly. Slowly in the sense that some of the food came at the same time the bottles of Mai Tai came. We discovered early on that drinking this Chinese edition of Moonshine was very dangerous on an empty stomach. This Mai Tai was their secret weapon to subdue foreigners. Other banquets we had attended were long on the Mai Tai and short on food. But this one was different. The little hors-de-oeuvres that began the meal were tasty and generous. We had little dumplings, both steamed and fried that were filled with the most delicious stuff.

Then they brought out the thousand year old eggs. After a month there, I could eat those black eggs; I wouldn't touch them at first. Someone told me that they were really eggs pickled with vinegar which turned them black. But the one dish I never was able to deal with was the sea cucumber, or sea slugs.

Every other course was perfect. The duck, the chicken, the vegetables looked and tasted great. The food just kept coming; mounds and mounds of it. Apparently, it is a Chinese custom to overwhelm your guests with food and drink. Although we could match most of them drink for drink and toast for toast, Mr. Mu turned out to be the senior undisputed champion at drinking and toasting.

We left to concoct our proposal. They went home to plan the next "battle" in their revolution. Everyone was playing his or her role to perfection.

Chapter 6 – Designing a Chinese System

London Times Apr 21, 1977
"LEONARD WOODCOCK APPOINTED AMBASSADOR TO CHINA"

Jimmy Carter was sworn in as the 39th President of the United States in January 1977. He celebrated the event by walking the entire route of the inaugural parade. No modern day president had ever done that, they all rode in a car along the same route. I guess President Carter wanted to impress everyone with the fact that he came from a humble beginning. Kind of like "of the people". All kinds of new and different things were happening. More important to us was how he was going to handle the situation with the Peoples Republic of China. It was not encouraging to hear him proclaim that he was just a peanut farmer from Georgia. Peanut farmers worry about the weather; we needed someone who would worry about relations with China. Although that was on the grand scale of things, we had a more immediate problem. Our China consultant was angry with us!

After we returned from China, without saying a word to John, Ken requested a meeting with Charlie, John's boss, to discuss IBM's relationship with our Chinese purchasers. I don't think he wanted to talk about President Carter's activities nor the nuclear energy program in China. The fact that he had not bothered to ask John first really annoyed John. Ken interpreted

John's treatment of him at the meeting with Wu and company in Beijing as a professional slight. John had told him, in front of the Chinese, to sit down when he objected to something I had said. My refusal to take his advice and give in to Mr. Wu's suggestions that we provide Chinese language contracts was a personal affront to him. Because of that, and several other instances of not taking his advice, it seemed that his nose was out of joint. He interpreted all these things as professional insults rather than differences in opinion. In particular, he did not think that I should be dealing with the Chinese. He was incensed that his direction and advice were ignored during the discussions with Wu and Co on several occasions. Charlie agreed to see him. Charlie told me the story some time later.

Charlie asked Ken, "What's up Ken? How was the trip to China?

"Charlie, your guys are not listening to me." Ken came right to the point. The tone of voice told Charlie that Ken was not happy.

"Oh, why not?"

"Because Joseph is telling them something different; Charlie, he's wrong for this job. He's not sensitive to the Chinese." Ken went on with chapter and verse of the session in Beijing. As he described it, his voice got shriller and shriller. Charlie could see that he was very upset.

I can just visualize what was going through Charlie's mind as Ken told his tale of woe. He, Ken, was recommended and hired through the auspices of the Treasurer of the IBM organization that Charlie was in. Ken was connected to David Rockefeller. David Rockefeller had spoken to our Chairman Frank Cary. So, he had a lot of connections inside IBM. Charlie had to assume that Ken wouldn't restrict this story to him. If his complaints were accurate, then he might have to move John and I out of the negotiations with the Chinese. If his complaints were less than accurate, he might have to fire Ken and then explain all of this to the higher-ups. So, Charlie had to be sure to hear Ken out. Such is the nature of bureaucratic actions; looking over your shoulder while looking into the future becomes habit. Only the facts would do in these circumstances. It was a typical middle management dilemma; you're damned if you do and damned if you don't. Then he called John in and asked him for his opinion.

Before Charlie called John into his office, John and I were discussing what our next step should be. Neither of us started out with any concrete way of handling this deal. The fact that the Chinese were not forthcoming about their client and what his needs were didn't help us one bit. We were stymied. At that moment, Charlie called John.

Charlie repeated each accusation just as Ken had told him. To his absolute surprise, John confirmed each and every one of them. I think that Charlie would have expected a difference of opinion on what had happened; then he would have to decide whom to support. But Ken's story had been accurate; John confirmed that. So, his decision was easy. I had to be removed from the team. That way, he wouldn't have to defend his actions to his management.

John, to his credit, adamantly refused to remove me from his team. Charlie, to his credit, ultimately agreed with John. Ken, to his credit, never went to China with us again. However, he, again to his credit, was paid continuously for his non-attendance for the rest of the year. The only work I am aware of that he did as our consultant was an excellent China briefing for IBM executives that he and Charlie gave nine months later in Tokyo.

While we were involved with these distracting turf wars, President Carter wasn't helping us either. Judging from the absence of any public statements in the media, as well as his failure to appoint anyone with a pro-China bias or experience to significant posts, he had little or no interest in what was going on in the Peoples Republic of China. My government was caught up in an impasse over official diplomatic relations with China while maintaining military ties with the Chinese on Taiwan. On top of that, China had exploded several nuclear test bombs;

how could you ignore a large country that possessed or would possess nuclear weapons? The news reports from China did note that Mao's widow was vilified in the Chinese press; while the counterpoint of Deng Xiao Ping's gradual ascendancy was continuously hinted.

Aside from the in-fighting, some decisions by the government were necessary because the Chinese wanted to buy the biggest and the newest computer for a plant somewhere. How would our government respond to an application for an export license? What kind of computer? How was it going to be used? What services, in addition to the computer were necessary? These questions were coming from our management. They would be the same questions we would have to answer for the U.S. government. In IBM, answering these questions was a significant part of primary sales training. The biggest question was which computer model could we export? In addition, would we get a license at all with the political instability in China after Chairman Mao's death? The "$64,000 question" was the one the Chinese were interested in, i.e., would the U.S. permit the export of a computer to the Peoples Republic of China? John, Charlie, and I were the little people who were trying to make a living while being pushed around by worldly events.

John was big on planning. If he took off his jacket while we were discussing our problems, that was the signal that he considered the matter very serious. This time he said, "Let's quit worrying about things we can't control and take care of the ones we can." His jacket came off. He was going to have a plan come hell or high water. "What are we going to propose to the Chinese?"

Our discussions lasted hours and hours over many days. We filled up chalkboards in the conference room where we met. We wrote and erased constantly. John would take a turn at the boards while I tried to think aloud. Then I would take my turn at the board writing down his thoughts. Then we would go over the ideas and eliminate the ones that made no sense to both of us. Finally we were able to summarize our "to do" list.

The results of this process, i.e., the specifications of the various units comprising a computer system and its software would become very important in later stages of our proposal process. Each piece of equipment would require education for the Chinese to run and maintain it (there were about 20 different pieces of input and output equipment in the system). Each unit of equipment would require a spare parts module to enable maintenance since IBM couldn't maintain the equipment so far away. Each computer application or control programming would require extensive education in the program's structure, purpose and code, etc. A price calculation was required for each of these components. Estimated delivery schedules were required before we would be done.

We agreed on the principle, "Don't propose it if we can't deliver it." The first objective was to find out which computer and software and what services the U.S. government export-licensing people would allow us to export to China. Even though the government was closed mouthed about computer exports, perhaps someone in Washington might help. The second objective was to find out what computer software applications a Chinese manufacturing plant might use. The answer to that question was in China. No matter which one came first, these objectives were key. However, at that moment, we were flying blind on both subjects.

For example, we did not know that President Ford had approved the sale of two of Control Data Corp's older computers to China three months before. But that deal had never come off. Those computers were not delivered; we never knew the reasons. No computer system had been exported to China in the last fifty years; a modern sophisticated solid state computer had <u>never</u> been exported. China had closed her doors to the West when the Communists took over in 1949. Then President Eisenhower and his embargo put locks on the doors in 1950. Now, more than twenty years later, since Nixon and Kissinger's visit, everyone envisioned a booming Chinese consumer market because of the size of the population. Business leaders were hypnotized by the size of a market not dominated by Americans.

Another problem was the amount of knowledge that John and I had about possible computer applications in a Chinese (or anyone else's) factory. We attempted to question the Chinese toward this end, but we were not sure what questions to ask. The sum total of knowledge for the both of us about computer applications in a factory wouldn't fill a thimble. If we could figure all this out, we could combine the results to prepare a proposal to the Chinese. We got to work.

A reading on the COCOM embargo as it related to China was the first order of business. I called a friend of mine, Ike Lewis, who worked in the Washington Government Liaison office of IBM. He could start the process of finding out what computer model our new administration would license for delivery to the Chinese. He could make some telephone calls to ask some questions. This was not as easy as it sounds. My own experience with our government's computer export policy and practice came when I was working in Russia. The U.S. government had approved the export of a large computer and software for the INTOURIST organization in Moscow for use in the Olympic Games in 1980. My group in London was conducting classes in Moscow for INTOURIST programmers who were modifying the IBM international airlines reservations system. The airlines reservation system was used as a base to create an all-Russia air, hotel and train reservation system for the influx of visitors to the projected 1980 Olympics. About a year after their approval, and well into the implementation and installation of the system, the American government committee asked for a status report on the modifications and installation. We had to recall one person from Moscow and another from London to attend this meeting in the Pentagon along with me.

The first part of the meeting went fine. My people reported exactly what they were doing, how far along the contract they were and what they still had to do to finish our contractual obligations. The members of the committee seemed to be bored until that part was over. Then we got to the question and answer part. They did not ask a single question about a subject covered in the presentation. They wanted to know about the Russian technical abilities (CIA work) ; they wanted to know the names of the Soviet students and their managers (more CIA work); they wanted to know who had access to the computer (more CIA work!); they wanted to know if one of our people was on site in the computer room whenever the computer was on (national security issues!). I objected to these questions because I felt that "spying" was not our business. Their response to my comment was that our customer, INTOURIST, particularly outside of Russia, was a hot bed of Soviet spies. Their logic meant we should be spies as well. In fact, the U.S. had just refused an entry visa for the Deputy Director of INTOURIST because he actually was a General in the Soviet Secret Service, the KBG. I put that information together with the fact that Mr. Zoloyev (my counterpart) sometimes was addressed as "Colonel" in my presence. If I agreed, my programmers and analysts would begin keeping notes of all the info the Pentagon would like to have. I didn't like the whole affair and I told them so!

Although some of the committee members had changed over time, this was the very same committee (and, some of the same people) that would examine our application to export a computer to China. I would be dealing with them again. The only difference was China being the subject, not the Soviet Union. These people came from various concerned Executive Branch Departments i.e., Commerce, State, Energy and of course, the Pentagon. These were the people we needed to question about China.

I asked Ike to set up some exploratory meetings with the committee representatives in the Commerce, State, and Defense Departments. Our approach had to be humble and discreet. We had to avoid a perception of IBM as a corporate "giant", but at the same time get some dependable advice. Any advice was better than no advice. This would be the first computer system export to China by any western company. Public opinion in this country was split on the subject of Communist China. If an anti-China group got wind of what we were planning, we could easily lose the public relations battle. IBM management would back away from the sale. If a pro-China group got wind of our interest, they might tout it as the grand "opening" of China to the entire Western world! IBM management would back away from that as well. Their attitude might be "let someone else be first!" It would be hard to be rational in the face of any public relations blitz, either pro or con.

Ike suggested that we go to each department separately and quietly. Although our activities were not in the "secret" category, if information of those activities got into the newspapers, it would be counterproductive. John remembered Ralph Pfeiffer's admonition about publicity of any kind. In Washington, for different reasons, Ike wanted to avoid any intra-governmental posturing that would result from each department's knowing what the others were doing. "Divide and conquer" was the policy.

We met with the Commerce representative first. I can't remember his name, but Ike told me that the traditional role of Commerce in these affairs was to be on the side of the exporter. The motto, "What's good for business is good for the country" was their guide. His office was on the inside of the building without any window. I wondered if the office location was an indicator of his importance. I had to wonder more when we entered his office. I noticed all the pictures on the walls of this gentlemen with various and sundry business and political giants. If this guy needed all those publicity photos to boost his ego, he couldn't be high up in the Department ranks. After we sat down in his office, Ike turned to me and said, "Tell him what we are thinking of doing."

I told him about the Chinese request the previous year for computer information. I described the computer and applications seminar in Beijing in October 1976. I told him of our visit in February 1977, who we met with and what they told us or, more to the point, what they didn't tell us. I told him that we were going to propose a computer and some applications software to go with it, but were unsure of the specifics at this time.

He listened very attentively. It was impossible to read his face. I couldn't tell if he was bored, or if he was interested in what we were doing. I concluded that was a standard "Government Issue" pose; don't let anyone know what's in your mind until you're sure that you're not alone in your thinking. That way, you are not responsible for anything. Besides, President Carter had not yet given his Cabinet their marching orders viz-a-viz China.

"Sounds great to me.," he said. "What system are you going to sell them?" That put my mind at ease a little; he had heard some of the things I said.

"We don't know yet. A lot will depend on our reading of the export situation as well as what computer applications we think the Chinese require. The application load will be a big factor."

"What applications are you thinking of?" This gentleman was beginning to impress me. He was smiling and his question was on point.

"We are thinking of an application in inventory control, manufacturing management and things like that." I made that up on the fly. I intuitively did not want to tell him that we didn't know a thing about computer applications in a compressor factory. If I had known, I could have told him about Deng's plan for compressing natural gas for the domestic market to replace the oil they would sell overseas. That would have impressed him!

"How was the weather in Peking?" The sudden change of subject caught me short. For a moment I didn't know what to say, my thoughts were still on the computer street; he had turned off on to some side street.

"Cold as hell", I answered.

"I've never been there. If we ever get off our duff and establish an embassy there, maybe I'll get the chance." It sounded like a sincere desire.

There was some more chitchat like that and then he said, "I would suggest that you don't come in to license something that needs an exception. Keep it under the current limits. That way a COCOM vote won't be required." A very positive statement bolstered by a very solid reason. This man was definitely on our side! I mentally took back all the negative things I had been thinking about him.

"Well, suppose we came in at the current limit?" I asked. Maybe a little pushing was in order. I had to get something concrete; something we could depend upon.

"It would be better under the limit." He wasn't going to give an inch ahead of time. Nevertheless, he didn't say "no" to a computer at the current acceptable limit of technology.

He asked me a lot of questions about what I saw in China. I answered as best I could. I didn't want to admit that we had spent most of our time either in the hotel, a taxi, negotiating with the Chinese or sleeping We had some coffee and after a while ran out of things to talk about.

Ike spoke up, "We have another appointment we shouldn't be late for. Thanks a lot."

Our host stood up and wished us well. He asked if we had seen any other committee members. Since his was the first appointment, we could honestly answer that we had not. In any event, what difference would it make to him? His question left me with the distinct impression that he, as well as anyone else, did not want to appear in the front of the pack. Better to stay with the pack.

We made out farewells, he wished us luck and we left. On the street, Ike told me, "That was a good meeting. He didn't put up any walls; he didn't take an absolute position. Now we go to the State Department."

I asked Ike "Any instructions?" These meetings had reached no conclusion. The responses we received were empty. This kind of answer, an empty answer, was not my cup of tea. I needed help.

"Nah, just keep it cool. Commerce would always be in favor of an export; State should be as well. I think that they'll do anything that will make us look friendly. The whole government bureaucracy is waiting for the first signs of direction from Carter." Ike was very matter-of-fact about the whole thing. Monumental things to me assumed different proportions inside the Washington beltway,

"We'll see"

I had to defer to his experience, but I wasn't so sure. The Commerce guy was so nonchalant about the whole thing, it unnerved me a little. After all, we were talking about giving China a modern computer, more or less, and that seemed like a big deal to me. I concluded that I was over-emphasizing this deal a little; I was being a little emotional about the prospect of being involved with what I thought to be an historic act. It was quite apparent that it wasn't such a big deal to Ike; he did this kind of thing every day of the week.

We took a cab to the State Department building in "Foggy Bottom". We didn't have to wait long for our appointment with their representative on the committee.

"Good Morning. How was it in China?" He already knew that we had been there. I had no idea where he got that information; news of our visits, if they were news, had successfully stayed out of the newspapers.

I told him that it was cold in Beijing and the smoke really got to you after a while. He agreed.

Ike said, "Tell him what you want to do." He sat back and waited.

So I launched into the same monologue that I had given over at the Commerce Department. When I finished, he asked,

"What's your impression of the Chinese?" It was as if I had just walked into his office. He was very nonchalant. My story had not impressed him one bit. He was toying with a pen on his desk while he asked.

I said, "My impression is that they are very pragmatic. My concern is they buy from us and not from the Japanese." Ike and I both understood that we had no hint that Japanese computer manufacturers were involved with the Chinese. As a matter of fact, as I discovered later on, the Japanese would be the last people the Chinese wanted to deal with.

"Oh, are they in there?" He perked up. The Japanese got his attention. He stopped toying with his pen.

"I think so."

"We don't want the Japanese to get this order. What did Commerce tell you?" This was the first hint of the standing intra-departmental competition in Washington. How did he know we had visited Commerce an hour before? He picked up his pen again. The pen movements in his hand were his body language.

"The Commerce gentleman was noncommittal."

"That's typical," he answered. More bureaucratic nonsense! I don't think that these people hated one another; it was just intramural disputes. "Well, you know that we are all tied up with the Chinese in Taiwan. Some people in Congress really believe we shouldn't have anything to do with the Communist Chinese. We have this treaty with the Republic of China." The pen was really shaking again.

I began to wonder where all this was going. Why should I care about what was going on in Taiwan so long as they weren't shooting at each other? I certainly didn't want my deal to get tied up in anything political.

I said, "We have a separate company on Taiwan. They have nothing to do with this deal. This deal is with the U.S. Company in New York, not Taiwan." I really didn't know what to say. I pictured the water getting a little murkier. We had to get the conversation back to the subject at hand.

So, I asked him, "Do you people have any suggestion for us? Areas that we should stay away from, subjects we shouldn't bring up?"

"I really have no suggestions. I think you are doing the right thing. Go for it."

Again, as at Commerce, we did the script about the weather in China and how he would like to serve there. My impression was that the people in Washington are completely bland about anything outside of Washington.

We made our farewells.

I asked Ike when we got to the street. "Is it always like this? All he wanted to know was what the Commerce guy said and did. He didn't give a hoot about what we sell or didn't sell."

"He's always like that. He wouldn't know a computer if he ran into it. So he just passes the time of day. Nevertheless, we can always say that we told him what we were going to do. That's important around here."

"Are all these people so blasé' about all these foreign matters?

"Absolutely; most of them at this level worry about how their inaction will be perceived by their bosses. The real policy action is much higher up the line. But, if the upper echelons did NOT want to deal with China, these guys wouldn't see us or talk to us."

I thought to myself. This is probably the only time that I would have to be sensitive to the absence of negatives. I was used to dealing with the absence of positives; you become sensitive when you don't hear the word "Yes" loud and clear. But this was new; you had to become sensitive to silence. During the IBM sales school that I had attended, they spent a lot of time teaching you how to recognize a "Yes" in any form.

The next stop, after lunch, was the Defense Department. We took a taxi over to the Pentagon and eventually found our way down to some sub-basement of another sub-basement. Our meeting was held in a windowless room that looked like the

back room of a saloon. Old beat-up chairs were set around an
even older beat up table, all Government Issue slate color. We
were ushered into the room by a civilian secretary. We had
to wait a little for our meeting. It was very claustrophobic.
Finally, a gentleman in an Army Colonel's uniform came.

"Hiya Ike" He was all business while he shook hands.

"Colonel, I'd like you to meet Allan Joseph. He just got back
from China."

"I'm pleased to meet you, Colonel."

"Tell him what we are planning to do in China."

I did my routine. This was the third time today; I had it down
pat. I gave him the whole story in about 10 minutes.

"What system do you think you'll offer to them?' he asked.

"At the moment, I'm not certain of the specific model. I do
know that it will be technology at or below the COCOM approved
level." I was repeating what the Commerce Department meeting
this morning had produced.

"Will the system have disc drives?"

"For sure; I don't know what model yet." IBM hadn't
delivered a system without disc drives in the last five years.
There were fast ones and there were slow ones. The control
programs for the computer resided on these disc drives. No
disc drives, no computer from IBM. He knew that, why did he
ask?

"Those random access disc drives are powerful stuff." Where
was this leading? He stood up as he said this. I thought we were
done for.

"Uh huh;" I didn't know what else to say.

"Do you know you're dealing with the enemy?" he said with
an absolutely straight face. His eyes turned hard, he spat out the
words. I looked at Ike. He shrugged. We both looked at the
Colonel. He didn't need any answer.

"Do you know that you're giving the enemy a very powerful
weapon they could use against us?" Again, the Colonel had a
straight, very hard, face. This guy was deadly serious. I didn't

know what to say, but instinctively I knew that no answer was the best answer.

He went on. "I was up in Korea when the Chinese came over the border and knocked us on our asses. I AM NOT JUST ABOUT TO GIVE THEM ANOTHER WEAPON TO HIT US OVER THE HEAD WITH!" His face got red and he slammed his open hand on the table. He wasn't going to get an answer from us.

This tirade went on for another couple of minutes. After he calmed down a little, I said,

"Colonel, we aren't giving the Chinese anything they can use as a weapon. At the moment I don't know for sure what kind of computer we'll try to sell them. And, I certainly appreciate how you feel."

Ike added, "Colonel, you can be sure that we will not do anything that either bends or breaks any law".

There was silence for a long time. I think he was embarrassed. We needed to get up and out. Ike motioned to me with a nod. We both stood.

Ike said, "I'll get back to you with the details as soon as I have them. Thanks for your time. He was talking as we were easing out of the room. I felt that anything I might add would trigger another blow-up.

We left. Neither of us said one word until we were out of the Pentagon. Neither of us breathed normally until we were on the street.

"WOW" I exclaimed.

"Double Wow", Ike answered.

"Is he always like that?" I sure as hell wouldn't want to deal with him on a week-to-week basis. Everything was either black or white, there was no gray in this Colonel's world. You were either with him or against him.

Ike said, "I've never seen anything like it. He went ballistic about the Chinese. We sure know how he will vote in the committee."

I agreed, "We sure know where he stands. Is the whole Defense Department like him?"

Ike answered, "Who knows? We'll find out." Without knowing it, Ike was like some of the others we had met. It was okay to be non-committal until the big guy makes a commitment.

On the plane back up to New York, I thought about the day. If everyone had equal weight, we were ahead 2 to 1. Not bad for the first shot! The real question was "Did they have equal weight?"

Because of this foray into the thicket of Washington, D.C., we decided on a computer with specs that were a little <u>lower than</u> the embargo limits. Those limits were set by the last computer export that was approved for export. That decision automatically meant that the China was not going to get the newest and biggest computer. Now all we had to do was convince the Chinese!

About the time that the Colonel at the Pentagon was laying us out for dealing with his Chinese enemies, there was an announcement in China that the 50-year ban on Beethoven and his music had been lifted. I should have sent that note to the Colonel to see what his response would be. If that wasn't enough to lift his spirits, a Congressional delegation visited China accompanied by President Carter's son and Shirley Temple, a visit that subtly presaged open friendship and preparation for a formal exchange of ambassadors later on. Speaking of ambassadors, while we were in China, John played tennis with the former Chief of the U.S. Liaison Office George H.W. Bush at the International Club in Beijing. The Liaison Office was not like full diplomatic recognition with an embassy, but allowed the countries to talk to one another in the meantime. Regardless of how the Colonel felt, friendly relations were in the cards!

Meanwhile, the next step was to figure out what computer applications we should offer. Without significant input from the Chinese, it was going to be difficult to find a good match between what was needed or wanted and what IBM had available. Had we known of the real Chinese intentions we could have avoided all this work! We went back to the application specialist, John

Makaapi. He had been with the group in China the previous October.

His advice was twofold. We should try to find a similar customer in the U.S. After finding one, we should query their IBM representatives to find out what they were doing with their computers. Then we should do the same in Europe. In addition, IBM had a specialist group in Germany that was working on all kinds of manufacturing applications. We should query them. And, of course, we should try to find out what was going on at Nuovo Pignone in Milan Italy. His suggestions became our immediate plan.

After several days of disappointing telephone calls to IBM regional and branch offices, I found there was a company in Milwaukee that sounded like it had the kind of factory we were interested in. The regional IBM man described the factory as a compressor manufacturer. I asked the local IBM sales rep on the account to see if they would be willing to talk with me. I told the sales rep that he could tell his customer I was from IBM headquarters. I was interested in seeing how they used our computer in their factory. That was necessary to avoid any leaks to the newspapers about China. He said that he would call them and find out if they were willing to talk to me. The sales rep called back the next day to tell me that I could come out the following week.

I flew out there in the morning hoping that I could have the meeting, turn around, and come home the same day. However, by the time I rented a car, drove to the IBM branch office, picked up the sales rep, and then drove to the factory, it was already one o'clock in the afternoon. Even with the time difference with New York added to the day, this wasn't starting out too well. I probably should have come out the night before. I asked the rep why we weren't taking this gentleman to lunch.

"We don't usually do that."

"Why not; he's going out of his way to give us something; he's entitled to a lunch if only as a ground breaker."

"We don't do that out here."

From that response, I presumed that the sales rep was not a buddy of the gentlemen we were on our way to see. He was only doing this because I came from IBM headquarters. He couldn't think of a good way to refuse my request. This was not a good omen.

At the meeting, the computer supervisor was cordial and helpful. He explained exactly what applications he had installed, which ones he was proud of and which ones he was not proud of. He described how they received a particular part from this plant; this particular assembly came from some other plant, etc. His computer program kept track of all these parts and the plants from which they came. He described how the management used all the reports in their day-to-day activities. He told us how important and difficult it was to stay ahead of the factory production schedule. It wasn't too long before I realized that his factory was only an assembly plant: they didn't manufacture anything. It was very interesting, but a little off target. I had to sit and appear interested for a couple of hours. I ended up missing my flight back. I had to stay over that night at a motel at the airport.

If the sales rep knew a little more about his customer, I wouldn't have made this trip. So it goes!

After a couple of more days on the telephone, I had to conclude that either there was no company in the U.S. that manufactured compressors from scratch, or if there were, the company was not a IBM customer. Many, many months later I discovered my conclusions were correct!

We turned our attention to Europe. I started by calling the manufacturing industry specialist in the IBM headquarters for Europe. Although I heard all the "cooperation" words from him, he was very light on the specifics. Everything was good and great. He sounded like a "Go, Go" guy, but he failed to mention where we were going. After several conversations with him, most of them about this "great" customer or that "great account"

I deduced that he was new to this job, just promoted from sales representative.

I did learn something that was very interesting. There was a French subsidiary of a U.S. manufacturer of compressors and their parts. At my request, he did some research for me and discovered that it was the Dresser-Clarke Company. They manufactured oil field equipment; compressors were just one of their products. Interesting! They were not IBM customers. My former sales representative totally redeemed himself. He also told me that if I came there, he could help me get more info about the company.

I did not know at the time that this company, Dresser-Clarke Company, had been one of the bidders for the Shenyang modernization program. Again, if I had known then what I know now, life would have been different. Any information was better than what we had!

One other thing my French friend told me. He had heard that IBM was working on some advanced manufacturing application programs in Munich. Although we couldn't market their work (their research work was not products yet), the people involved were the most conversant and knowledgeable on those subjects in the company. He thought a visit to them would be very helpful. As soon as I hung up from his conversation, I called there to make an appointment to visit.

The IBM Manufacturing Center in Munich had system engineers from all over Europe and the U.S. I was lucky enough to speak to an American who was there on temporary assignment. He gave me a lot of interesting information. We scheduled a visit. John would join me at the Center in Munich. Then we would both go to Milan to take on Nuovo Pignone, the Italian company that already had a contract with our Chinese friends. Off we went!

In Munich, I had a dazzling explanation by my host of the world-to-come in factories. The wave of the future, according to my new source, was computers running all the machines in the plant. The machines became robots, the only manual labor involved was getting the work pieces moved and mounted from one machine to the next. It was fascinating! All of the machines, my host told me, were run by computers attached to the machine itself. Right now, my guide told me, many machines are controlled by people.

Previously, if the machine got too hot, it was tough luck if no one was watching. All the set- up time for the tool operation would be lost and the work piece would probably be ruined. In his world, the computer was watching. It was just like a Buck Rogers movie; all these machines running like robots, acting and reacting as if they were intelligent. It was a wonderful presentation!

While I was waiting for John to join me, I thought about it. What a coup if we could present something like that to the Chinese. However, I realized there was no way that my government would allow us to export such advanced technology And, when I really thought about it, I realized that the systems engineer had mesmerized me with all that future stuff; there was no current product involved. We had nothing to sell. I ended up with a pleasant afternoon in "never-never" land and still didn't know what to propose to the Chinese. I had to go back to the drawing board!

Over dinner that night in a Munich hotel John and I compared notes. All we had to offer at the moment were these factory information collection systems. If we couldn't find something more sexy and exciting, we would have to propose that "old hat" stuff to the Chinese. The only redeeming feature was that what was "old hat" to us might be brand new to the Chinese. We gave up and went back to enjoying the dinner and the beer.

John and I decided on Thursday evening to meet in Milan and then drive to Florence to visit or see the famous Nuovo Pignone plant on Monday morning. I was going to Vienna to visit some friends for the weekend. John was going to drive over the Alps in a rented car and meet me at the Milan airport.

John was busy with something so he asked me to rent a car for him. I went straight to the concierge's desk in the lobby.

"I would like to arrange for an inexpensive rental car tomorrow morning. It will be returned in Milan on Monday morning. Is that possible?"

"Of course, sir" the concierge said. That was all it took.

We both had a pleasant weekend. John turned in his "over the Alps" car at the Milan airport and rented a much cheaper one for the ride to Florence. He almost had a hemorrhage when he discovered that the hotel in Germany had provided him with a Mercedes at $75.00 per day. He tried unsuccessfully to change it, but it was impossible at the late hour. So he motored over to Italy in total comfort and style, all the time worrying that he wouldn't be able to put the car rental fees on his expense account. As soon as he could, he turned the car in replacing it with a small Fiat; that is to say, a sardine can on wheels. We met at the airport as planned.

"Did you know that you rented a Mercedes for me?" he asked.

"No. I asked for the cheapest car they had. What happened?" I said

"They gave me a $75.00 a day car. How am I going to put that on my expense account?"

"Tell Charlie the truth. I rented it, you didn't know." John worried about things like that. As it turned out, when John discovered that any alternative method of getting from Munich to Italy would have cost more, he cooled off a bit.

After we put all our bags in the sardine can, we turned on to the Autostrata for the drive to Florence. Autostrata is Italian for speedway or maybe it means "Autos go as fast as they can". Even though we got our sardine can up to 120 kilometers per hour, with only one wheel left on the ground, cars were passing us like we were standing still. The first time we saw a wind sock on a pole next to the highway, we thought there was an airport close by; the second time, we thought that distressed airplanes could land on the highway if they had to; the third time, we realized that it was for the cars! The cars were moving so fast that wind direction was important to the drivers.

We had a harrowing car drive from Milan. There were times during that drive we felt as if the Fiat was flying with no wheels on the road. We took a little time to find the hotel in Florence; we saw the famous DaVinci statute of David and we stopped at the big cathedral in the center of town. We washed up and John went off to find the local IBM office. I went out to do a little shopping for leather goods. Florence is not only known for its statuary and cathedrals, but also for its handmade leather articles. While I was loading up on presents for my wife and kids, John was meeting with the IBM manager who handled the Nuovo Pignone account. My Florence foray was much more successful that Johns'.

John waited a long time to meet the manager of IBM's branch in Florence, who had forgotten that he had this meeting with John. When they got that straightened out, the manager told John he had arranged to meet with some people at the Nuovo Pignone plant. The branch manager admitted he didn't know much about what was going on in the computer room at the plant; he thought it would be much better if John asked his questions directly. So, off they went. It quickly became apparent that not only didn't he know what was going on in his customer's shop; he didn't know how to get there. He drove John around and around Florence, all the while pointing out the tourist spots, but never arrived at the plant.

John finally told him that we had reserved time during out stay in Florence for sightseeing, but right now he was interested in seeing the Nuovo Pignone people. The IBM manager admitted that he had not been to the plant in a long time and wasn't sure how to get there. After a stop in a gas station for directions, they got on the right road and arrived quickly.

We thought we could find out what the Nuovo Pignone people were selling to the Chinese ("technology") and use that information to design our proposal for the computer equipment. The theory was flawless; the reality was the opposite. John found that the Italians at the plant were evasive and very hesitant to discuss their "secret" sale to the Chinese. John tried to persuade them. He mentioned Mr Wu. John couldn't tell them the name of the Chinese plant since Mr. Wu had neglected to mention it during our talks in February. Maybe the Italians thought we were trying to undermine their deal. Maybe they thought their sale was illegal and they weren't going to discuss it. Whatever the reason, John couldn't find out what the Chinese had bought from those people! We were back to square one.

At dinner that night, I told John, "I got a lot of beautiful leather presents for my family. I bought a pocket book for my wife, and I got the kids leather carry-alls for school." John was not impressed.

"The branch manager here was a loser," he said, "We wandered all over Florence looking for the Nuovo Pignone factory. He didn't know where it was." He took a sip of his cocktail before going on. "Then when we got there, they really didn't want to talk about China."

I answered, "So our trip here was a big waste. The only good thing was the presents I bought."

"Right", he said. "I didn't even get a chance to go shopping. I was with that dingbat all day. C'est la vie"

We would have to go with a proposal for gathering up a ton of daily factory information and distilling it in the computer. Then, the computer would spew out reports by the basketful that told the factory people what they had accomplished the day before. We had fancy names and acronyms for that process, but that was the essence. We were not happy, but that was it!

As if to top off our visit to Italy, we witnessed a scary thing on a flight to Rome to connect with a flight to New York on some internal Italian airline. I don't remember the name. The cabin consisted of double seats with a central aisle. We were among the first to board so we sat up front. We could see out the pilot's windows when the entrance to the cockpit was open. After we were airborne, the steward served a delicious Italian cocktail of some kind. Most of the seats behind us were empty. John and I were discussing what we had not found in Florence. As we were talking, the steward moved up the aisle and into the cockpit. He was carrying on a lively conversation with the two pilots when he leaned over the man on the left and began pushing levers and turning knobs. At the same time, the airplane banked to the left and the engines slowed down perceptively. I poked John and said jokingly, "I think the steward is piloting the plane." John looked up into the cockpit and said, "He is piloting the plane!" The steward continued talking, pushing and turning. We grabbed the armrests and went knuckles white. We did not enjoy the rest of the flight. Before landing, the steward returned to the passenger cabin as if nothing was wrong.

In Rome, we put together all the information we had collected and left for home. We consulted our factory computer specialist and wrote up the specifications for our computer system. Based on our specifications, the computer maintenance people put together a program to train people to maintain it. They also put together a spare parts list to keep the computer running. The software staff at Headquarters put together a training program for the Chinese who were going to install and run those computer programs. The pricing department calculated the prices for all these things; we typed it all up. We were ready to return to Beijing!

President Carter finally gave some hints regarding the direction he planned for China. Perhaps it was Zbigniew Brzezinski, his National Security Advisor, who dealt the cards. Who knows? The appointment of Leonard Woodcock, a seasoned labor negotiator and former President of the United Auto Workers union as the head of the U.S. Liaison Office in Beijing was a clarion call for negotiation and movement in our relations with China!

We simply did not know that Nuovo Pignone had sold them engineering programs that ran on their IBM computers. The

Chinese from the factory simply wanted a duplicate. The Ministry in Beijing, on the other hand, wanted the largest system we could export. We didn't know that either! We put together a proposal for a system that could churn out all kinds of factory production information data. Had we known, the system, the spare parts and the training programs could have been much smaller; small enough to handle those engineering programs. BUT, we had a set of equipment that would pass COCOM's inspection; we could price it out for delivery in China and we could detail all the training and maintenance stuff that was required.

During all this time, we had no hint of the true reason the Chinese government wanted this computer. All these efforts could have been eliminated had we known!

ON TO BEIJING...we had to rejoin Deng's industrial revolution in progress!

Chapter 7 – Bargaining with the Chinese

London Times, May 24, 1977

"MR. TENG LAYS DOWN TERMS
FOR REHABILITATION"

When Mr. Wu and Ms. Ma met John and me at the airport in June 1977, he hastened to tell us that he had been unable to get us rooms at the Beijing Hotel. Instead, he said, he had reserved rooms at a better hotel called the Minzu Hotel, also located near Tienamin Square. John didn't respond. Mr. Wu kept repeating that it was getting more difficult to get rooms since so many American companies wanted to send representatives to China. If you listened closely, you could infer that for some reason we (the Americans) were to blame for the absence of space at the Beijing Hotel.

At that time, the Chinese had only a few hotels where Westerners were put up. The city government owned and operated all the hotels. We did not qualify for the hotel used for "overseas" Chinese, the Chinese who lived in foreign countries, There was another hotel, the Oriental Hotel, that was used for foreign reporters and/or journalists; we didn't qualify for that one either. The Minzu and the Beijing Hotels were for the rest of us. The Communist government built hotels for foreigners; perhaps there were other accommodations for domestic users. Where were out negotiating partners staying? We never knew.

Although the Beijing Hotel had a very large capacity, only half of it was available for foreign guests at any given time. Something was always being fixed. That seemed to be typical for hotels in Socialist countries.

The Minzu faced the same street as the Beijing Hotel and was almost as large. They were about three blocks apart. The Beijing Hotel was east of Tienamin Square, the other on the opposite side of the square. We had not been inside it. This was our chance!

The car arrived at the front door. We should have been a little suspicious. There were no guards at the door, either to keep the Americans in or the Chinese out. The check in, with Mr. Wu in attendance went smoothly. The lobby was no better or worse than the Beijing Hotel's. We were told that we were assigned a suite containing a living room and two bedrooms, each with a private bath. So far so good! Mr Wu remembered we did all of our work between negotiating sessions in our hotel room.

We said our "Good Nights" to Mr. Wu after arranging the schedule for the following day. We carried our bags, including boxes of computer manuals, up to our suite.

After opening the door, I had to grope through the darkness for the light switch. When I found it and turned it on, the only light that went on was a little lamp on a table near the door. There were other tables nearby that also had lamps on them. John and I turned all ten of the little table lamps on.

The living room, once all the table lamps were lit, was very large. Not only was it large, it was also well stocked with furniture. There were the ubiquitous overstuffed sofas and chairs all over the room. Each chair or sofa was covered with tan slip covers. Each chair or sofa had its share of doilies on the arms and back rests. There was so much furniture in the room that we had to navigate carefully from the living room to our bedrooms. We could only take one piece of luggage with us at a time without bumping into the furniture. It was an obstacle course!

And, there was not a regular table or desk in sight although there were many little side tables next to all those chairs. We had been put into a furniture storeroom, not a hotel room. We looked for a telephone on all those little tables; there was none to be found. We somehow got ourselves and the luggage into the bedrooms and fell into bed. It had been a long and exhausting day. It was after 1:00 a.m. and nothing further could be done. The question still remained. Where were we going to work?

Normally, when we returned to our hotel rooms after a day's discussions with our friends, we would sit down to review and write out the agreed changes to our contract/treaty. The process required some desks where we could do that. We never knew what the Chinese were going to bring up so we had material on every subject in the proposed contract with us. It made quite a pile of paper. We kept it organized by spreading it out on various tables. We would be unable to do any of that in this room. During the past visits, we were in rooms that contained desks and a telephone to the outside world. We wrote and re-wrote the sections of the contract/treaty that we covered in our talks each day. We were on the telephone to New York almost every morning and every evening.

In the morning, we re-packed all our bags and left them by the door of the suite. I told John there was no way we could work in this room for six weeks. If we couldn't do that, there was no point in meeting with the Chinese. We talked it over and decided if we couldn't get a better arrangement, we should leave. No meetings, no discussions; no nothing. It was not an easy decision for us. Back home, without the facts, some of our critics would find it easy to paint a different picture of two guys who demanded the best hotel. But it wasn't true at all. We had no place to work!

We got our taxi and went to Er Li Go. We took our seats in the meeting room and didn't say a word about the hotel. Mr. Wu introduced the subject that he wished to discuss that morning. He explained that his clients (whom he finally identified), the Shenyang people, were waiting to see our new proposal.

After he finished, I stood up and moved my seat away from the center. This signal really startled Mr. Wu. For that rare moment, he had a worried look on his face. The change in our table positions was a first. Mr Wu knew something very important was coming. John assumed my seat. He began speaking in a very serious tone.

"Mr. Wu, I am afraid that we cannot begin our contract discussions today. We have something far more important to discuss." As Ms. Ma translated this, Mr. Wu's worried look got even worse. He did not have a clue as to what was coming. He looked at Ms. Ma as if she knew what was coming.

He said, "Fine". At least that's what Ms. Ma translated.

"Mr. Wu, we cannot resume our contract talks until our accommodations are changed. It will be impossible for us to conduct any normal negotiations when we cannot work in our hotel room before and after our meetings. You do your work in your offices; our hotel rooms are our offices." It was the voice of death!

Mr. Wu replied through the translator. "You actually mean you will stop our meetings because of your hotel room?" We could even detect the disbelief in Chinese. He looked at Ms. Ma as if he was questioning her translation.

"Yes"

"Because of the hotel room?" he repeated. I don't think he or Ms. Ma believed what they were hearing. The Shenyang men sat there with their mouths open. They heard and understood the Chinese side of the conversation; the English side with all the explanations was lost.

John went into a long explanation of the problem. Even when he finished, their expressions told us of their disbelief. It was real cultural shock! We had not taken this decision lightly; he wanted to impress that upon them. We needed someplace to work!

Mr. Wu said, "They told me at the hotel that there were no other rooms available. I tried the Beijing Hotel and they had no rooms available either." Cultural shock notwithstanding, he had to keep these talks going!

"I'm sorry to hear that" John was adamant. This was not a bluff; he meant every word that he uttered.

"Let's continue our discussions, and I will try to fix your problem as quickly as I can."

"Mr. Wu, I'm sorry. There is no point to our discussions if we cannot work in our hotel rooms. It doesn't even make a difference which hotel.'

"I promise that I will fix your problem." Wu said. That answer wasn't good enough.

John said, "We will return to Beijing when suitable rooms are available. Now we have to conclude this meeting because we have to arrange for airplane reservations to Tokyo"

At that, Mr. Wu began to believe what he was hearing. He may not have understood the "why" of the situation, but he clearly understood our reaction to it. John had convinced him of our intentions. He had to do something to keep us in Beijing or lose a great deal of face. If we left because of something his bosses thought he had control over it would be a disaster for him. There was no doubt in our minds that he would have as much trouble explaining our departure to his management, as we would have with our management. The Shenyang people hung on every word. Inside their eyeballs, you could see their computer floating away because of a hotel room. Mr. Mu stared at his friend Mr. Wu. I imagined that he was sending all kinds of subliminal messages.

He said, "Please go for your midday meal and return here. I will try to do something."

We left. When we came back, Mr. Wu took us in a car to the hotel and helped us collect all our baggage. Then he took us to the Peking Hotel where we moved into a suite on the ninth floor. It took us the rest of the day to unpack all the stuff we had brought with us.

Our new rooms in the Peking Hotel were more conducive to working and sleeping. I moved into Room 929, a corner suite with balcony consisting of a large living room (with a desk, several chairs, a couch, and a television) a separate bedroom with twin beds and a bath. We put all the cartons in the corner of the living room and asked the room boys to get us a large table and chairs for the center of the room. That became our office. John had a separate room down the hall. These were very grand accommodations; I don't know how Mr. Wu arranged to get them.

The next day we arrived at Er Li Go ahead of time. We had a lot of paper shuffling to take care of. The new contract/treaty proposal had to be put together for their translation. The form of our contract/treaty was entirely new and according to Mr Wu's specifications. The IBM lawyers had balked at his specifications. The IBM sales contract was as immutable as the Bible; it was pre-printed in many languages for use by IBM companies around the world. They would brook no changes, substantively of course, but in format as well. Mr Wu's specifications were an affront to their legal community. But we prevailed since the Chinese had not asked for any substantive changes, at least not yet. We felt we were keeping our eyes and efforts on the target, i.e., selling and installing the first computer in Communist China. Other items, like whether a paragraph was indented or not, or if the terms and conditions of our treaty/contract were stated separately from the product descriptions were minor.

As requested, we were prepared to go through the technical parts of the contract first. That covered the machines, programs and the education services that we were offering. We had two sets of contracts with us. They were duplicates except one copy didn't have prices shown while the other one had all the prices included. It was our intention to give the Chinese the copy without the prices since that was to be the subject of a later discussion. But our copy required prices so that we could follow any changes made during the discussions by our own private review of the price impact.

The hotel subject was never mentioned. It was as if nothing had happened. The Shenyang people had big smiles on their faces.

As before, we gave Mr. Wu the contract/treaty proposal. We had anticipated that he would arrange the translation overnight, so we gave him several additional copies. He handed one to Chen. As he did, I apologized to Chen for the length of the document. I knew that he was going to work through the night to finish the job. He said, "It's nothing, it's my job." Mr. Wu handed a copy to Ms. Ma. The third one he kept.

"Before we leave, I would like to say a few things about our proposal. Is that convenient?"

Mr. Wu answered, "Of course."

"Our proposal is as complete as we could make it based on the information we received during our last visit. Inasmuch as we have not seen the physical facilities and operations of the intended user, we have assumed many things about the computer configuration, the software and the engineering training that will be required to install and operate a computer system. Our hope is that these talks will resolve all our assumptions. But we should all remember that if we add or subtract anything from the items in this proposal it will cause a change in our price calculation."

When the translator said the Chinese word for "price", Mr. Wu's expression changed dramatically. That word was really his "hot button".

"We will discuss prices AFTER we finish these technical discussions."

"Of course", I said. "But it's important to remember that when we change things in this proposal, we change the price as well."

"That's not important right now. We are going to talk about technical matters first." Mr. Wu was not going to let me get the last word.

I responded. "And that's what we are prepared to do. This proposal contains computer and terminal configurations, spare parts for those configurations, control and application software and technical training for the programmers and maintenance engineers. All the technical requirements are there."

At that moment, I felt like our consultant, Ken Morse would have gone ballistic had he been in the room. Here we were telling the Chinese that we couldn't, wouldn't, separate price from content. To us they were one and the same; his thoughts would have been kinder to the Chinese.

"We'll meet tomorrow at 9:00 a.m.". With that, Mr Wu stalked out of the room. I thought that he considered our constant pressure on the subject of price and content had begun to annoy him, particularly in front of the Shenyang people. So be it! However, we forewarned of our position on price the first day we met. He did not like to be reminded of it; we did not want him to forget it either.

Everybody left. John and I gathered up all our papers and went downstairs to try to get a taxi back to the hotel. One came up rather quickly. As usual, we did not talk much in the taxi. We both had become obsessive about being "bugged".

After lunch, we decided to go for a walk. It was the beginning of summer, the weather was warm and the sun was shining for a change. We crossed the street in front of the hotel, turned left and headed east toward the Temple of the Moon. The street was crammed full of bicyclists. A brown and Mao blue mass of men and women, obediently stopped at the traffic lights and then moved off as one when the lights changed.

We turned right a couple of blocks down. We could see a large building at the end of this street. A lot of people were scurrying in and out. We walked towards the building and as we got closer, it became apparent that it was a huge train station. It stretched quite a distance to the right and left. We crossed the street and stood in front of the entrance.

Many people were in front of the station. Some of the crowd began to stare at us. Many who were looking at us had never seen a foreigner or a westerner, and, compared to all them, we were, indeed, rather strange looking. We went inside.

"John, are we supposed to be in here?" I was apprehensive. Courage, or stupidity, in the face of the enemy was not my forte.

"Sure, nobody has stopped us." That didn't prove a thing at that particular moment.

"Yeah, I know. But we kinda stand out in this crowd."

It was true, both John and I stood head and shoulders above all the Chinese. John was even taller than I, so he towered over the crowd.

"Let's look around."

"Okay." I answered even more hesitantly. This was crazy.

The central concourse was filled with people. It was about half the size of a football field and had the very high ceilings common to railroad stations all over the world. We didn't see any ticket sellers or information counters, just a lot of people. On either side of the concourse, there were entrances to the train tracks. As we moved towards one of the portals, the crowd of children around us got larger and larger. I was getting more and more scared. I kept thinking of Gulliver's Travels. I couldn't get over the thought of what happens when "big guys" get inundated with thousands of "little guys".

"John, let's get out of here."

"Wait, I want to see the locomotive."

"John, we'll ask Wu to take us to a locomotive. C'mon."

"The engine is just down here. It won't take but a minute." I would have left, but I did not want to leave him there alone.

We moved down the track side to the steam engine he had spotted. It was immense. I had to look up to see the top of the wheel things on the side. The parts we could see were so clean they sparkled. I could see my face reflected in a part that had no paint on it. John was in heaven. He just stood there and looked up and down at that monster. If any machine ever portrayed raw power, that locomotive sure did. Even I was mesmerized by the sight.

While we were looking, a man in a blue uniform with a white leather belt and a white hat came up behind us. He didn't say anything until he touched my sleeve. When I turned to tell the kids to go away I saw who it was. In less than one second, I had visions of a Chinese jail cell on some remote island with a bowl of rice and a glass of water each day. The policeman spoke softly to me. I grabbed John and pointed. The policeman continued speaking.

I had no doubt he was asking us "What the hell are you doing here? or Let me see your papers! or come with me!"

John said quietly, "Show him your passport." He was sure taking it all very calmly.

So, while the policeman was still talking, I took out my passport. John gave him his as well. The policeman looked through them. I don't think that he could read English, but he looked at our passport pictures and then at our faces. He found our Chinese visas in the passports. At least he could read those. He continued talking. Meanwhile my thoughts had moved from the jail cell to a scene showing us being escorted in handcuffs to the airport for expulsion.

Suddenly he stopped talking. He put the passports behind his white belt. He took John's sleeve in one hand and my sleeve in the other. Very gently, he maneuvered us away from the locomotive and back the way we had come. This time, movement was an effort. A large crowd had gathered around us and the policeman had to push and shove them aside to make way for us. He got us out to the street in front of the station. He took the passports out of his belt and made a final comparison of our passport pictures to our faces before he handed them back to us.

We made our way back to the hotel nonstop. We didn't know it at the time, but there was a lot going on that the police were worried about. Deng Xiao Ping was rattling the cage of the government, and the posters were up on the walls of the Palace. I am sure that the police were taking notice of any congregation of more than three people. The fact that we had gathered a large crowd at the railroad station must have caused the policeman to take notice. We stayed in the hotel the rest of the day. John took his third bath of the day while I tried to bury myself in one of my detective stories. We never mentioned this to Mr. Wu.

The next day we began the technical discussions. In about two weeks, we whizzed through all the units that made up the hardware system, all the specifications of those units and all of the software that they required. Our Chinese friends took nothing for granted. They wanted us to explain every specification for every computer unit. Each gentleman must have felt obligated to ask something; and they did. They had at least five questions about everything. We explained what each item was for, why it was there and how it operated. I think we literally gave them an electrical engineering course in computer construction and operation. There were very few instances where we couldn't gain agreement with a explanation of the whys and the wherefores of the situation.

If Big Mu wanted a faster model of the same machine, we said fine. If he wanted a larger capacity machine in the same model group, we said finc. The only time we had to hesitate was if, and when, an upgrade in performance pushed against or went over the COCOM embargo limits. Thankfully, that only happened once. Big Mu wanted high performance disc storage devices. The minute he raised that question, I had visions of the Colonel back there in the Pentagon. If he were here, he would simply go nuts!

We tried to talk him out of them by using an old argument. When configuring a computer system it is always desirable to have the input and output units' performance values in balance with the central computer unit's performance value. If the central computer unit was fast, you could have equally fast input and output units. If the central computer was medium fast, the same logic held. We told Big Mu that the high performance disc drives were too fast for the central unit. He didn't believe us; he insisted that they must have the fastest devices.

Unfortunately, high performance disc devices were on the "no-no" list of embargoed exports. They were also on the "no-no" list of my Colonel friend back there in the Pentagon. Although I could sell them, there was no way I would ever deliver them. Since the balance argument had been refused, we had no option other than to tell the truth. I really wanted to tell him about my Colonel in the Pentagon, but I was sure he wouldn't care and Wu would have another fit.

"Big Mu, I can sell them to you, but they will never be delivered."

"I don't understand" Big Mu had a quizzical expression on his face; he really did not understand. There were others in that room who did understand.

"I will never be able to get an export license from the U.S. Government for these disc drives."

At those words, Wu looked up. His expression changed from bland to furious.

He said, "We don't want to hear anything about "export licenses" during these discussions!" He even raised his finger and pointed at me.

Wu knew exactly what I was talking about. If he were to allow me to discuss embargo restrictions on computer exports, it would appear as if he recognized that China had to accept the facts of the embargo rules in regard to this contract. This was a political position he would never, ever, ever endorse.

He went on in a very stern voice. "If there are any other parties to this contract, they should be at this table. If they cannot appear, then we will adjourn these talks until they can. Big Mu does not need the high performance units. Continue!" That was it! No discussion, no nothing.

We all found out the hard way that there wasn't going to be any mention of export licenses or any related subject. But the subject was always there. One of the other requirements for an American license was a contractual monitoring requirement. The US government required all computer exports covered by the embargo to be inspected by the vendor (IBM) periodically to determine if any military usage was evident. We had not mentioned this yet, but we knew when we did the proverbial "perfect storm" would ensue. But we still had some time.

In the meantime, we did come across a few unrelated points that caused many days of discussion. Sometimes IBM's blatant bureaucracy created those disagreements. The first time that we presented a contract to Mr. Wu, it was in the "standard" IBM format and style. The lawyer/authors had sequenced the paragraphs the way they wanted; to a western bureaucratic lawyer it was perfectly logical. When we discussed changing that contract to Mr. Wu's required format, "technical" content separate from "commercial" content, the lawyers in our headquarters really got their noses out of joint. We had several rancorous telephone conversations in the middle of the night. Neither John nor I saw any merit in sticking to any particular format, but we had had to fight with Mr. Wu for a day or so before we were able to agree to modify the style and format of our contract. Charlie, back in our headquarters, had come to our aid in circumventing this unnecessary bureaucratic obstacle. This was one of many turf battles Charlie fought.

The incident over the contract format illustrates another international negotiating dictum. "Never agree (or disagree) too quickly!" You convey the wrong impression if you give in to quickly. The credibility of your response, and, sometimes your own general credibility, is at risk. Quick responses indicate a lack of thought to the proposal.

In the middle of these negotiations, John had to leave the meeting a little early to take care of another turf battle. Ken was in Beijing negotiating with Han Li Fu and another Chinese organization. Some weeks previously, Ken called to tell John he (Ken) had sold an IBM cardpunch to Han for some institute in Beijing. During these talks, Han brought up the subject of this IBM machine and Ken wanted to please him. John had drafted a one page contract for the machine (a minor one) and gave it to Ken for Han's signature. Ken took the contract back to Han. Han changed one of the provisions of the contract; regardless, Ken signed it on behalf of IBM. John was apoplectic when Ken showed him the completed contract. John fumed, "Ken, you can't modify a contract that I give you! And, you sure as hell can't sign one on behalf of IBM". He tore it up right in front of his eyes. "You call Han and tell him we have to see him as soon as possible, today, if possible." They both went to see him early the next morning. John told Han that Ken does not represent IBM in any way shape or form. He brought the original version of the contract, which both signed on the spot. Weeks later, John told me Han wanted the machine; no parts, no manuals, no education, no nothing. John thought it was a clear case of the Chinese wanting to reverse engineer the unit. We no longer manufactured new ones, so we didn't care.

That cardpunch machine came back to haunt us about a year later. Han told Mr. Wu that he wanted to see someone from IBM. Wu told me. I called and made an appointment. Han Li Fu wanted to order a single part for a card punch. I knew nothing about a cardpunch and Han had to explain the whole story to me. I answered that I had to know the parts group to which it belonged, as well as the part number itself. Some parts are common to many machines so which machine it is for could be important. Although my response could indicate knowledge on my part, I can assure you my knowledge of cardpunch machines was less than zero. But there was no way I would let Han know that. He took me to the Institute so that I could see the machine.

We went into a room on the first floor. The parts of the cardpunch covered the floor of the room. I was looking at a bone fide attempt to reverse engineer the machine. They had taken it all apart so that individual parts could be copied. Now they were having real trouble getting it back together again because they had mangled one of the parts in the disassembly. I thought to myself, they have one hellava nerve to call me for a part that

154

would help them make a copy of our machine. On the other hand, it was a cardpunch. IBM was refurbishing them in India at that time, but it was not a major product that I wanted to worry about. So, I helped them find the part and group number and I ordered a replacement. In the process, I insisted that they purchase several replacements at the same time.

Embarrassing moments, either for the Chinese or for us, came up a couple of other times. We had a IBM factory management expert in town to speak to the Shenyang group. Remember, this computer application was our story for our export license application. One Sunday when we were not working, he went for a walk down the shopping street, called Wan Fu Gin, next to the hotel. He was carrying the standard American tourist's equipment, his camera. That's one of the ways you can identify an American overseas. As he told us later, a limousine stopped in front of a department store. The driver dressed in some sort of uniform, hopped out and went around to the passenger side to open the door. Our guy had never seen a chauffeured automobile in Beijing before. As the military General, in full uniform, got out of the car, our expert took his picture. The General, who knows, he could have been a Field Marshall or a Lieutenant, saw what happened and he said something to the driver holding the door open. The driver ran over to our man and grabbed the camera. Our man resisted, but only for an instant. He told us he thought at that moment that he would never get home to his wife. The driver fumbled with the camera for a couple of seconds until he found the catch for the film magazine. He took the film out of the camera and put it in his pocket, gave the camera back, and returned to the car. Our man tried not to run back to the hotel. Another lesson learned!

After several weeks of haranguing with Mr. Wu and Shenyang people, we welcomed any kind of diversion. One Friday afternoon, Wu asked us if we would like to see a Minorities Show. Neither John nor I had any idea of what a minorities show was, but we were both game, ready for anything. After a while twelve-hour days with little sleep makes one a dullard. Wu and Ms. Ma picked us up at the hotel directly after dinner and off we went.

Let me tell you, that show was something. We sat through about eight dance numbers that were supposed to be characteristic of a Chinese minority represented by each group of dancers. According to the show, there are 11 Chinese minority groups although only eight were represented in the show. Each group's costumes were more colorful than their predecessors, but to my ignorant eye, many dances appeared to be the same. Some of the dances had some heavy political overtones when one or more of the dancers gracefully carted a very large picture of either Chairman Mao, or Chairman Hua Go Feng around the stage. I asked Ms. Ma what some of the dance titles listed in the playbill were. I was told that several of the dances were entitled "Ode to our Chairman" or something like that. I guess I should have known.

During an intermission, I asked Ms. Ma, "Can you translate any of the lyrics of the songs?"

She said, "Of course. Which one would you like?"

I pointed to one of the lines in the program. "That one,", I said.

She translated "We love you, Chairman Mao" followed by "We want our lives to be like yours, Chairman Mao," with an absolutely straight face.

As politely as I could, I said "Thank you" and decided not to ask for any further translation.

Most of the women dancers were lovely. Some of the men were handsome. I could see some differences in physical appearances, but many of the cast looked the same to me. Most of the dances were unimpressive, but the ones performed by the Mongolian minority were good. They did some numbers that looked just like the Russian Cossack dancing that I had seen in Moscow. All in all, it was a very pleasurable evening.

AUGUST 1977 - ENTERTAINMENT AT NATIONALITIES SHOW IN BEIJING

On our own, we tried to find things to do to relieve the boredom. A trip to the "Friendship Store" always did the trick. The "Friendship Store" was a government super market (Chinese style) that sold foodstuffs and other things for foreign currency, especially dollars. Foreigners were the only customers allowed. In fact, your passport had to be shown to gain entrance. I often wondered if you came from a country that China was not happy with, would they exclude you from the "Friendship Store"?

The Friendship Store reminded me of the "free" markets in Moscow where farmers and trades people sold all kinds of farm foods and where any and all customers were accommodated. My favorite there was what we call sour cream, but fresh sour cream made that morning. It's an acquired taste I had acquired it from my Russian father. It's called "Smetana' in Russian. We used to go on a Sunday morning to get a farm fresh breakfast rather than the hard boiled eggs in the hotel. But this was China; there was no Smetana, although you could get any kind of bird's eggs you might desire.

I wouldn't have purchased anything in the meat department of a Chinese "Friendship Store" because their unrefrigerated and un-butchered chickens, goats and beef were, to say the least, unappetizing. Since butchering American style is not practiced west of Hawaii, the cuts of meat were totally unfamiliar to me. Their dry goods, like cereals and grains were interesting, as were the 50 gallon drums of sesame oil and other frying agents, items not found in American supermarkets.

One of the most interesting, and to us, funny, things sold there was their beautiful acupuncture kits. Acupuncture, at least at that time, did not enjoy a place in the medical lexicon in the U.S. For a few dollars, I think it was $8.00, you could get a complete assortment of acupuncture needles along with two large drawings of the human body, one for the back and one for the front. On each of these drawings, an "x" was placed where a needle (also specified) could be inserted to correct some sort of problem. The human diagram was filled with 'x's" and accompanying Chinese characters denoting something or other. Unfortunately, I couldn't read the Chinese. But who cared; any problem lower down on the body would be cured by the needle poke above it. Armed with those needles and charts, I fantasized going into the acupuncture business in the U.S. I actually purchased a kit and brought it home. After some years, the novelty wore off when I discovered you needed a license to practice acupuncture in the U.S. The kit disappeared.

Unfortunately, we had to go back to the negotiating table. The peace treaty between IBM and the Peoples Republic of China was waiting

The American tendency to tell all got us in trouble as soon as we were finished negotiating which computer was required. American marketing people and lawyers cannot refrain from telling their prospective customers everything they know. Relevance is never considered. It's as if the human talking mechanism takes control of the mind, everything spills out. That propensity is evidenced in our written sales proposals as well.

The contract people had put a phrase in the proposal that we gave to the Chinese that read as follows: "some of the machines included in this contract may be reconditioned..."

The proposal went on to state that reconditioned or not, the machines were unconditionally guaranteed to function as they were supposed to. But it was a fact that some of the machines wouldn't be of original manufacture. This was due, as was so much of the deal, to the embargo restrictions we were facing. New machines were entirely newly manufactured and usually newest technology; older technology meant that some units were already out of new production. Newest technology was prohibited from export to embargoed countries.

Mr. Mu picked up on the "reconditioned" word very quickly. I don't know how the Chinese language handled that particular sentence, but he was very unhappy with it. He said to me, eyeball to eyeball, "Reconditioned machines are not acceptable." This was one of the few times that there were no niceties and no formality to his statements.

"We can only accept new machines in China." This was getting worse by the sentence. That pronouncement sounded a little political.

Big Mu piped up. "You must guaranty that all machines and parts are newly manufactured."

Wu came back with his entry in the fray. "We can only contract for new equipment." They were ganging up on us.

"Gentlemen, how am I going to do that when I know that some of the units might be reconditioned? Please remember that our warranty covers all the machines, all of them, no matter what they are. If they don't work, we will replace them."

"My government will not allow me to accept used machines." Mu said.

"In one sense, all the equipment has been used before. Every time we run diagnostic tests on the equipment, it is used. That's why my company doesn't use the word "new", because the equipment is not "new", it's been used before." I had deliberately taken the word "new" out of the proposal, accidentally leaving the word "reconditioned" in.

"Why don't you just take the words "reconditioned" out of the contract?" Wu said. Ever the negotiator, he could always come up with an alternative.

I thought to myself, that's the first time that any customer I ever dealt with wanted something <u>removed</u> from the warranty. Putting those words into the contract was a gratuitous gesture that some lawyer thought would avoid a lawsuit. If I was able to take the word out, I would be avoiding a confrontation that I wasn't sure I could win.

"Let's take a break." I responded. By this time, I could say that in passable Chinese.

John and I walked down the hall outside the room. I told John that we were in a box with no easy way out. We had deliberately written the warranty without words like "new" and "unused" so that we guarantied functioning machines only. A functioning machine was a machine that passed our diagnostic tests. To me, "new, used or reconditioned" were irrelevant. That reconditioned word got by our review in Tokyo and now we were suffering from it.

If we could get away with just removing the one word we could get by. We couldn't add the word "new" as they requested. We would be right back where we are right now. So, "reconditioned" had to go.

John would have to spend hours on the telephone that night with Charlie. Charlie had to go back to our lawyers and convince them that we wouldn't be sued if we were to remove the "reconditioned equipment" phrase from the warranty. I only had to go back in the room and get the Chinese to agree to its removal and not to add the word "new" in its place. "Functioning machine" was a term I had dreamt up to cover IBM in the place of "new". I thought John had the harder job convincing the bureaucrats back home. Meanwhile, we had to go back to the table and press on.

We went back to the table.

"We have to review this situation with New York. However, in the meantime, I propose that we re-word the sentence to remove the words, 'Some of the equipment will be reconditioned'. The rest of the warranty mentioning "functioning machine" will remain the same.

Surprisingly, Mr. Wu said, "OK." On every other occasion where we had to use this tactic, he would respond with some statement about getting all the relevant parties to the contract around the table. This time he didn't. I wondered why.

No sooner we had solved the "reconditioned "problem; Mr. Mu mentioned that we had to discuss the shipment of the computer system. This was an old subject so we couldn't imagine what new twist he was going to test us with.

During the discussions in February, Mr. Shu had mentioned that they wanted the computer to be air shipped to China. They didn't want to wait for a sea shipment. The IBM traffic people had determined that the newly opened international airport in Peking was an acceptable port of entry from IBM's point of view. All of the normal international documentation, insurance and handling would be effective to Peking. In fact, there was no closer air port of entry at the time.

Based on that information, we had to have someone in IBM, we didn't know who, arrange for all the various pieces of the computer system to be air shipped to our plant in Japan. There, in a very unusual step, we arranged for the system to be put together and tested. It was unusual since IBM's practice was to assemble the computer right at the customer's site. That was the most cost effective way. The various boxes and units normally would arrive during the same week. We couldn't do that in China. Beijing did not have normal daily air service to many locations. We had to avoid multiple handling and the risks associated with packing and unpacking the units many times.

Unfortunately, and for all those reasons, we couldn't follow the normal practice in this case. In fact, there was nothing normal about the whole project. Some units of the system were old; they were coming out of storage. Other units of the system were reconditioned. Most importantly, some pieces originated in Europe, in South America as well as in Canada and in the U.S. It would take days, even weeks, locating all the units we needed and arranging to get them. We were concerned about sabotage in some of these places by folks who did not agree with trading with China or giving them a modern solid state computer.

All of these problems were caused by the embargo on computers using state-of-the-art technology. We had to find each of the units that we wanted to sell wherever in the IBM world we could. So, we decided to assemble the whole computer system in Japan. There we could test it completely and ship it as a complete and operating system, a la our warranty. Probably the most important thing of all, we could positively guarantee the whole system.

There was no commercial airfreight service to China. We planned to charter an airplane to pick up the whole thing in Japan and take it to Beijing. Willy, our maintenance angel, had also arranged that the same maintenance people who assembled and tested it in Japan would do the same thing in China. We covered the sabotaged angle and the warranty angle with one shot. The only thing that the Chinese had to do by themselves was to transport the system from the Beijing Airport to the factory in Shenyang.

Mr. Mu threw a monkey wrench right into our well thought-out plans.

"We want to have the computer air shipped to Shenyang." He has his little notebook open in front of him. He was still smiling (that was good) but he was clutching the notebook rather tightly (that was bad). The mere fact he raised this point should have put us on notice higher-ups were involved. He was asking for a foreign airplane (possibly CIA) to fly over previously forbidden Chinese territory and land at a previously unmentionable airport. WOW! We were so naïve.

"Shenyang? How are we supposed to do that?" I answered. All I knew was Shenyang was north of Beijing, it didn't have a commercial airport.

"We will arrange it." The smile was slowly leaving his face. This was serious stuff to him. He looked at Big Mu for a little encouragement. Big Mu didn't even blink.

"Arrange it? There is no commercial airport in Shenyang. Are there freight handling facilities in Shenyang?" I asked. I was getting a little annoyed with all these things coming up after settlement of this issue weeks before. How come they could open closed books, but we couldn't; particularly a closed price book. The IBM Traffic Department warned us that they would take no responsibility for handling and delivery if their suggestions (?) were not taken. This threat is the ultimate bureaucratic threat; do it our way or else!

"We will arrange it." Mr. Mu insisted.

"How?" Mr. Mu now knew that I wasn't going to simply agree with him and let the issue slide. He had to give me a reasonable answer. Flying over territory that had not been opened to commercial aviation started wars.

"There is a military airfield in Shenyang. We will ask them to allow the airplane to land." He replied. Insofar as he was concerned that should be the end of my concern. It was only the beginning!

I had thoughts of telling the people at the Defense Department in Washington that the computer they didn't want us to sell to the Chinese was being delivered at a military airfield. My Colonel friend would go ballistic! Maybe now was the time to tell them about my Colonel friend at the Pentagon. Then again, maybe I shouldn't. They probably had their own "Colonel" friends who did not want anything from the U.S., much less a computer.

"Do they have forklifts to take the crates out of the airplane?" I was trying to approach this thing in a reasonable and logical way.

"We don't know. We will find out."

"You will have to tell us the proper air route the aircraft must take. We don't want it shot down. Hah Hah." I tried a little levity. I remembered the first non-scheduled stop we had made somewhere around Shanghai when we first came to China. Mr. Mu was clever at reading us; if I stopped with the very pointed questions, he felt he was going to prevail.

"We will find out" No laughter at my joke. Again Mr. Mu looked to Big Mu.

"Now, how are we going to say all of this in the contract? Our warranties will only go as far as Tokyo. If anything happens after we put the computer on the plane, it's your risk." That wasn't exactly true, but in negotiation, facts sometimes get a little bent.

"No, no. According to the proposal, your warranty runs for up to 90 days after the computer is installed, not shipped." Mr. Mu came back.

"Yeah, but that's only if we ship in the normal way to a recognized international airport. Military airfields don't count!" That was also not exactly true.

"What difference does it make to you? We are paying the shipping expenses"

"I know that. It's not the shipping expense, it's the cost of the computer if it is destroyed or lost."

"If the computer is destroyed, it is one computer out of the thousands that you sell each year. If we lose it, it is the only computer that we have. The loss is far more significant on our side."

"I understand that. Let me see what I can do." He had me. Mr. Mu was very clever. We had to find a way to ship the damn thing to Shenyang.

Mr. Wu and Mr. Shu recognized my last phrase as the beginning of an agreement on the subject. We had to make up some rationale that would pass muster back home. The only stickler was the label "military airfield". John felt that if we could avoid using those words anywhere, we would be okay. We agreed that we would use the label "Shenyang Municipal Airport" instead. A bent truth to be sure; two of the three words were correct - Shenyang and Airport. .

We discovered much later our "Shenyang Municipal Airport" was the site of a Peoples Liberation Army air base and headquarters. Planes were sited there even before the Korean War.

Our discussion on air shipment illustrated what came to be a very common method of resolving issues that arose. Sometimes we were able to address it in a positive way that the Chinese could accept. Sometimes we had to stand fast and they would cave in. And, sometimes, as in the shipment issue, we both agreed to sidestep the issue at hand and trust each other to do the right thing.

Mr. Wu was sensitive to our personal situation. Working 6 days a week, very long hours, sometimes made us both grouchy and stressed. John would take a bath and soak the stress out that way. Sometimes, he took several baths in one day. I read myself into a stupor with nonsense detective novels. When my eyes refused to function, I would fall asleep for a couple of hours. When the weekend came, Mr. Wu would suggest a tourist outing for us. Once it was a trip to the site of the discovery of the Peking Man. This was the skull of some prehistoric being. But he explained that the skull wasn't there, someone had taken it out of the country. The ride there would be interesting; he and Ms. Ma would accompany us in one of those little cars for 4 hours outbound and 4 hours inbound.

We decided to take a pass on that invitation. An immediate problem arose. How could we diplomatically refuse the invitation in a way that wouldn't shut off any future invitations? We established a sickness routine. On one occasion, I would be sick and unable to go. On another, John would get sick and be unable to go. Since they didn't want to separate us, no one would go. Our problem was keeping track of who was sick last.

Another time Wu took John and me to an evening outdoor anniversary celebration of the Revolution. It was held in Tienamin Square. Bleacher stands for foreigners had been set up against the front walls of the Forbidden City. They faced the half-finished Mao Mausoleum. The seats were separated from the mass of people in the square by rows and rows of soldiers. As we walked past these soldiers to our seats, I marveled at their size, demeanor, and "spit and polish". My previous impression of pajama clad Chinese solders melted away at the sight of these 6-foot West Point "copies". This was Chairman Mao's renowned Honor Guard.

For the next hour and a half, we viewed the most magnificent fireworks displays we had ever seen. It was stunning! The vivid displays originated to the east, north and west of the city. We couldn't see their origin. All of the buildings lining the Square were outlined against the background of the rockets, sprays and waterfalls of the fireworks. The colors were the brightest I had ever witnessed. First we looked to the west, followed by a display to the north, followed by bright lights to the east. It went around and around. The sky filled with smoke and the smell of cordite was everywhere. By the time Mr. Wu led us back to our hotel nearby, my neck was totally bent backwards. It was impressive; we spoke of it many times in the following days.

We had almost reached the end of the technical sections of the contract. We had gotten over some hurdles. Everything had been continuously moving and it seemed like we were going to finish up that section of the contract/treaty rather quickly.

Wu smiled and said, "We have to talk about an acceptance test."

As soon as those words were out of his mouth, Mr. Mu perked up. He had been sitting quietly for a couple of days while we covered things which didn't interest him. This subject must have been close to his heart.

Mr. Mu said, "We need to put some words in the contract so our technicians can run our acceptance tests. The words should come right after the part where it says that IBM engineers shall install our computers."

"Why in the world do you want to test after we have finished installing the computer? I asked him.

"Oh, it's our normal practice with a new machine."

"But this isn't a machine tool, it's a computer. When our engineers finish the installation tests, the machine is yours. You can run any tests you want, for as long as you want."

"No, no. Before we can sign any acceptance papers, we have to run the tests ourselves."

John whispered to me. "Do they mean that they could hold up payment until they run installation tests to their satisfaction?

"You got it." I whispered back. "The tests themselves wouldn't take a lot of time, but they would simply keep running tests until they are satisfied the machines met the technical specifications that were listed in the contract."

I turned to Mr. Mu. "Mr Mu let me be sure that I understand what you want. After our engineers finish installing the computer system, you want your technicians, who just finished <u>our</u> classes, to repeat the installation tests, as well as your own tests, so that you can accept the machines. Is this correct?"

He wasn't going to be intimidated. He said, "Yes, that's right"

He wasn't averse to trying a little intimidation himself. He then said, "Our leaders and the people in the Technology Bureau of the First Ministry require us to do this." His reference to his "leaders" and this brand new "Technology Bureau" should have put us on notice of higher-ups involvement; this never was mentioned before. Again, we were so naïve!

."Well", I said, "you want the students to run the same diagnostic tests we taught."

"Yes." He was sticking by his guns. He wasn't even smiling; this was serious stuff for him.

I raised my voice a notch. "Who or what are we testing? The students, to see if they learned to do the diagnostics test properly. Or, are we re-testing the machines that our engineers just finished assembling and testing?"

Mr. Mu came right back at me. "It seems very strange to me that even though you are certain your machines are running properly, you do not want the very people you trained to run the same tests and prove the very same results."

"Not exactly true. Your technicians can run those diagnostics for as long as they like; BUT, not as an acceptance test. When our engineers finish their entire test and turn the control of the computers over to the Shenyang Blower Works, they are installed as described in our contract."

He still didn't like that one bit. We went back and forth for the balance of the day. Neither side budged one inch. In Mr. Mu's world of machine tools, acceptance testing was normal. His technicians tested every tool he had ever purchased before they accepted it.

IBM, with its history of leasing its equipment, did not allow customer tests before acceptance of a machine. Whether for that reason, or some other, we couldn't agree to allow payment and title to a machine to be dependent on someone else's test. The precedent that would be set, not only in China, but elsewhere as well, would drive our lawyers absolutely wild. Even I could understand that.

The next day we began again right where we left off. Mr. Mu repeated his requirement of an acceptance test. We repeated that there would be no acceptance test in contract.

Mr. Wu entered the discussion. "Is there some language that we could use that requires Chinese technicians to witness the tests that IBM engineers perform?"

The word "witness" struck a chord. "Absolutely" I said. I smelled the beginning of a resolution.

"How about our technicians watch as the diagnostic tests are run? After completion of those tests, the IBM engineers can complete their installation documentation."

I could have kissed him right then and there. I agreed without any hesitation. Mr. Wu saved the day. He saw the middle ground that had eluded all the rest of us. Another hurdle crossed. The only technical subject left was the computer training classes IBM would provide.

The education that IBM usually provided was broken up into two pieces. One piece covered courses on the maintenance of the equipment. A second piece covered all the software and programming involved.

For educational efficiency, the maintenance education people (yet another bureaucracy within a bureaucracy!) wanted to limit students in any single class to multiples of four. They insisted on putting a cap on the number of students in each class. For maintenance people, study in the classroom itself was kept to a minimum; hands-on training was emphasized. From the educator's viewpoint, when the students were working inside a computer unit, there was just so much physical room. Available space limited the number of students the instructor could handle simultaneously. Add in the requirement for translation and you had some real educational problems. We were told, at least a dozen times, the training was intended to make each maintenance worker completely self-sufficient; he rarely would require somebody else to help him do his job.

The printed prospectus for the maintenance school pronounced:

THE COURSES PRESENTED HEREIN REPRESENT THE BEST EDUCATION IBM OFFERS FOR ENGINEERS RESPONSIBLE FOR COMPUTER MAINTENANCE.

WE ARE PROUD TO PRESENT

THE IBM MAINTENANCE RECORD OF EXCELLENCE

Our Chinese friends were very impressed with that statement.

For obvious reasons, the pricing people wanted to adjust the price as the number of students increased. If there were four students, the price would be "X". If the number of students doubled to eight, the price would be "2X". But if the number of students were five, or six or seven, the price would still be "2X". When we attempted to come up with a more logical formula, it wasn't only the pricing people who gave us a hard time; it was the maintenance education people as well. There was no way we could have IBM's formula changed for China.

When we were asked to add a single student to IBM's magic number, we explained our dilemma to Mr. Wu and Mr. Shu. We tried to get them to understand the situation with machine maintenance education, hands-on training, and the physical problems. I believe they understood, but they, like us, had the problem of convincing their leaders. After all, this was the first western computer in China and the more engineers they could get trained by IBM, the better it would be. Little did we know that they had seven (note the odd number) electrical engineers waiting to become students.

We thought that the Chinese answer to this problem was to call some of the students, "students" and others "translators". We were very wrong. Their translators were just that and nothing more. Not one of the translators who went to IBM classes ever became a specialist in the subject of those classes. Nevertheless, at the time, our pricing people considered "translators" just another label for "student".

On the systems and programming side, the situation was quite different. For these subjects, classroom lecture and study was the mainstay of the curriculum. There was hand-on training, but compared to classroom time, it was relatively minor. There was no physical limitation on the number of people in the class, only the room size itself.

After many days of discussion, we agreed to provide computer training for a total of eleven people who were to do the programming and operate the system. Typically, in the United States, where software education was ostensibly free, the number would have been half that. However, since the Chinese were paying for the education (our pricing people had said that classes for the Chinese would be separately priced) as well as the travel and living expenses we accepted the increased number. Keep in mind the Chinese were supposed to attend classes already designed and taught, and, sometimes, already scheduled for other customers in a specific location. Under those circumstances, the cost to IBM for those classes was already factored into the overall costs of the locations involved. Charging the Chinese for those classes was a distinct "win-win" proposition.

"Let's review what we have all agreed to." I proposed, "The primary classes will be held in Hong Kong, all the others will be held either in the United States or in Canada, depending on the schedule. Is that ok?"

Mr. Shu answered. "Yes, that is okay. But we want to be sure that most of the classes will be held in the United States. This is very important to us. We want our people to learn the latest in the U.S. technology." There was a political component involved. Deng had expressed "Western technology was the key to China's modernization". His point was particularly important to the Ministry, but it was to become a problem for us. At that time, Canada had diplomatic relations with China for many years; the U.S. did not. It wouldn't appear too strange for a large group of oddly dressed Chinese to be in an IBM Education center in Canada; the U.S. was another matter. Many people in the U.S., and some in IBM as well, would not take kindly to finding a large group of Chinese in their midst.

I said, "We will try for United States classes even though the course content is exactly the same in Canada. Since you do not want your people traveling back and forth from China to attend a single class, we have to find the classes that will ensure a continuous schedule. We have promised to do the best we can." Schedule and continuity was more important than anything else. Neither we nor the Chinese wanted to have 10-15 Chinese visitor/students sitting around doing nothing no matter what country they were in.

"Okay" Mr Mu spoke up. Everyone was getting into the act.

"There is a strong possibility that there will be some traveling required within the United States or Canada, but we will try to avoid any long gaps in the education program. However, I am sure some gaps will occur."

"That's fine. Thank you."

I tried to finish the subject. "OK. There will be five classes for your three System Programmers, seven classes for four application programmers and two classes for four operators. I hope you understand that eleven students are almost double the number of students that we normally recommend for training. Both John and I realize that it is important to you that as many people as possible get original training."

Neither John nor I recognized foreign training as a key ingredient for the Chinese. We did not realize these "students" would become the "teachers" almost as soon as they returned to China. The Chinese were having us "teach the teachers", normally we teach the workers! Maybe its psychological, but I now know the Chinese believe foreign education is better than local education on the very same subject.

"Thank you". Mr Mu responded.

"And, lastly, I told them, all of the classes are the normal and regular classes that IBM provides for our U.S. customers in IBM Education Centers. They will contain the same material and be taught by the same teachers who normally teach those subjects. Oh, and by the way, all the classes are taught in English. I believe that is all that we have agreed to."

Mr. Mu was jotting some notes in his notebook while the translator was going through all of this. When the translator got to the last sentence, he quickly looked up at me and spoke.

"Wait a minute. There may be a problem."

"What's that?" I asked cautiously. I was weary; I wasn't up to another long discussion.

"Translation." Mr Mu said.

"What about translation?" We had already covered that. I looked at John. He was turning pages in his notebook to find where we had covered education translation. He found it quickly. He shook his head up and down.

"We need translators." Mr. Mu continued.

I answered quickly on the basis of John's message. "No problem. We have provided for a translator in each class."

"We don't think that will be enough." Mr Mu responded.

"Why won't one translator be enough? There is only one instructor in each class. One instructor equals one interpreter!"

"Wait, you don't understand." He was smiling; this was important, but not life or death or political. Big Mu usually showed agreement with every word that Mr. Mu uttered. It was obvious that he was in total agreement with Mr. Mu on this subject.

The minute I heard that phrase in translation, which, by the way, I had begun to understand without translation, I knew what was about to happen. Mr. Mu wanted something from us that had not come up before.

I would admit privately that I had never had experience with a translator becoming knowledgeable in a technical subject. I knew that the translating itself was hard enough without trying to absorb the content, but I wasn't about to admit that publicly. In addition, we had the pricing people breathing down our necks to increase the price without increasing the content.

Mu went on. "The people we are sending with the students to act as translators have only recently been trained themselves."

"So?" I had no intention of making it easy for him.

"During these classes, they will be trying to learn all new computer words and terms that they are completely unfamiliar with here in China". This time he wasn't looking at his notes. I felt this was coming from his heart.

"Mr. Mu, that's the whole reason <u>everyone</u> is going to these classes."

"I know. It will be difficult for any one of them to keep up with the teachers day after day. They must have some rest."

Now it was real easy to anticipate what he was going to say next. Mu wanted to get more students into the classes without having to pay for them. We had spent a lot of time on the subject of changes to the content affecting the price. Mu clearly understood that. He was about to ask for a change in the number of students under the label of translator. That way, he could claim he was not asking for a change; therefore there should be no change in the price.

"And?" I was waiting for the other shoe to drop. How big was this change going to be?

Mr. Mu said "We estimate that we should have a total of six translators in our delegation. With that many we could arrange a work schedule that would allow for rest between each class session." He put his notebook down. This was it!

"Mr. Mu, that's almost a translator for each student. You are doubling the size of each class. You don't really mean that, do you?" Maybe I could intimidate him a little.

"Yes, we do. We take this matter very seriously." There was to be no intimidation.

"So do we. As we said before, changes in the class size have to be considered when we complete our pricing for this phase of the contract." I couldn't fold so quickly. If I obligated IBM to more "translators" our pricing brethren would jump up and down attempting to increase the contract price.

"We are NOT doubling the class size. These people are translators, not students." He insisted.

"It doesn't make any difference what you call them. There are more people listening to the instructor." As I said that, I was becoming tired of my own line of reasoning. At that moment I was leaning towards just agreeing with Mu.

"Mr. Mu how about if we do this? We will put some language in the contract that states that only one translator at a time would be allowed into the classroom. I don't care how many translators are in the delegation. Some can rest in the hotel on their days off, but not appear in the classroom. The individual instructors can then determine if more than one translator can sit in the back of the room." As I said this, I kept as stern an expression as I could on my face.

He did. He said, "We agree." He was all smiles now. Since he was ahead in the game now, he took another shot. "There is one other point we should make before we leave the subject of education."

"What is that?" I answered with a big sigh. Here we go again.

"We would like a phrase in this section to read that IBM guaranties that all students shall <u>learn</u> instead of merely guarantying that IBM will conduct the classes, their length, and their subjects as described."

I answered quickly. "How can I possibly guaranty that <u>your</u> students will learn? I don't even know who they are or where they come from or what kind of education they have had previously."

At that moment I couldn't think of any way I could write a clause like that into an IBM education contract. Even the public schools in the U.S. are never asked to warrant that their students will learn. In fact, learning was a major problem. They guaranty to teach, nothing more!

"All are capable of learning the subjects that you are teaching." He knew that there were seven graduate electrical engineers waiting in Shenyang; I didn't know that.

"Mr. Mu, I will be glad to make that guaranty if you will guaranty that each student has the equivalent of a U.S. college degree and finished in the top 20% of his class in college."

"I cannot give any such guaranty." Mr. Mu said.

"Then I can't give the guaranty you are asking for."

"You don't understand." I could even understand Mu's Chinese by this time.

There it was again, the "I don't understand" routine.

He explained, "When my suggested language is translated into Chinese it really doesn't sound as rigid as it does in English. Here in China, such a statement is in every college handbook. It usually is stated that if you attend such and such a course of study, you will be able to do the thing that is studied. For example, if you study engineering, you will be an engineer."

"Mr Mu, that's probably how it is stated in the U.S. as well. That statement is not the same as a guaranty. In any event, the schools give the students many, many tests. Then the government gives the candidates for those titles a test. Everyone is sure that the students have learned what the Professor has taught them. There are no tests in the IBM classes. We have no way to determine whether the student has listened and learned".

"Well then, you can give our students an examination."

"We are not equipped to do that during our scheduled classes. If you really want us to do it, we can arrange for your students to be tested. And, we will have to add the cost of preparing, giving and grading those tests to our proposed prices in the contract."

If my argument didn't hold up, I would have to come up with another. IBM would never put a learning guaranty in a contract. Neither would I for that matter. Our lawyers would visualize enough lawsuits to keep them busy for decades.

The expression on his face told the whole story. He was caught between a rock and a hard place. He wanted the "student will learn" statement in the contract to satisfy his Chinese audience, but was not prepared to pay extra for it. On our side, we were not running college courses. If a customer sent one of their employees to our classes and he didn't get anything out of it that was their problem, not ours.

We adjourned for the day. Deng's industrial revolution was slowly taking shape and form, albeit in fits and starts.

One thing was becoming obvious. We had to have an American translator on our side of the table. During these talks, the only translator we had was the one on the Chinese side. On an earlier trip we had Mary Wadsworth a Chinese speaking consultant with us. We discovered that discussions moved a lot faster, and disagreements based on semantics appeared to be fewer when we had a "Chinese as a second language" person on our side of the table. We didn't need a business consultant, we didn't need an expert on Chinese politics and government, but we did need someone who understood and spoke Chinese <u>with an American mindset</u>.

Some Chinese translators, like the one who worked during our initial seminar, often interposed themselves into the discussion. If their vocabulary was threatened by speakers using words they were unfamiliar with it might take many, many minutes to get back on course. If we didn't realize what was going on, we might lose hours. Expressions containing words like "could" or "would" and "shall" or "will" caused us no end of trouble, particularly when we became lax and used them interchangeably. Expressions containing computer jargon or IBM acronyms (which were particular favorites of some of speakers we brought to make presentations to the Chinese) drove all of us crazy.

We decided to bring our own translators with us on our next trip. Although there were a great many Americans of Chinese descent working for IBM, any one of whom would literally jump at the chance to go to China, we didn't like that idea. John, rightly or wrongly, felt that there might be an element of competition there that wouldn't be helpful. The only place I knew Americans who spoke Chinese were at the University of Michigan. My daughter, Maria, was a student majoring in Chinese at the time. Maria's major professor at that time was Professor Michael Okensburg, a China expert of renown. In fact, at the conclusion of the, 1976 spring semester he left the University of Michigan to become a aide to Zbigniew Brzezinski, the President's National Security Advisor. Later on, he was instrumental in the U.S. drive to formally recognize the Peoples Republic of China. Whether the need for an American translator started in my head with my daughter, or whether the idea ended there, I thought it would be a great idea if she came and acted as our translator at these talks. John agreed with great trepidation. Nepotism was not practiced at IBM in any way, shape, or form, at least not at the lower levels of management. I arranged for her to accompany us on our next trip. There was no way we could change horses during the current talks. I fully believe that the selection of my daughter to translate and be there was instrumental in creating very positive Chinese perceptions of our credibility.

The following Sunday afternoon, usually a time when John and I slept or bathed as the case might be, or simply thought nothing in reaction to a week of hard thinking and talking, we were treated to a visit to an amusement park set up in the Forbidden City Garden in Peking.

Mr. Wu and Ms. Ma picked us up at the Peking hotel and took us to the park. It wasn't very far. We walked around looking at the various booths. There were games for the adults and kids. As usual, everyone stared at us. Big tall Westerners weren't common on the streets of Beijing that year, so some people enjoyed looking and pointing at us. It didn't take long for a crowd of children to surround us, gawking. I played with them and we all had a laugh.

The sun was out and the usual smog was absent. We passed a gallery where the kids were trying to hit what resembled milk bottles with little balls. We stopped to try, and of course a crowd quickly gathered around us to see if the "round eyes" could hit the target. It was prophetic that we didn't, but we had fun anyway. Anything was better than the hotel room ceiling for another day.

We came to a gallery that consisted of a mounted toy machine gun. It was aimed at a little model airplane that moved down a wire across the booth from right to left. The idea was to hit the airplane with the pellets from the machine gun and knock it off the wire. As we got closer to the booth, I was stunned to see that the airplane had a big "US" insignia painted on the side. The children were using that as a target.

I called John over and showed him. Mr. Wu and Ms. Ma followed.

"Now you know why we are the enemy to all adult Chinese," I whispered to him. "They learn it as children."

"Yeah, isn't that something?"

Mr. Wu hurried up to us and saw the US flag on the plane. The look on his face showed his embarrassment! He gently pulled us away from the booth and said, "I didn't know that was going to be here" I am sorry" he said to us. We were too.

Wu took us back to the hotel. We rested for the rest of the day. I'm sure that John took a bath. He always took a bath when we had a moment to ourselves. I went back to reading my mystery stories intermixed with trying to get something on the short wave radio. I could pick up the Far East Network of the U.S. armed forced in Japan, and the Voice of America relay station in the Philippines. Our radios were the only outside contact we had.

The following week was comparatively docile. Perhaps it was because of the incident in the amusement park. It served to remind us all that both sides were still far from being "true" friends; we were still very close to enemy status. Maybe Mr. Wu and the people from Shenyang didn't feel that way, but the general population certainly did. Maybe subconsciously Wu and Co, and John, and I thought that we had to work at being friends. It didn't come naturally. Whatever the cause, there were no further blatant disagreements during that week. We concluded all the technical subjects and were ready to construct a contract to deliver and install all the computer hardware and software we had agreed upon.

About this time, we were honored by the visit of John's boss Charlie and his wife. I was not aware of his visit until John told me he was coming to scope out the subsequent visit of some IBM executives.

I said to John, "What the hell does that mean?"

In his imitable way, John said, "Calm down. He will only be here for a couple of days. There won't be enough time for any trouble." When it came to deal with our executives, John had no equal.

I was worried that another voice at the negotiating table would seriously disrupt the progress we had been making. Maybe I was expressing my own turf ownership or something. If I were the Chinese, I would grasp at any IBM executive above these negotiators to attempt to reverse any agreement already made. If I were the Chinese, I would bring up the discount price subject with as many people from IBM as I could. The Chinese are pragmatic; nothing ventured, nothing gained.

John explained to me that the IBM Board of Directors were having their quarterly meeting in Tokyo the coming September.

After that meeting, four senior executives with their wives were planning to tour China as guests of the Foreign Minister, Mr. Huong Wa before returning home. The fact that the most senior executives, Chairman, President, Senior VP and VP, were traveling together was a first. Something, or somebody, very high up must have caused this. We never found out the reason. Remember, at this junction, there were little or no formal connections between the U.S. and China. They did not have diplomatic relations yet. A new Liaison Ambassador was named, but he had not been confirmed by the U.S. Senate.

Anyway, to prepare for these executives, Charlie had convinced Ralph Pfeiffer an advance review of the itinerary and accommodations was necessary. The plan was for Charlie to make all the arrangements right on site in Beijing with the National Tourist Office right across the street from our hotel. Then, after all the arrangements were scheduled, Charlie and his wife would actually test the itinerary and accommodations by doing the tour themselves. I thought of the word "bureaucracy" to describe this scenario, but it really doesn't do justice to the event. Who ever heard of "testing" a sightseeing tour?

Charlie did a magnificent job of planning for their trip-his trip as well. I will say more on this subject later. Since Charlie was in Beijing, it was necessary for the Chinese to host a banquet in his honor. They dragged Mr. Wu's boss and his Director, along with the normal assortment of helpers to one of the better restaurants in Beijing. I thought Charlie and his wife did rather well. Being thrown into one of those banquets, whose purpose was to foster friendship and drunkenness, not particularly in that order, was a test for all. The translators were kept busy on all sides and the toasts were rampant. There were no gaffes at dinner. However, on the way out of the restaurant it was different.

We were walking down the hall with Mr. Ma, Mr. Wu's immediate boss. He spoke English. We passed the open doors of other rooms where other banquets had just concluded. The dessert for the evening was delicious watermelon, regular watermelon like you get in the U.S. of A. complete with ten thousand seeds. The Chinese custom is to spit out, or place in your hand, the seeds that you didn't swallow when eating watermelon. Then they threw, or spit them on to the floor, the tablecloth or wherever. Our hosts didn't do that at our banquet, probably out of deference to us. It was not so at the other banquets. In the rooms we passed, there were watermelon seeds everywhere. The floors, chairs and tables were covered with watermelon seeds.

Charlie's wife commented to Mr. Ma that it looked like her children had eaten there. The translator told Mr. Ma what she had said in Chinese even though it was obvious he understood what she had said.. Mr. Ma, with a completely straight face, turned to her and asked her what she meant. She didn't sense the trap he set and gaily went on to describe how her kids would have left watermelon seeds, food scraps and other dirty things all over the place for someone else to clean up. She had no intention of insulting the Chinese. It was a limp little joke. If we had an American translator, nothing would have happened. Mr. Ma didn't say a word. He looked at the translator as if he had said an obscenity. Remember, he could understand the English as well as the translator. He just moved in front of us all and practically ran down to his car. To this day, I have no idea what was in his mind. Charlie and Co got out of town on schedule.

Back in Beijing finishing up the technical specifications and the education program I realized we were getting more and more tired and irritable. Even though I had spent a little time touring other parts of China, it was still China. The treadmill of eat, sleep and work was taking its toll on both John and me. Not only were my daily naps lasting longer, but it was harder and harder to get out of bed in the morning. Mr. Mu's questions were beginning to irritate us while at the same time Big Mu's passiveness also somehow annoyed us. We had to work at listening to the Chinese while watching their impassive faces to detect any nuance. It was getting more and more difficult. We all had to have a little change of scenery and language.

John and I had planned to take some vacation time when we had finished the technical discussions. The talks had been long and arduous. The subject matter was complicated and translation requirements caused major difficulties. The compromise process also was stressful. Upon arrival in Tokyo from China in September 1977, we put our vacation plans into effect. He planned to spend some snooze time in Hawaii and then join his wife in Santa Barbara, California. While John was in Hawaii, he made arrangements to have a IBM contract writer meet us in Tokyo after our vacations. Alice Nadich, from the Contract Practices department of IBM, got the job. Alice was an excellent choice; she had lots of experience dealing with cultural contract requirements that arose around the IBM world. John and I were extremely happy with her selection. She was to join us in Tokyo to help us put the document together that we would subsequently give to the Chinese. Everything was set.

I planned to have my wife join me in Beijing for a couple of days of sightseeing then move on down through south China for the sights there and then home. It just happened that our supply of American food (which I brought with me in the spring) was in short supply at the time of her visit. These American foods were essential to our health and well being. During one of my telephone calls arranging her visit, I asked her to bring large jars of peanut butter and grape jelly. You'll see why this is important in a little while.

My poor wife had all kinds of trouble. The flight from New York to Beijing at that time required a stop in Tokyo, Japan to change planes; an overnight stopover preventing total exhaustion from an 11-12 hour flight. The Japanese had just completed their new International airport at Narita, 70-80 miles east of Tokyo. The airport location and the airport construction had angered a group of farmers (or agitators, depending on your point of view) whose land and livelihood had been disrupted. Consequently, they had besieged the new airport in an attempt to either dramatize their plight, or get the damned airport closed. I often wondered which was true and finally concluded that dramatization was the objective; they could never get the airport closed.

The day before she was to leave to join me, the travel department at IBM called. They told her that her flight was cancelled because of the troubles at Narita. So she unpacked and waited for the next telephone call. It came rather quickly, later that day. The plane was rescheduled and would leave in the morning. The bags were packed again.

Upon arrival at JFK the next morning, she was told that the flight was delayed. This time the message came from Japan Air Lines, who should have known. It was delayed all right, for about eight hours. The plane got off the ground late in the afternoon. Of course, the once-a-day flight from Narita to Beijing had already left by the time the New York flight took off there. Nobody told her. She arrived at Narita in the middle of the night, and, in the middle of mayhem.

The Japanese riot police had the airport surrounded and closed. There were armored cars all over the place. There were barricades everywhere; it was like a war zone. The air outside the terminal was white with tear gas even though the farmers (agitators) were outside the airport. If the flight from New York had not been in the air for so long, they would have sent it elsewhere. The passengers were herded off the arrival ramps into a corner for protection. Here is my little wife, clutching her handbag and a large shopping bag filled with peanut butter and grape jelly. The riot police, with their helmets, large plastic shields and Billy clubs were frightening. They pushed and shoved everyone down corridors, up stairs, down stairs trying to keep the farmers (agitators) from seeing them, or possibly the reverse. Ultimately, they got everyone into busses for the trip to the overnight hotel.

We thank the fates because the hotel was outstanding. It was far enough from the airport to avoid all the noise and lights of the battle going on there. She had a large room, took a bath and tried to get a good night's sleep. Her clothes were a shambles. So, as they say, she grinned and bore it.

The next day, the hotel and/or Japan Air Lines, we never found out which gave her a sumptuous breakfast and sent her back gratis on the bus to Narita. At the airport, chaos was still the theme. The cops pushed and shoved. During one of their pushes down a flight of stairs, my wife stumbled and fell. Thankfully, nothing was broken but a bottle of grape jelly and the heel on one of her shoes. By the time that this happened, the grape jelly had been warmed by the constant jigging and jogging and was a little less jellied than usual. Consequently, the grape jelly spilled all over my wife's clothing. Meanwhile the police, not very mindful of the jelly and the broken glass problem, were still prodding and pushing to get the passengers on the airplane.

The flight to Beijing was uneventful. We all were waiting for her at the Beijing Airport

Mr Wu, Mr Mu, the translator Ms. Ma, John, my daughter Maria, and I were waiting. The Beijing civilian terminal building had a concourse above the airplane gates where you could wait and watch the airplanes coming and going. We were all up there when they wheeled the stairs up to the flight from Tokyo. We had no inkling of the events in Tokyo. The Chinese newspapers had no pictures of the goings on. In any event, international news was not available in Beijing. We could see her come down the stairs, kind of limping. Then as she got closer, the full color version of her clothes came into view

I hollered down, "Are you okay? What the hell happened?"

She looked up at us. She said nothing.

We got the whole story while we were waiting for her baggage. If it were not that she looked so sad and bedraggled, it might have been funny. But it wasn't, she had been scared half out of her wits. Our Chinese hosts couldn't understand out peanut butter and jelly requirement. Why would anyone want to carry jars of that stuff 8000 miles? They all kept very sad looks on their faces. Another one of those culture shocks!

After a couple of days, my wife recovered completely. To celebrate her recovery, we went on a sightseeing tour of China. But before we left Beijing, we had an incident that demonstrates some sort of cultural bias. It started like this:

It was the season of the ripe lichee nuts. These dimpled brown fruits, about 1 to 1 ½ inches in diameter contain one of the sweetest fruits known to man. China is, or was, the only place in the world where you could get them. The Chinese consider them a delicacy. When they appeared in the markets there was usually a rush to purchase them. Lines would appear and everyone would happily get on line to get a little of this sweet fresh fruit.

My daughter Maria was a blond college student about medium height. When she came down the street and the lines formed for buying lichee nuts, she quietly assumed a place at the end of the line. The people in front of her noticed that there was a blond foreign girl amongst them. The woman directly in front of her motioned that she should move in front of her; each person in the line did exactly the same thing. Before you knew it, Maria was at the head of the line. She asked, in Chinese, what the price of the lichee nuts were. The vendor, his mouth hanging open, replied. He had very little, if any, experience with a Chinese-speaking foreigner. Maria completed her purchase and came back to the hotel to join us.

After hearing her story, we all attributed the politeness and deference to customary Chinese treatment of a guest. We all dove into the lichee nuts and devoured them. Later on, my wife decided that she wanted some more of the nuts. She asked Maria the location and price of the fruit. Off she went! An hour later, she returned with the nuts. She told us that she didn't get to the head of the line, she had to wait and wait and then have an argument with the vendor to make him understand. After a heated discussion about age, gender, politeness and Chinese culture, we concluded that it was the 'blond' thing, not the foreigner, and certainly not the female attributes that made the difference. My wife is a brunette.

Our sightseeing trip was a total success. We enjoyed every minute of it. We visited China's Grand Canyon, a place called Guai Lin. We visited all the big cities, Canton, Shanghai, and Wushi. In a place called Loyang in central China, we saw something that knocked our socks off. As we were riding down a street with our guide rattling off the successes of the local Communist government, we passed a flat bed truck. Two police officers were holding a third person. His hands and feet were tied. He had a sign hanging from a cord around his neck with some Chinese characters on it. He was also wearing a pointed cap, something we would call a dunce cap.

I asked our guide what was going on. He was visibly stumped. Prior to becoming an English language tour guide, like two weeks before, he was a schoolteacher. He told us that the local tourist bureau had given him some tour materials to read. When he had finished reading, they announced that he was a tour guide. My question, unfortunately, was not in any of the materials that he remembered reading. So, he was stumped and didn't know how to answer. He was in a difficult situation. If he told us the truth, it would differ intensely from the Communist success stories he had just been mouthing. If he did not tell us the truth, we might figure it out and tell someone else of his performance. He decided on a story that was kind of in-between truth and fiction.

First, the person on the truck was a criminal who had stolen from his neighbors, so the sign on his chest said. Second, he was on exhibition to the citizens of Loyang to show them the result of stealing from your neighbors. At that time this was a very plausible and acceptable story. We watched the truck slowly make its way down the street until it turned a corner and disappeared. That evening, I asked the clerk at the hotel about the incident. He told me, with a very straight face, that a criminal had been executed that day for killing someone. He said that everyone knew about it. He told me the normal practice, in that event, was to parade the perpetrator in front of all, with a sign that told of his misdeeds. This was to make sure that others wouldn't do as he had done. Equally plausible! The question remains, did we see the poor guy on his way to his execution?

The rest of the sightseeing tour was confined to geography, animals and the arts. My wife and I ended our tour of China and went to Tokyo, then to New York. .

There was an important thing I had to do while in New York. John and I had been troubled during our prior sessions by the fact that neither of us had a great deal of computer maintenance experience. In fact, none! That fact, coupled with the fact that the Shenyang people were all engineers of one kind or another, left us doubtful that we should be discussing this subject as experts. Both he and I couldn't give adequate answers when simple maintenance items came up. We decided that we should have a real computer maintenance engineer at the table with us to keep us honest. However, we were hobbled by our Ralph's edict not to enlarge the staff as they did in the IBM Russian operations, so we had to beg, borrow or loan people that we needed from other functions within IBM. Although it wasn't difficult to get almost any resource we needed (a free two week trip to China, plus a tour after is a great inducement!) it took a lot of time to keep going to the well. A more permanent solution was required.

I went to the Headquarters section that commanded the computer maintenance troops. I gave them my specifications. In no time at all, they had a candidate. This time it was a young man, named Willy, actually William O'Leary, who until I met him, was maintaining the very machines we were offering the Chinese. He was, literally, right off the streets of New York. I drafted him immediately. He had never been outside the U.S. before. In fact, maybe not even outside of New York. Perfect! I thought he would fit right in with the Chinese; they would adore him. I told him to get his passport, apply for a Chinese visa and meet us in Tokyo. He actually took this accelerated hiring process right in his stride. I have no idea what he told his wife that night, but I am willing to bet it took her breath away. "Honey, I just got a temporary job in China. I have to pack and leave in a couple of days. I'll call you when I get there."

Willy later proved to be one of our better decisions. However, we quickly discovered that while you can "take the man out of New York", you can't "take the New York out of the man". Our first hint was at breakfast Willy's first day in Beijing. He didn't like the coffee or the bread or the eggs (which smelled fishy). We had become so hardened that we no longer noticed. Then at dinner that night, we really got a surprise. Remember, we were in the best hotel in Beijing, maybe even all of China. We were surrounded by the most authentic Chinese culinary artists one could ask for. We had the most exotic as well as the plainest Chinese cooking available in the entire country. Willy looked at the menu for a while and then read out loud the pidgin English titles for some of the more exotic Chinese dishes presented. He asked if there was another menu. We told him he had the only one available. He settled on a dish called Russian beef with boiled potatoes which probably was a holdover from the Russian advisor days. If it weren't for the fact that the hotel was built and staffed while Russian influence was at its peak, Willy would have been sorely disappointed. He would have been forced to eat the Chinese cuisine. He was lucky there was a beef and potatoes mixture on the "international" menu. Since China is not noted for its beef, or its potatoes, one can only wonder where these came from. He gravitated to that dish, not only that night, but every succeeding day and night for the next three months. I believe that he set the record for not eating Chinese food while in China. From that moment forth, Willy only ordered and ate the boiled beef and potatoes. Every noon, every evening, Willy had his beef and potatoes dinner (like the good Irishman he was) and never, at least in our presence, touched the Chinese dishes

Chapter 8 – Putting the Deal Together

The London Times, July24, 1977

"REINSTATED DEPUTY PRIME MINISTER LIKELY
TO PURSUE GOAL OF MODERNIZATION; NO
INHIBITIONS ABOUT TRADE & TECHNOLOGICAL
LINKS WITH FOREIGN COUNTRIES"

On the way back to Tokyo through Hawaii, I visited the Ala Moana Shopping Mall at the end of Waikiki Beach to pick up some things I had forgotten at home. As I was passing through the lower level of the mall, I saw a hobby store that had a beautiful display of model boats in the window. As a kid, I had built a couple of model boats. I was attracted to one kit in particular. It was a four foot long powered model of an ocean-going freighter. There was enough detail to keep me busy but not enough to drive me bananas if I couldn't finish it. I went into the store and bought it along with all the supplies needed to complete it. The whole thing came to quite a large and expensive package costing $400. Remember this was 1977. Even at that, it was still missing the motors and the driving mechanisms needed to make it operate in the water. I didn't care. I had to have something to do when I wasn't working. I simply couldn't read any more lousy detective stories. I would put it on my expense account.

I carried the whole thing back to Japan. Going through Japanese customs became a chore. The model had been manufactured in Japan; it clearly said that on the side of the box. The customs official did not seem to understand why someone who was coming to Japan would buy a Japanese product to bring to Japan. I tried to explain that I had this feeling in Hawaii and on the spur-of-moment purchased it. He thought he could charge me duty but couldn't figure out how to calculate it on a Japanese product returning to the Japan. In the end he gave up and passed me through.

That night in our Tokyo hotel, I showed the model to John and told him what I was going to do with it, particularly the part about the expense account. If he didn't agree, I would pay for it myself. At first he was aghast, but quickly recovered. He well understood the purpose of the boat. It would give us (now I included him in the work) something to do at night and on the weekends. Otherwise, we both would go nuts! Once I had his agreement it was easy to get him to come with me to the hobby store in Tokyo to get all the missing parts. We bought little electric motors, little model winches, lots of paint and glue and every tool I could think of. They cost another $200.We now had a $600 recreational toy.

Unbeknownst to me, that night John called Charlie to warn him of an unusual expense account on its way. John thought he would have to make an impassioned plea for exceptional treatment of yet another very unusual expense account item for the men working in China. John knew that when we submitted expense accounts accompanied by Chinese language receipts no one could read anything but the numbers! This time, however, the receipt was in clear English. Model boat and $600.00 would stand out like a big "red" flag. Charlie cut him short with a quick "OK".

Many months later, Charlie told me that he was called to task for allowing us to put the model boat on our expense account. The English language receipt and the amount did indeed raise a "red" flag. Charlie not only defended us, he questioned the questioner, putting him on the defensive.

Charlie had approved the purchase, but that still wasn't enough to fend off the bean counters. The bean counters were busy counting beans while we were facilitating Deng's revolution! What nonsense. Nevertheless, while we were in New York in between China sessions, some accountant from the Controller's department couldn't let it die. He called John to question him further.

"John, what the hell is this model thing on Joseph's expense account?"

"We bought a model boat in Hawaii that we are building while we are in China. Charlie approved it".

"What the hell are you talking about?"

John repeated his explanation without explaining the motivation. John was a believer in telling only what was absolutely necessary. The questions and answers went into revolving door mode without any exit.

"I'm going to have to pass this up the line for approval. I don't think you can do this."

"Go right ahead." John wasn't going to be bluffed by the threat of a higher accountant disapproving the money for our boat.

"And, by the way, tell Charlie to make an appointment with Bill Eggleston (the President of our unit) for both of us. Just let me know when it is so I can be there."

That trumped the accountant. When they went back to Charlie with the problem, he told the bookkeepers they should try living in a Chinese hotel for a couple of months at a time. Nothing more was said, there was no big executive meeting on the subject; it died a natural death

When we went back to China, the boat came to China with us. When Mr. Wu picked us up at the airport and saw this big box, he asked what we were bringing with us.

When I told him a model boat, he said "A little boat for children?'

I said, "No, it was for us."

193

He looked at Ms. Ma, his translator, and she looked at me. I really don't know what he said in Chinese, but that was how she translated it. She also gave him the "I don't know what he means" expression and raised her shoulders just a little bit. Even though he was thinking in Chinese, the expression on his face told me in English that he believed that either I was insane or this was another western trick.

We all had to get working on Mr. Wu's contract and play our continuing role in Deng's revolution. We had about two weeks to get the contract together in Tokyo. Normally we would have used a "standard" sales contract and merely filled in the blanks. IBM had a lot of those form things. The "standard" IBM contract, when we had showed it to Mr. Wu, didn't fit his definition of what a contract should be. He wanted all the technical details in one section and all the commercial details in another. That way, it would conform to the Chinese idea separating the "commercial" sections (the responsibility of the foreign trade organizations) and "technical" sections (the responsibility of the user). The IBM contract people objected at first but we were able to quiet them down after a while. We didn't want the format of the contract to become contentious, so we agreed with Mr. Wu right away. The cutting, fitting, pasting, and most importantly, the editing, of clauses from our standard contract into Mr. Wu's treaty/contract format was a major effort. That's what caused all this work in Tokyo

We hadn't been at that work for more than a couple of days, when the first (and only) dissension occurred. Alice, our indispensable contract writer, worked for the Director of Contract Practices Pete Palmer. He liked to be involved in the minutia of her work. As a result, she had to report to him on a daily basis. Alice, during one of her telephone reports back to her boss, had told him what we were doing. She also told him of our plans to present this "new" contract to Mr. Wu when we returned to China ten days hence.

He asked Alice, "Do you have a visa for China?"

"No." Her face dropped. She knew that neither John nor I had said anything about her going to China with the contract.

"Why not?" Even over the telephone from 8,000 miles away, his annoyance with her answer was obvious. Alice knew that everyone in the room could hear her side of this conversation. His question clearly indicated he didn't like the answers he was getting.

"No one has mentioned anything about a visa for China." Alice whispered. This was getting embarrassing for her.

"Hmn" Peter said. The conversation continued until Alice ran out of things to tell him. She hung up.

We were all in the same room. We heard her end of the conversation. Except for the words "No one mentioned anything about a visa..." the rest of the conversation had no meaning or impact on us. We did not intend to add someone else to the negotiation team. Insofar as we were concerned, her answers were statements of fact; no further explanations were necessary. We all went back to work.

Minutes after she hung up, the telephone rang. The ringing telephone surprised everyone. No one knew where we were, or what we were doing. This was in keeping with the rules of engagement laid out by Ralph Pfeiffer. It was Peter asking for John.

"Hi Pete." John and Peter had known one another for many years. In fact, we all knew one another. Peter, John and I were on assignment in Japan 1969-1974. For a while I worked for Peter; John was working for Charlie.

"John, how come Alice doesn't have a visa for China?"

"She doesn't need one." John's face tightened. He knew the visa question was a side issue.

"John, she is a contract administrator. She not only prepares contracts, but if there is going to be any give and take with her contract, she has to be at the table."

"Pete, let me call you back." Although we couldn't hear both sides of the conversation, we could see that John was getting angry. He left the room. Alice and I looked at each other. We both knew what was coming; we went back to work. Although we couldn't hear the specifics, the tension of the conversation was evident.

About an hour later John returned and went back to reviewing the work we had completed. Five minutes later Alice was called to the telephone in the other room. John didn't say a word to me. He didn't even look at me. The Japanese girls that were doing the typing couldn't figure out what was going on. For days everyone had been simply working; no telephones had rung; no visitors appeared. We had been deliberately isolated. Now, in the space of two hours, Alice and John coming and going and the telephone never seemed to stop ringing.

Fifteen minutes later, Alice returned. Her face betrayed the devastation she must have felt. We all knew that she had been talking to her Boss.

"I have to go back to the States tomorrow. Something urgent has come up." She was upset. Her eyes were wide; she nervously picked up the papers that she had been working on.

I said, "I hope it's nothing personal. Can we do anything?"

"No. Pete just said that I have to come back as quickly as possible."

I looked at John; He just shook his head and sent me a message in body language that said, "Drop it!"

At dinner that night, I asked John what the hell was going on. He told me that Pete insisted that Alice come to China with us so that there was a "contracts" person at the table with us. John told Peter that would happen only over his dead body. That's where it was left; a major turf war between a staff manager and the line troops. There was no question; Charlie would have to get involved.

Aside from "managing" us, one of his major functions was protecting us from staff nonsense while we went about our job.

The only bad part wasn't that she was not going to China, but that she wasn't superintending the preparation of the contract document. John or I were well able to defend the contract, or even change it during verbal combat with Mr. Wu but we realized that if our headquarters staff didn't bless it going in, we would have nothing but continual aggravation. A stupid turf war would put us on the defensive; facing both the Chinese and our home base. We would be fighting a war on two fronts; a perfect plan for disaster! John said that he was going to call Charlie to get him to put Peter back in the box.

We didn't learn the details until much later, but Charlie really went to bat for us. He went directly to the Ralph Pfeiffer, our CEO. Charlie laid out the ground rules that John and I were working with in China. He told the CEO that you couldn't have two people negotiating the same thing at the same time unless they were identical twins. It was as simple as that. They called Peter into the meeting and the CEO laid it out for Peter. That was the end of it.

The only person who suffered from all of this nonsense was Alice. She flew back and forth from New York to Tokyo twice in one week. Alice returned from New York about four days later. We continued cutting and pasting and revising until the very last moment. With Alice's help, we were done on time. I think it's safe to say that we wouldn't have had a China-IBM peace treaty without her assistance.

We took the opportunity in Tokyo to prep a couple of technical speakers that we had arranged for. Some of the technical things in the contract are better described by a technician familiar with the subject. One such subject was the computer room site that the Chinese were advised to prepare. Although the Chinese were not required to provide a "clean room" for the computer, we told them it was a good idea. At that time, smog, thick smog, was ubiquitous in Beijing. If the air quality in Shenyang was similar to, or worse than, Beijing, we told them they had better have one. Mr. Mu knew it was far worse in Shenyang because of the immense amount of soft coal that was burned in the factories there. What John and I knew about computer rooms and computer environments could be put on the head of a pin. Willy, our new maintenance guru, wasn't familiar with the subject. But, he sure knew where to find these experts when we needed them!

Mr. Mu had specifically asked us for information regarding the construction of earthquake resistant computer rooms. He had read about them somewhere. We didn't even know such things existed. Many years later after I had visited the Shenyang plant, I could only wonder at Mr. Mu. The Shenyang plant had machine tools, massive machine tools, some costing much more than our computer, sitting on earthen floors in the workshop. Why bother with an earthquake resistant room for a computer when the same protection is not afforded these machines as well? The only answers I came up with then were the mystique surrounding the computer; the lack of experience with a computer. Later I realized the real answer was that the computer belonged to the Ministry; the factory was just the caretaker. The Ministry people had experienced the Tentsien earthquake just months before the contract negotiations! Those people in Beijing wanted their investment protected.

I put Willy to work to see if IBM had earthquake resistant computer room expertise. In nothing flat, Willy located someone who was IBM's resident expert on the subject in our branch in San Francisco. That was great. We had a computer room construction and environment expert all rolled up into one. His bosses had agreed to let us pay for his trip to China to give a presentation to the Chinese. In fact, we never were bereft of people for whom we could buy an airplane ticket and a two week stint in China. We had to fend them off at times.

We had mixed experiences with American technical experts that we brought to China. Some of these experts tended to be pedantic and dogmatic and the Chinese audience felt it. Our particular concern was the inadvertent habit of some to respond to questions with rambling answers. They wasted a lot of time and ultimately lost credibility. A question became a jumping-off point to exhibit the speaker's knowledge of the science. Sometimes the presenter never answered the question.

Sometimes the speaker answered, but his answer was to a question that had not been asked.

We were all in the conference room at our Headquarters in Tokyo. We were scheduled to leave for Beijing in two days. We were using some of our time in Tokyo to try to help this particular specialist (I only remember his first name) make his presentation. We wanted him to be cogent and concise. His time for the presentation in Beijing was very limited. We wanted to be sure that he used the time effectively.

"Steve [our computer environment/construction expert], when someone asks you a question, I suggest that you wait for the translator to finish their translation. When the translator signals you that he is finished; you take a deep breath then repeat the question to the translator. He, or she, will tell you if you are repeating the question accurately."

"Why don't I just answer the question?" His face betrayed his confusion. He was probably thinking "What kind of direction is that?" I didn't want to tell him that some people have difficulty in answering in a straightforward manner.

"We have to be sure that the translator interpreted the question accurately. If you repeat it to him, he gets the opportunity to check it out in his own mind. At the same time, you get the chance to think your answer through."

"It'll take forever to get done." A logical and correct reaction when you don't need a translator to get your words across.

"Don't worry, they have plenty of time. Once you get the rhythm, it goes fast. The audience is really interested in what you have to tell them. After you and the translator agree, then answer it."

"That seems like a big waste of time." He was bending just a little.

"It will be a bigger waste of time if you don't answer the question they asked. And, the audience will think that you don't know what you are talking about."

"Well . . . OK."

"Then be sure that you answer the question that was asked of you. You don't have to tell them all that you know about the subject. Don't wander off the question with an answer to some other question. Be Specific!"

"Yeah, but I may think of something that I forgot to mention before." I began to think that I was facing one of those scientific guys who wanted to share <u>all</u> his knowledge.

"Never mind that, just answer the question. Nothing else!"

"But suppose the question really reminds me of something else that's important?" We could see that Steve was having a lot of trouble with this sort of discipline. He really wanted to tell them everything he knew just like he did in San Francisco.

"Just answer the question. Make a note on a piece of paper if you think of something else you want to tell them, but don't bring it up in answer to a question."

Steve kept telling us that he understood what we were trying to do. We stayed with him for about an hour and half. By that time, he was going to respond either correctly or not. The time was up.

When he actually made his presentations in Beijing, the morning sessions went smoothly; the afternoon ones were more difficult. I guess he got tired. That's par for the course!

One last thing that we had to do in Tokyo was to get the names of several construction companies who specialized in computer rooms. Raised floors, air conditioning, ductwork, fire suppression systems were all necessary. Mr. Mu wanted the computer installation to be completely first class. He did not want to put a brand-new (remember our discussions about "reconditioned" equipment) American computer into a Chinese built room. Even the room had to be imported! Today, I would guess that he was following the desires of his mentors in the Beijing Ministry. So, Willy got the names of several contractors from his counterparts in our Japanese company. We had everything.

We really did have everything. In addition to the boat, we had purchased a whole bunch of food stuffs to make our stay a little more comfortable. We had peanut butter and jelly; we had dried American soups in a variety of flavors; we had peanuts, Coca Cola; we had short wave radios to listen to American news, we had music tapes. John even brought several cans of tile cleaner and a brush to clean his bathroom with. Since he took many, many baths he was very concerned with the condition of his bath tub.

We had many cartons of these life-giving things. In addition, the IBM Medical Department back in New York had gotten into the act and forced several cartons of medical supplies on us. Included in their supplies was a case of sanitary napkins even though there were no women on our team at that time. Some doctor in the bowels of the IBM headquarters building had put together his list of supplies needed if you were going to be out of touch with humanity for six months. John had really blown his cool over that, but higher authorities had prevailed. We could have opened a colony on the moon and survived until the next shuttle came along.

When we left the hotel to go to the airport, there wasn't enough room in the taxi to hold us and all the supplies. So, we simply hired another taxi to carry the freight. We also had a little problem with John. He had broken his arm while playing tennis on vacation and needed a little extra room to sling his cast around. Later, some accountant questioned Charlie why we had to pay two taxi fares to the airport (at $75.00 each) as well as why we were bringing all that supermarket stuff to China. Now I believe the accounting department in our headquarters had some guy solely assigned to question our expense accounts. Charlie, in his inimitable way, even when he didn't know exactly what we were doing, took care of questions like that. We were a good team!

We had our contract, we had our experts and we had our boat. We had our supplies for the long haul. It's off to Beijing.

Mr. Wu, here we come! Deng Tsao Ping's industrial revolution was moving ahead at top speed!

While we had been beating ourselves to a pulp to produce the treaty to Chinese specifications, the Chinese were really moving. Their entire bureaucracy was singing from the same hymnal. As usual, we knew nothing of their preparations for the computer that we had not yet sold. Twenty of their engineers were already in Florence, Italy at the Novo Pignone plant learning how to design and manufacture high-pressure compressors. Assigned to the various factory departments, they would reproduce the observed processes in Shenyang. Even though, at that point, no one could be sure that a computer would eventually end up in Shenyang; and even though, at that point, we couldn't be sure that we could get an export license, the Chinese were betting on the outcome. They would be ready, no matter what!

Chapter 9 – Battles with Mr. Wu

London Times July 15, 1977

"NEW YORK BLACKOUT!"

New York Times July 23, 1977

"TENG RETURNS TO POWER"

Finally, we were starting the long awaited "commercial" negotiations. Mr. Wu had promised us, threatened us, repeatedly, that the "commercial" negotiations were his bag. He was only involved in the "technical" talks as a sort of referee, letting the people from Shenyang, the users, do most of the talking. The only hint we had of what his "commercial" negotiations meant was when Mr. Wu interrupted a conversation with the Shenyang people. He told us this particular subject was not to be discussed with them, ergo; it was a "commercial" subject. Even though the Shenyang people were most immediately impacted by those "commercial" subjects, they had nothing to say about it under the Chinese Communist system. Inevitably, the subjects chosen by Mr. Wu were the very same subjects that IBM lawyers made their living making inviolate, i.e., payment, delivery, warranty and similar ones. The very subjects that Mr. Wu wanted to China-ize were the same subjects over which, theoretically, we had no control. But we were game to try anything

That July 1977, we had quite a group in Beijing working on the contract. John and I were there. Our new interpreter, Maria (my daughter) was there, Willy our maintenance guru was there, and Steve, our temporary construction expert from the San Francisco IBM office was there. We were all anticipating the "commercial negotiations" with a great deal of trepidation. Before we were able to get into the meat of the matter there were some loose ends that we had to complete. One of them was satisfying Mr Mu's request for more information on the construction of a computer room. Normally, that subject would come up, if it came up at all, much closer to the anticipated delivery date for the computer. Here in China the subject arose even before we had a signed contract for the computer, much less a delivery date. If I knew then what I know now, as the saying goes, I would have recognized that something unusual was going down. On the other hand, our friends never had a computer before; they wanted to give it the best home they could. It turned out that a new building, not just a computer room, was going to house this computer! This had never happened in either John's or my experience.

As we finished up that subject, a major political event began to take shape under our very noses. We had no idea of the magnitude of political, cultural and economic changes that were beginning. We went to work every day ate our meals in complete isolation from the rest of China. July 21, 1977, however, was different. The political impact of the demonstration we witnessed that day only dawned on us much, much later, but it made us sit up and take notice.

The evening of the day our construction expert finished his presentation, we were all hanging out in our suite on the ninth floor of the hotel. John, Willy, and I were doing our thing on the model boat. Maria, my daughter/translator, was somewhere; she was due back soon. Our San Francisco expert was examining the insides of the television set that was in the room. We had turned it on for five minutes the first day we moved in and had never bothered with it since. It seems that 8 hours of Chinese per day was 7 ¾ more than enough. Watching and listening to more dancers carrying pictures of their leader and singing praises to his name was really more than we wanted to hear. However, he was fascinated by something inside of the set, what I don't know. He had it turned around and was trying to figure out how to get it out of its case.

Our suite was near the northwest corner of the building. The windows faced on to Chung-An Street, the main east-west street in Peking. If you looked to the west from the balcony, you could see a much of Tienamin Square as well as a long stretch of Chang'an Street. We could see all the area directly in front of the main gates to the Forbidden City. Since it was on the same side of the street as our room, Chairman Mao's twenty-foot portrait atop the entrance to the Forbidden City was outside our visual range. From that spot, he could see everything. The Square spread out like a huge concrete tiled village green without trees. It was big! The buildings around Tienamin Square obscured the southerly portion of the square where Chairman Mao's Mausoleum was still under construction. Construction activity had slowed down that week. His memory was in disrepute at that time.

The wall posters changed every day. Although we couldn't read them, the fact that they were different each day was apparent even to us. Some were torn in half; others disappeared from one day to the next. Someone told us that one poster said, "Deng is Back!" That meant nothing or close to nothing to us at the time. We were focused on our impending treaty/contract, so that, short of a bomb going off outside the hotel, we felt unaffected. Little did we know Deng Tsao Ping was almost solely responsible for the changes that brought us to China! Something was going on, but we had no way of finding out. Neither Mr. Wu nor any of the people of Shenyang gave us any hint of what was going on in the streets outside the building. Our overseas American news broadcasts (Voice of America) from the Philippines told us nothing. Insofar as the broadcast was concerned, the only news was that today, July 21, 1977, followed yesterday, July 20th.

The number of people on the street increased dramatically just as darkness fell. I opened the door to the balcony to get some fresh (almost unpolluted) air. As I looked out to see what was happening, the bicyclists had disappeared, replaced by a tremendous number of people on foot. The street from the hotel to Tienamin Square, two long blocks, and beyond was filled with people milling back and forth. The street lights lit up little pockets where we saw the heads of people packed together. It was frightening. We joked back and forth that maybe another revolution was under way.

John and I went out on to the balcony. Outside you could hear the roar of the crowd, but it was not an angry roar. It was more like a happy hum. We asked Maria to see if there was something on the television. When she went over to the TV to turn it on, it didn't work. Our expert had done something in the back of the thing. We hollered to him to fix it so that we could find out what was going on. He did, and Maria then quickly reported to us that some leader named Deng Xiao Ping had been returned to power and the people were celebrating. None of us knew who he was.

It was scary. Down on the street and up in Tienamin, it looked like a beehive. There had to have been several thousand people within our sight. There had to be several more thousand beyond. They did not appear to be moving in one direction or another, just swaying in the breeze, but there was no breeze. The only areas we could see clearly were under the streetlights, but there were not that many of them.

July 21, 1977 Honoring Deng's Rehabilitation

We continued looking. Steve, our San Francisco expert, was so enamored of the Chinese television set he wouldn't come out on to the balcony to see what we thought was a live revolution. It's amazing how ignorant he, and we, were. The rest of us couldn't take our eyes off the spectacle before us. Up the street, on the edge of Tienamin there were two very large circles of lights, much brighter than the streetlights. Maria called us to the television. On the screen there were pictures of wildly celebrating people in the Square. We went back to the balcony and saw that the TV pictures were what we could see from our vantage point. It was thrilling. This spectacle went through the night. We went to bed about 2 in the morning while it was still going on unabated. Since we were nine stories up, we didn't get too much crowd noise bad unless we went out on the balcony. I was reminded of the picture of Times Square on VJ day in 1945 that I had seen. This was similar, but there were ten times more people covering an area that was much larger.

The next day, in fact for the next two days, the celebrating continued. There was no way for us to go to work since there were no taxis and even if there had been, there was no pavement for them to ride on. The street, and the sidewalks, remained jammed with people all day. Then after lunch, the parading began. Lines and lines of people paraded down Chang'an Street from the west through Tienamin and past our hotel. Many times groups were headed by comrades carrying banners which we were told said, "Long Live Chairman Deng" and similar commemoratives. Many carried large posters with Mao's, Hua Go Feng's or Deng's picture.

Since there was no way to go to work, Maria and I went down into the happy crowds. We were able to walk through and among the folks who were parading. It was great fun! Everyone was smiling and appeared to be very happy with what they were doing. The marchers were spread far enough apart so that we could walk with them, or actually cross the street through them. John had stayed up in the room. He told us later that he saw us walking and marching with the demonstrators. On the street, I thought to myself, "Isn't it wonderful that everyone got up in the middle of the night somewhere beyond the downtown parade route, lined up and started down this wide and very long street so that the rest of the world, Communist and noncommunist, could see a public outpouring."

Wait a minute, I thought to myself. Deng came to power just last night or so I thought. (I cannot imagine how naïve I was!) Here it is less than 5 hours later, and I'm watching an organized parade complete with printed signs and pictures. This is no impromptu outpouring of public sentiment. Well, it might be an outpouring of public sentiment but it sure wasn't impromptu. Organizing all these people into disciplined groups, equipping them with signs and transporting them to wherever this parade originated took a lot of planning. Either it was planned weeks ago, or someone worked like the dickens all last night. Either way, you had to admire the result.

I had read somewhere about a similar outpouring of public sentiment when Chairman Hua Go Feng assumed power in September or October, 1976. The descriptions I read of the size and scope of scene paled into nothing compared to what I was seeing. All this noise was for Deng's re-appointment as Deputy or Vice Chairman, not Chairman. He was only the assistant, not the chief. I knew that I was missing something, but what never dawned on me until years later. Some aspects of Chinese politics remain peculiarly Chinese while others are just universal politics. Deng was easing into power, insofar as the public was concerned. There was to be no abrupt change in the power structure, just a smooth transition from one leader to the next. Pretty smart! And, these events happened to be positive and happy. I wondered what would have happened if there had been an event with a negative twist requiring an outpouring of public sentiment. One hundred thousand people milling around in a controlled dance of happiness is one thing! I don't think I would want to be around for an uncontrolled dance. I wonder if that is what the Chinese leaders felt about the Tienamin demonstrations in 1989? Who knows?

After a couple of hours it became boring. The people kept coming. That night and the following day it continued unabated. We thought that we saw the same banners a couple of times. I told John that I thought the government might be carting people from the end of the parade route, out of our sight, to the beginning, also out of our sight. It was obvious the government was very conscious of the public impact these images would have. Imagine people marching almost day and night for three days! Three days with 100,000 people demonstrating is three times more impressive than one day with 100,000 people! At the end of the third day, the demonstration kind of fizzled out.

We were able to get back to work. Amazingly, there was not one iota of reaction, or even comment, from the Chinese across the table when we got back to work. From the number of people involved in this demonstration and from its location (in the downtown government area where our talks took place) they had to have known and/or even participate in the demonstrations. There was not one word! Years later when I asked, they told me political matters did not concern them. To my mind that was a limp reason. Mr. Mu, particularly, just did not want to talk about it for some reason. I found that curious because I thought he was, of them all, the most politically savvy person. It could be they habitually did not make public political statements, especially to foreigners.

Our meetings resumed. The subject of the demonstrations of the last three days was never mentioned, or even alluded to. The first thing that Mr. Wu brought up was that the Peoples Republic of China couldn't accept wording in a contract that included the word "nuclear". We had learned that whenever he started throwing the expression "the Peoples Republic of China" around, he was deadly serious. For the same reason, we rarely, if ever, mentioned "our government" or the "U.S. government". If we did, it was only in connection with an export license, a subject that Mr Wu adamantly refused to hear.

The IBM "standard" contract negates our equipment guaranty when the computers are near or passing any nuclear device, power plant or other emitting source. Big corporations like "standard" things, particularly contracts. Lawyers, who are more expensive than sales representatives, wouldn't be required to sit at every contract signing to interpret the "small print" to customers. Standard, in a bureaucracy, also meant that changes couldn't even be requested. They were simply not permitted. The whole system would break down if a change were suggested and made.

Changing a word was bad enough, but the worst thing a sales representative could do was to think the warranty was modifiable. Here we were, 8000 miles from the center of the IBM universe, gaily getting ready to defend statements in a warranty. To us the reasons for a nuclear exclusion appeared logical; the Chinese did not share our definition of logical.

Wu warmed up to his subject. He couldn't and wouldn't have a contract with those words in it. China has no nuclear power. Therefore, those words have no application in this situation. In retrospect, his vehement objection was just a lot of hot air. China had been exploding test nuclear devices for several years. We knew that. Although we did not know it at the time, China had run a particularly dirty test of an atomic bomb just a few months before. The fallout from this particular bomb had reached the Western Hemisphere. Under the internal Chinese news restrictions, however, it is quite possible that Mr. Wu didn't know of that atomic test, or any atomic test for that matter. It is equally possible that Mr. Wu was chalking up another future "give" on his "fairness in negotiation" scorecard. In my naiveté, Mr. Wu appeared sincere in his objections; I never made any of these connections.

We were very leery of making any changes to the warranty statement for lots of reasons. Logic and relevance were not among them. First, a full corps of lawyers spent their careers with IBM designing the warranty. It covered every possible liability into which the company might stumble. Second, if we were to request any change in the warranty, even one as little as a comma, red lights would go on all over the legal community in IBM. Instead of convincing one lawyer of the necessity and desirability of making the suggested alteration, we would have to convince a troop of lawyers. Third, we would be asking our division lawyer to agree with us (which was problematical). If he did take the argument up the legal line he would be putting his judgment and abilities on the line. Therefore, we had to sidestep Mr. Wu's simple and logical request as quickly as possible.

We asked why he wanted it removed. If it didn't apply, why bother with it at all? If there was no nuclear power around, the clause did not apply.

He said that the words, when translated, would confuse and anger his bosses.

The phrase "when translated" really illustrates a basic issue. Even though we were contracting in English, the Chinese translation had to mean the same thing. The two languages are ideologically different. In one, the words are all important; in the other, the thought is all-important. Reconciling them was a monstrous all-consuming continuing task for both sides.

The statement, he said, had no rationale anyway, since they had no nuclear power plants or emission sources. We thought that this probably meant that if they agreed to such language, it was an implied admission that the Chinese government had a nuclear capability of some kind, somewhere. Half of the population of the earth knew that already. Obviously, we couldn't touch that one with a ten-foot pole. We were trying to write a commercial contract, not a nuclear proliferation treaty! I need to note here that within eight months of Mr. Wu's statements, somebody else in China succeeded in test firing yet another nuclear device. I don't know what that proved, but it sure was interesting.

Our answer was that surely they understood that if nuclear (and therefore, magnetic) emissions were near to the computers, they could irrevocably damage the sensitive components. They couldn't longer replace or repair them. It could have the same effect as if you passed a very strong magnet next to the memory unit of the computer which, at the least, would destroy the data stored there and at the most, could melt and fuse the metallic elements of the unit together.

On top of all that, we had previously agreed to send the airplane carrying the computer to the "Shenyang Municipal Airport," a very thin reference to the military airfield near the plant. I had visions of our computer being carried alongside a nuclear bomb depot at that airport. There was no way, however, that I could mention something like that publicly; in fact, I shouldn't have even been thinking like that.

We had been haranguing each other on this subject for the better part of a week. It was summertime in Beijing and had there been any trees along the streets, it might have been cooler. It was hot. The entire Gobi Desert had moved eastward into the city. The normal sooty grey sunrise was replaced by a golden hued sunrise. Everyone was tired. We had been trying to come up with a set of words in English and Chinese that would satisfy both of us. Our friends across the table absolutely refused to have the words "nuclear" in a contract . . .

Their position had to be political. Mr. Wu was fighting over some sort of principle imposed on him from above. It was a tough point for them and an equally tough point for us.

We had tried at least ten different expressions and synonyms unsuccessfully. We tried "emissions", we tried "waves of energy", and we tried "fields of energy". We were just as adamant that a warranty exception for radiation had to be in the contract. Each side had long explanations for their position beginning with the words "You don't understand . . ."

The process worked in the following way. At least four and sometimes six men and women were on their side of the table.

Wu seated them in what we came to realize was a significant order. The most important person would be in the middle, the other people in order of position, arrayed on either side of him. If the point made was really important or really critical, the person in the center would do the talking. In fact, you could judge the priority of the topic by who was speaking.

To begin, Mr. Wu opened his notebook (as if his entire speech was written there). He looked us straight in the eye. I thought that there must be a negotiator's school in Beijing where the first lesson was staring your listener right in the eye. It seemed as if he was looking right through you, never blinking, and never moving his eyeballs. He would then straighten up his body, adjust his seat and then begin. During his speech, he wouldn't look back at his notebook once! What a memory! His mind had sucked up the entire notebook in one gulp.

By this time, I guess he thought we really understood every Chinese word that he uttered. He would go on for what seemed like twenty minutes, but I'm sure it was much, much less. Their translator, Ms. Ma, would be jotting something down in her notebook. Every time he paused, she would translate what he had said. If our translator had a problem with the translation, she would whisper a correction in my ear.

Our translator, Maria, seated next to me, did some jottings, but mostly listened. I guess the English language is less flowery, or more precise than Chinese. Sometimes, a five-minute Chinese speech would come out in English in about two minutes. Maybe, Ms. Ma spared us from what she thought to be inconsequential. Sometimes, the reverse would be true. A minute of Chinese turned into five minutes of English, as the translator groped her way through the idea.

Anyway, during this particular harangue Maria whispered to me several times that Ms. Ma was adding some of her own logic to Mr. Wu's. I said, "OK," and kept looking directly at the Chinese speaker. That way, I wouldn't insult him through obvious inattention. At these meetings there was both speaking and listening etiquette. Several more times, Maria told me Ms. Ma was really adding a lot of her own comments to those of the speaker.

I truly lost my temper. Maybe it was the heat, maybe it was the boredom, and maybe it was the stress of hearing the same subject over and over again. I held up my hand so that the Mr. Wu, who was still talking, could see. He stopped speaking instantly. This was a monumental breach of etiquette.

I said, "Ms. Ma. Could you please just translate what Mr. Wu is saying? It's difficult enough to respond to one negotiator. Two of them are impossible"

Silence. No one said a word. The Chinese who did not understand English had quizzical looks on their faces. The ones that could understand English (never admitting to it, however) looked stony-faced. That was how you figured out that some of their people understood English; their "no response" was really a response. The Shenyang people stopped breathing.

I poked Maria. Even she was jolted by my interruption. She quickly translated my remark. Up to that point, Ms. Ma could have handled this criticism without most of her comrades understanding what I had said. Once Maria translated my remarks, "no response" was out of the question.

Ms Ma got red in the face. Then, still in English, she said that even though she was translating at this meeting, she was as much a part of their negotiating team as anyone else and therefore was entitled to comment. Her voice rose. She said her comments were important to the explanation of their side's position. Then, like a bolt out of the blue, she said,

"Here in China, everyone is equal. Everyone on this side of the table is equal. Women are equal and take part in all negotiations" That statement immediately escalated the situation into a red zone.

Then she turned to her boss and repeated, in Chinese, what she had said to us along with some justification for doing it. At least, that was what I think she was saying. Then she began crying.

I looked at her boss and just raised my shoulders. I repeated to him what I had just said to Ms. Ma.

"Mr. Wu, I am not commenting on her right to speak her opinion. I am not commenting on her position in these negotiations. I am merely commenting on her repeated additions to your statements in your name." Maria translated my words.

"Ms. Ma is just doing her job." Maria translated Mr. Wu's words.

"I don't think so. You did not make half of the remarks that were attributed to you." Maria was still translating. Ms Ma had not said one single word.

Maria spoke very, very slowly. She knew we were treading on dangerous ground. I told Wu again I was not commenting on her right to speak her opinions or her rights as a member of the Chinese delegation. I was merely commenting on including <u>her</u> opinions in the translation of <u>his</u> words. If I did not have my own translator at all, our side would have assumed that her words were his original words. Maria repeated that to the Chinese.

They were in a quandary. Mr. Wu knew full well that my comment, regardless of its motivation, was correct. He also knew that if he did not defend Ms. Ma, there would be a tremendous loss of "face" on their part. Part of what she had said was true, the part about being a member of the team. The part about interjecting unspoken comments into the negotiation was an enormous error. Therefore, he took the only way out.

Mr. Wu abruptly adjourned the meeting until the next day. The men from Shenyang just sat there transfixed by these sudden events.

While we were packing up all our papers, the Chinese group left the meeting room quickly. We left and went downstairs out into the summertime heat of Beijing. Luckily, we found a taxi quickly and returned to our rooms at the Beijing Hotel. Then John started in at me.

"You were wrong", John told me.

"Maybe, but I'm a little tired of hearing her opinions on top of his. In fact, I'm tired of this whole subject. We've been at it for a week." I knew that was a weak excuse.

"Tough, you still shouldn't have insulted her." John had no mercy for me. Many years later when he and I spoke of this, he admitted that he, too, was annoyed at the time. However, I was the negotiator; our ground rules prohibited him from interfering at the table.

"All right! All right! I'll apologize tomorrow."

The Chinese response bothered us. Maybe my error was bigger than we thought. It was most unusual for the daily discussions to be suspended in the middle of the day. It was most unusual for the daily discussions to be aborted by the Chinese (usually, we would get tired first); it was most unusual for all the Chinese to troop out of the room in a body (usually, the Shenyang people would leave by themselves followed by the Mr. Wu and the others from the Ministry in Beijing)

I resolved to apologize the next morning. John reminded me that I had made the point and if we said nothing, the Chinese had no easy way out of their dilemma. We had to regain the momentum of the discussions or we'd still be in Beijing for the next revolution.

So, we went back to the table the next day. I apologized for ungraciously interrupting Mr. Wu during his discussions; I apologized for addressing Ms. Ma with my unkind remarks and I apologized for causing the meeting to be cut short. I could see in Ms. Ma's eyes that she didn't believe a word I was saying. My apologies were directed to Mr. Wu and not to her. She couldn't respond to me directly because I was not talking to her. I ignored the impulse to say something directly to her. Wu didn't say a word; he just stared right through me. I thought that he had listened to my apologies with an almost imperceptible sigh of relief but he never acknowledged them. We immediately turned back to the subject of discussion.

We changed the word "nuclear" to "magnetic". Another day passed and another sentence was completed.

The next day began with nary a word about my fiasco. The new subject was the letter of credit to pay for the computer. The morning went by quickly. Mr. Wu wanted payment to be made inside China; we wanted to get paid outside China. Back and forth, back and forth, back and forth. We finished the morning session about 11:45a.m.--12:00 Noon. John and I went outside to wait for a taxi, which took about 2 minutes to never. Today was one of those days that took "never". At times, we thought that Mr. Wu turned the taxis on or off depending on the status of the negotiations. Today, they were off. I sat down on the steps of the building and leaned back against the facade. The sun, which was intermittent in Beijing, felt warm. What with the warmth and the sleep (or lack of it) and the adrenaline drain, I dozed off on the steps. At just that moment, the Chinese stepped out of the building on their way to lunch.

Maria tried to explain to them what I was doing. She thought it was very funny. They didn't think so at first. No one awakened me. They all just stood there, Chinese and Americans, looking down at this IBM negotiator sleeping on the sidewalk! They all waited either for me to wake up or for the taxi to come, which ever happened first. The taxi came, Maria wakened me and off we went. The Chinese were now laughing their heads off.

We finally got back to the hotel, had lunch (Beef Strong Hot, my typical lunch. This was shredded beef all spiced up and browned. It was delicious!), and went back to our room for a little 20-minute siesta, and then back down to the taxis and to Er Li Go. The afternoon session began around 2:00 PM, went to about 3:30PM. We took a break and then continued on to 5 or 5:30PM. We couldn't come to a resolution of the payment terms.

Our relative positions were clear. We wanted payment for the contract to be made through the Chase Manhattan Bank via a letter of credit. Mr. Wu wanted payment to be made through the Bank of China via a letter of credit. The Bank of China was their fiscal agent and the government wouldn't allow transactions through any other banking institution, or at least so he said.

When I worked in the Soviet Union, our contract there stipulated payment by the State Bank of the Soviet Union at their Vienna branch via a letter of credit. That bank held up a payment of $13 million dollars to IBM for over a year on some pretext or other that never would have existed in a western banking institution. It's a never, never land. The buyer had completed all the documentation and sent it to the bank. The buyer's bank said they have transmitted all the documents to the paying bank. Everybody was right, but the bill remained unpaid. Even though all the conditions of the letter of credit had been met, the bank still didn't pay. We did not want a repeat of that situation. I, and IBM, wouldn't accept the Bank of China as paying agent, no matter how trustworthy. The Bank of China is another piece of the Communist government. The Bank of China is completely subject to the same discipline any other part of the government enjoys.

Wu, grandly making a compromise, offered that the Bank of China in Hong Kong should be the paying agent, as if their Bank down there would be any different from the branch in Beijing. We had a problem. We would accept any bank with which Chase Manhattan Bank had a correspondent relationship. That covered about every bank in the world, except for most Socialist government national banks. Any bank accepting international rules would work; any bank under the thumb of a government, any government, wouldn't.

We suggested English banks; we tried European banks, all to no avail. Mr. Wu wouldn't move. The Bank of China was it. Our suggestions moved geographically west to east. We were on the telephone back to the States every night, seeking alternative bank suggestions from our Finance people. The Finance people were probably on the telephone with IBM's bank to get their suggestions. The Finance folks were beginning to get testy when every one of their suggestions was turned down. After many days, we tried the Bank of Pakistan. That bank was a national bank in a quasi-democratic country that followed international law, a legacy of British colonialism. Most importantly, it also had the required relationship with Chase. At the time Pakistan was one of the few countries that had diplomatic relations with China. We didn't expect to get a hit but we desperately wanted to get over this hurdle. IBM never had a relationship with the Bank of Pakistan, but we were willing to try.

Mr. Wu took our suggestion in hand. That should have been a clue for us. Every other suggested bank had been turned down immediately. Mr. Wu had not waited a single second before he refused. He would take The Bank of Pakistan under advisement. Maybe we had a breakthrough. We had to check back home as well. We had to be sure that the Bank of Pakistan would take Chinese paper. Both of us had to refer this issue to the higher ups.

We got our answer that night, almost immediately. Pakistan was okay. The next day, Wu reported that the National Bank of Pakistan was acceptable as a paying agent and holder of their letter of credit. It was touch and go up to that point since the Chinese attached political implications to most everything and particularly to banks.

We're over another hurdle; how many more? Deng's revolution had more twists and turns than a jig saw puzzle.

Even though we had disagreements at the negotiating table, Mr. Wu never forgot that he was our host in his country. He tried to make life a little easier for us. One of his suggestions was that we should use the International Club in Beijing for a little relaxation. He didn't put it quite that way; he just told us that such a place exists. We took a taxi over to the Club one late afternoon before dinnertime. Mr. Wu wrote the name for us in Chinese so that we could give it to the taxi driver The Club building was in the midst of the old foreign embassy section of east Beijing. The building was also one of the casualties of the government's "all foreign devils out of the country" edict. It had not been in use for more than twenty-five years and it looked it.

Workers were all over the place doing repairs. It was obvious that the Chinese were re-opening the "International" part of their existence and were getting ready for many foreigners. The tennis courts in the front of the building looked fine and ready for use. The swimming pool probably was next since there was scaffolding all over it. We met the "tennis pro". He told us, in sign language, that the courts needed some players. I say "tennis pro" only because he was dressed like one. He had white shorts, white polo shirt and socks. He had on a polo shirt with tennis rackets hand embroidered on the left pocket. If you changed the background scene to the Forest Hills, New York, Tennis Stadium, you might have thought that he was on his way to a tournament. John was ecstatic; he was the tennis player among us. Our tennis pro made it known that before we could use the courts we had to have a health examination. Health examination; what's that?

That reminds me of the cast on John's right arm. He had broken his arm and had a cast put on in the States. When it came time to be removed, he was in China. Mr. Wu arranged for him to go to the local hospital. The doctor, or nurse, or whatever, refused to cut it off. As Ms Ma translated, they did not want the responsibility of injuring a foreigner's arm during the removal process. However, the cast had to come off, it was long overdue. When John returned to the hotel, he told Willy and me this absurd story. I promptly accused him of making it up to get our sympathy. Willy, our mechanical angel in disguise, came to his rescue. He had a small electric saw in his tool kit. With great care, he cut the cast off; John kissed him in relief! Weeks later, when this visit to the International Club took place, John was ecstatic; he was going to play tennis again. But first, the health examination had to take place.

We went back to Mr. Wu the next day and told him that we needed to get a health certificate. We had no idea what that was. Mr. Wu came back to us after the lunch break. He told us we had to go the local hospital for a doctor's examination. We looked at each other. This local hospital had refused to take the cast off John's arm. This was getting serious. Every new thing took us deeper and deeper into the quagmire of Chinese administration. I went to the hospital at the appointed time. I took the precaution of taking Maria with me in the event the MD knew no English. And, of course, she didn't. We finally arrived where I was supposed to be. The way it worked was that Maria, a woman, stood outside the room where the lady doctor examined me with the door half open. As the doctor asked me questions in loud Chinese, the Maria would repeat them in English. Then I would answer in English and Maria would repeat them in loud Chinese. I was thankful that there were not many questions; the doctor was satisfied that I was vertical and apparently healthy enough to get a card for the International Club. It was all over in ten minutes. Maria later went back to the hospital with John at his appointed time and went through the same rigmarole again. John got his health certificate. He could play tennis to his heart's content.

The next problem that had to be resolved for our relaxation program was swimming trunks. I had none with me. I had visions of splashing around in the Club pool for the rest of the hot Beijing summer. But it was not to be. I tried to find swimming trunks in the department store around the corner from the hotel. Even with a translator's help, it was a losing situation. During a phone call with my wife back in the U.S., I asked her to mail me a set of swimming trunks post haste. The package arrived in due course. The Beijing post office sent a little chit to the hotel announcing the arrival of a package. However, I would have to pick up the package personally at the post office. The water was cool and delicious in my fantasy. I would jump in the pool as soon as I got my swimming trunks from the post office.

Maria in tow, I went to the post office. There was a special window and counter for foreigners. I stepped up and presented my little chit left at the hotel. The clerk disappeared for a couple of minutes and returned with a package. The package looked a little worse for wear. My explanation for the condition of the package was that it did fine until the border of China. When the Chinese postal system got their hands on it, everyone had to look at it. They did not handle many packages from New York to the Beijing Hotel. It was a rarity deserving examination by everyone.

The clerk asked me what was inside. Through Maria, I said "My swimming trunks." I don't know why he asked, the contents were visible through the holes in the packaging. Nonetheless, I repeated dutifully, "My swimming costume."

The clerk quickly responded. "Have they been used?" As soon as the translator repeated his question, I realized I was sliding down a slippery slope. The condition of the trunks screamed out that they had been used many, many times.

I said, "Yes, of course." Another wrong answer! Why all these questions about an old pair of swimming trunks?

With a very serious face, he announced, "We do not allow the importation of used clothing. We do not need them. I must confiscate this used clothing. You may not bring it into this country."

There was some chit chat back and forth, including the Chinese equivalent of "You've got to be kidding!" To no avail, my swimming trunks to this day, remain in the main Beijing office of the Chinese Postal System. As we were walking out of the Post Office I thought to myself that this must have been one of the ways the Chinese government accumulated all those foreign antiques back in 1949. I had to go back to hotel and work without the International Club pool.

At the same time we were trying to get into the International Club for sports, we were all very busy building our model boat. But when we wanted to test the hull in the bathtub, we ran into a major problem. We needed some weights to put in the bottom of the model to maintain the balance and depth. We couldn't think of any substitute material heavy enough to do the trick. So we took our problem to Mr. Wu.

John said, "Mr. Wu, could you help us get some ballast for our boat?" No sooner the words out of the mouth of the translator, we had another problem. The question, even if translated correctly, meant nothing at all to Mr. Wu. You could read that in his face.

"What do you want?" he said.

"Some material that is heavy and small so that it fits into the model boat we are building."

"What model boat?"

This went around and around a couple of times until one of the synonyms struck a chord with the translator and then Mr. Wu in turn. He remembered the box we had with us when he picked us up at the airport. Suffice it to say, a couple of days later Mr. Wu appeared at a meeting with several small pieces of lead. I thought John would kiss him. We never found out where the lead came from, nor did we ever ask. We just went back to the grinding talks.

Mr. Wu started the discussion of prices by making the blanket statement that our prices were too high and that we were taking advantage of the Chinese. He followed that up with a statement that he had proof we were overcharging simply because we were the only computer dealer in China now. Parenthetically, many years later, he told me he believed that IBM had lost money on that first contract. If that were true, it certainly didn't stop him from trying to have us lose some more. I thought he was making one of his speeches to his peers on his side of the table. He permitted no interruptions. He had a lot to say on the subject of prices and no one, particularly John and I, were going to prevent him from saying it. After a while I stopped listening to the translation.

I think Ms Ma, the translator, had heard all this before. She kept right up with him as if she knew exactly what he was going to say before he said it. Normally, speakers would pause to allow the translator to catch up. Not during this speech. He would slow down and reduce his volume a bit. She would translate in a loud voice.

Two days later, still on this subject, he brought a copy of something he called the "Red Book". He showed us the cover of his "Red Book". While waving the book in the air, Mr. Wu said, "This book contains the US prices of IBM data processing equipment in Boston, USA."

I said, "Oh?" I thought that Mr. Wu would like me to say something.

He continued. "Every model of your computer and every machine is listed in this book!"

Again, I said, "OH?" I looked at John quizzically. His look told me he never saw or heard of any such listing.

"Mr. Wu, where did you get it.?" He ignored me. He waved the book a couple of more times.

"Mr. Wu, how old is the information in the book? He continued to ignore me. He had a speech to make and my interruptions were not going to stop him.

Mr. Wu said, "I compared the prices of the units of equipment in your proposal with the prices in this Book. I find that your proposal prices are significantly higher." His Chinese audience was all beaming. Their smiles radiated from each face. Mr. Wu was making his grand play!

I said, "I would like to see the comparison." As soon as the words left my lips, Mr. Wu was ready with the answer. We were on some script each of us was playing by ear. I began to think I was intuitively playing the proper role in this play.

Wu said, "It is not necessary for you to see the numbers. I am telling the truth. Take my word for it."

That gave us the clue we were looking for. We had deliberately removed the individual unit prices of everything in the contract. The only number in the entire contract was the total cost. It was all or nothing. Since there were no unit prices in the contract, there was no way to remove a product and reduce the price by the amount of the removal. So how could he compare prices?

But we had to go along with his charade.

We said that our costs of doing business in overseas markets were much higher than in the U.S. and that our prices in the proposal reflected that. Mr. Wu was unimpressed. More of the same. Chit-chat---Chit-chat! I told him that the cost of this negotiation was in excess of $300,000 USD. How were we supposed to recover that? Hoping to get his goat, I said, "On the other hand, should we make a gift of that to China?" He ignored the remark.

I told him that we were not going to reduce the price in the proposal. If that meant not making a contract with them so be it. Wu was unimpressed. My remark was standard negotiating talk. He had heard it before

I said then that OK, in order to keep our discussions going I would change the prices in the contract to those mentioned in his book (which he did not allow me to see) However, I would also change some other provisions in the contract so that they would match his "Red Book".

First, we would make delivery of the computer in Boston; they could choose the address we would deliver it to. They would have to arrange for shipment from that location to anywhere else they wanted the computer to be.

Second, the computers should be packed as we do in the US in cardboard boxes, covered by a plastic sheet on a single pallet.

Third, we would install and run the computers at the Boston location to be sure that they would run and meet all specifications. Any further installation and tests would be the responsibility of the buyer.

Fourth, all risk of losses beyond that point in Boston for any reason whatsoever, would be the buyers.

As I was outlining these new conditions, the translator's voice rose higher and higher with each new condition. At the fourth one she was screaming. The situation was tense. We adjourned.

The following morning John took the center seat at the table. This was the third time he had done that. The Chinese recognized the signal that we were convinced the talks were ending. On the first occasion in June when we thought there was no further purpose remaining in Beijing for aimless negotiations,

John had written what we called his "Parting Friendship" speech. He actually wrote it out longhand. His speech consisted of three parts. In the first part, he said, "We love you, we like you. However we have reached a point where neither side can compromise any further. The best course is to keep our friendship and discontinue these talks". In the second part, he summarized our current dilemma and in the third part he said, "Thank you and goodbye." I had timed his speech, surreptitiously of course, at 22 minutes. John's recitation, right from his notebook, took 21 minutes this morning. He must have been a little tense.

We were to leave the following day. Our only way out was to price the entire package, which we had done. Changing that price was something John and I couldn't do while in China. We had to leave; Mr. Wu said if that was the way it was, then that was it. So long!

The Shenyang people sitting at the table visibly froze. The minute I moved out of the center seat and John sat down, they knew what was coming. If I could read their minds, they were thinking that their entire world was crumbling before their eyes. Mr. Mu's eyes were dull; Big Mu was slouched in his seat. Their revolution came to a screeching halt! Deng's grand plan for Shenyang dissolved before their eyes!

This was the supreme bluff; but not a bluff at all. No word change would suffice. Either we would have to change that price or Mr. Wu would have to accept the price we have given. Simple! Everyone stood up. No further words were spoken. As we were leaving, Mr. Wu invited us to a farewell banquet. If we were bluffing he would play his role! We left; they left.

We had similar exciting meetings with IBM pricing gurus in New York. Since this was the first prospective deal in China (again, the mystic of 1.2 billion people!), our executives had made it clear to us that they would be willing to price it so long as we didn't lose any money. We had to have some profit, but not necessarily the normal profit. The pricing people looked at it a little differently. From their viewpoint, if a contract did not bring its proportionate share of the profit, it was a loser. Those opposing points of view caused many, many arguments. The key issue was how to handle the marketing costs. Direct costing of products gave us the requisite bottom line. Apportioning marketing costs (for John and I, along with our entourage, we estimated it was on the order of $5,000 to $6,000 per week) would kill the deal. John's point back home was the marketing costs were developmental because we were reconciling IBM's western business practices with an isolated country. Therefore those market development costs should not be charged to this contract. We took Mr. Wu's point of view; the normal prices (with all apportionments) were too high. Twice our arguments brought us to the President's office. Only he could referee our battle; each time our position prevailed. Frank Cary, IBM's CEO had told Ralph Pfeiffer that he did not want IBM to come in second in this market. We never had to play the Cary trump card. Of course, there was no way we could tell Mr. Wu all of this; even if we did, I could imagine him responding with the Chinese equivalent of "So What!"

The situation was tense on both sides. We knew we had to go. We knew that there was no more flexibility in our pricing. Mr. Wu met with the Shenyang people after our meeting adjourned. I heard about the meeting years later..

Mr. Wu and Co. felt the price was too high (a knee-jerk reaction to all talk of price). Mr. Wu's job was to make that statement over and over again. He also felt IBM wanted this pilot project, first time sale in China etc. Mr Wu felt our traveling costs were being passed along to them. He told his colleagues he understood our pricing process. Decisions about price were taken at a high level in western companies. The Shenyang people were fearful that if we left, we wouldn't come back and their modernization plans would be shot to hell. In the background, the Ministry's plans would go down the tubes as well!

The situation was stretching the Communist system to its limit. The Shenyang people wanted the product at the price offered. The central government international purchasing authority, Mr. Wu, did not agree or maybe he couldn't agree. The modernization program; the first computer import, the new revolution was at risk. The computer programs from Italy were already in Shenyang without a computer to run them. No matter Mr. Wu thought we were bluffing; he thought even if we left we would come back.

While we were waiting in the hotel lobby for Mr. Wu to pick us up to go to the restaurant, I asked John what we were going to do with the model boat. It was about 90% complete, but the size and associated supplies created a baggage problem. Neither he nor I could figure out how to take the boat back home with us. It was too big and bulky to take on the airplane. We couldn't get it packed properly even if we could take it on the plane. Leaving it with the Chinese to be packed and shipped to us was asking a little too much we thought. So, the only option that came to mind was to present the model to the Chinese as our gift.

By this time, it was a beautiful model. John's constant repainting of the hull made it shine like a new black automobile. The name "S.S. Friendship" was John's inspiration. He emblazoned the name on the stern and bow. Somehow he had obtained tiny American and Chinese flags that he affixed next to the name. The upper works had enough detail to make one think it was professionally done. The motor and drive mechanism had been fully tested in the bathtub of the suite. The only problem was its size.

At dinner that night, not a word was uttered about our difficulties. The food at the restaurant was first class, but the amount of liquor was limited. We spoke of the weather in Beijing, our families, our friendship, but not one word about business. As the dinner was concluding, I invited them all to come to our hotel room/office. John and I had something we wanted to give them in remembrance of our talks. Mr Wu immediately objected saying that they were not permitted to visit foreign guests in their room. We insisted and he relented.

Messer's Wu, Mu, and Big Mu, along with Chen their translator, came to our hotel room at 10:00 p.m. that night. I had to wake Maria up to translate for us. We were busy packing up to go. It was the first time that the Shenyang people had been above the first floor in the hotel. It was the first time that Mr. Wu had been in any foreigner's hotel room.

I have to give you the background for the scene that followed.

We usually broke the cycle of negotiate-sleep-negotiate by working on our model boat I had purchased in Hawaii early in the year. After dinner each night, while we waited for the inevitable telephone call from the U.S. Willie, John and I sanded, shaped, glued and painted the model boat.

John was the hull specialist. He started out with the frame. Then he attached strips of wood to the frame, piece by piece, just like the construction of a real boat. He had a problem. He had to hold the strips in place while the glue dried. At the beginning, he just sat there and held the strips against the frame. That got somewhat boring. He could only hold one strip at a time. He tried to devise some way to hold many strips in place at the same time. First, he tried Band-Aids. That worked for about one evening. He used up our entire emergency medical supply kit. Then he tried Scotch Tape, but we only had one tiny roll. He tried thumbtacks; the holes were so big that a separate hole finishing technique was required. Then he thought of pins, little dressmaker's pins; the kind the tailor's or dressmaker's use to hold fabric in place. Great Idea! But, where were we going to get pins in Beijing, China?

We went to the Friendship Store, the store for foreigners and diplomats that accepted U.S. dollars. They had everything. We looked and looked. John came across a big display for acupuncture. The acupuncture needles were just the thing. They were narrow, very sharp and had a t-bar at the top for grasping. Perfect! We didn't know it, but we had become self sufficient, Communist style.

The hull was entirely black with a water line encircling it. Measurements were painted on the hull showing the depths (I think they are called Plimsol marks). The name was painted on both sides of the bow and on the stern. Each night John spent at least 30 minutes lightly sanding what he had painted the night before; then for another hour or so gently applying another coat of paint. At the beginning, it was very detailed work requiring a great deal of concentration; after the 20th time, it turned into mindless handwork. It filled up the evenings and the result was a brightly shining hull reflecting stars from the lights in the room. He did such a good job that when we put it in the bathtub to see if it leaked, it was perfectly sound.

Bill O'Leary, our Willie, the computer maintenance guru, was the engine and insides specialist. Both John and I had put aside the problem of powering the boat because we didn't know how to do it. Willie, on the other hand, was a mechanical expert. He mounted the batteries, the two little motors that drove the propellers and the propeller shafts that went through the hull. When he was finished, it looked like a professional job, which, in fact, it was. He spent hours each night fitting, testing and otherwise passing the time in the most constructive way. He used all of his IBM maintenance tools to do the job. When we put it in the bathtub to test the propellers and he turned them on, the boat went beautifully from one end of the bathtub to the other. You should understand that the model was four feet long and the inside of the bathtub was five feet; it didn't go very far. However, it went! We were all very proud.

S.S.FRIENDSHIP - THE MODEL THAT SAVED OUR CONTRACT

I was the specialist for the decks and superstructure of the model. Nobody wanted that part because of the myriad of tiny parts and intricate structures that were involved. Each of us was able to work on his part without interfering with the others. The entire deck came off the model in one piece so that John and Willie could work on their pieces separately. Willie had mounted the engines and batteries in such a way that the whole assembly could be mounted and dismounted from the hull as one unit. This allowed John to do his daily paint job. I could lift my piece out of the hull so I could work on it. It was great!

It was a regular evening ritual. After supper we would go upstairs to our communal room, turn on our record player, or the short wave radio to listen to the Far East Network of the U.S.Armed Forces Radio in Korea, and go to work. The room boys would sometimes come in to watch and, if Maria, our translator, were present, would offer comments on what we were doing. Adult model building was not a common activity in China. In fact, model building by anyone, was not a common thing. The room boys were enthralled. They were so interested that when we filled the thick pile rug under the coffee table with sanding residue, balsa scraps and paint drippings, they didn't say a word about cleaning it up every morning. My wife would never have been so accommodating if I had done that at home. Sometimes the debris on the floor was appreciably thick after a particularly active evening. Once, when we were all crowded in the bathroom with the model in the tub, the room boys applauded when the model moved from one end to the other.

Back to that evening...

The group entered our suite. We cleared away all the documents and manuals from the temporary table set up in the center of the room. We placed the four-foot freighter model on the table, front and center. The four Chinese were stunned at the sight. The model had a beautiful black, shiny hull courtesy of John's painstaking work most nights for several months. My white superstructure was replete with little details, pumps, wires, ropes all painted in their proper colors. Willy's bronze propellers and neat little engine room was a miniature ship's boiler room. All the time we put in that model showed in the professional result.

Mr. Wu finally made the connection between the boat in the box when he picked us up at the airport and John's request for lead ballast. Mr. Mu couldn't get the questions out of his mouth fast enough. "Who built this"? How long did it take to build it"? Who knows how to do this"? Big Mu wanted to know if it was computer controlled. We answered all the questions, one at a time. We told them about our problem of no recreation for weeks at a time. We told them that our model boat solved that problem. They were overwhelmed. The crowning achievement was the boat's name emblazoned on the bows and the stern. In a moment of sheer creativity, John had named the boat "S.S.Friendship".

The name really blew their socks off. "Friendship" is a peculiarly Chinese slogan very dear to them. Mr. Mu, particularly, couldn't believe what he was seeing; the whole idea was a revelation to him.

John cleared his throat to get everyone's attention.

"We would like to give you this model boat as a symbol of the friendship that we have developed over these months. Your friendship is a treasured thing. We want you to have the "S.S.Friendship" to remind you of efforts we have all made to achieve success".

Mr. Wu started to answer, but Mr. Mu stopped him with a hand on his sleeve. He spoke to him in an urgent voice even we could detect. As he spoke, his eyes became full of tears. He wiped his sleeve across his eyes and continued speaking in Chinese to Mr. Wu. Neither translator translated. None was necessary. Later we found out what he said. Mr. Mu insisted that Mr. Wu bend just a little bit to prevent us from leaving China and their negotiations. This was the first time that the user group was trying to influence the "commercial" side of their house. Mr. Mu told him the computer programs were in Shenyang, but they had no computer to run them. Mr. Mu told him it was obvious that we were sincere and honest. Why would they make such an obviously important gift if they were not sincere?

Mr. Wu came right out and told us. "Mr. Mu would like you to stay for a few days." I noticed that the request was attributed to the Shenyang people, not the Beijing people.

"What for?" I answered. I didn't even guess, or hope, that they were going to cave in over the price issue. Price was the essence of Wu's position. The process of getting a discount was the Holy Grail; the actual price itself was secondary.

Mr. Wu noticeably gulped. He said, "I will go to my superiors to discuss this price problem." His face mirrored his unhappiness with telling me that. "However, there is no guaranty that our position will change." The last was for the benefit of the Shenyang people.

I looked at John. I was always the optimist. John was the pessimist or realist if you choose. If he didn't want to stay, we were not going to stay. Agreeing to stay could compromise his departure speech of the afternoon. I think Mr. Wu's obvious discomfort got to him. He nodded to me.

We agreed to stay. Mr. Wu told us he had to wait until daylight to speak to his boss. The fact, as we later found out, that their strategy was to let us go was established at a meeting Mr Wu had with his leader before coming to our hotel. Everyone went to bed, or so we thought.

We didn't know it, and perhaps Mr. Wu never knew it either, but the Shenyang people had been meeting with Vice-Minister of the First Machine Building Ministry, Mr. Suen Yu Yu, at his home twice a week while we were negotiating. He was the Vice-Minister in charge of Science and Technology. A year before he had Okayed the whole modernization initiative that brought us to China. Mr. Mu told me that this kind of constant, twice a week, review was unprecedented. There were people in the Ministry who hewed to the Maoist line; they did not want any contamination of the Communist movement with modern Western technology. These Maoists were content to remain "self-sufficient" and not get involved with the rest of the world. There were others like Mr. Suen Yu Yu more inclined to side with Deng Tsao Ping and look forward to Western introductions. With a contentious atmosphere, the leaders had to be sure that their plans were not thwarted in action; hence the continuous reviews were necessary. Normally, the people at the bottom of the ladder received a task passed down to them from Beijing. Periodically, i.e., once a month, they reported on the progress of the task. Remember, all plans are successful plans. No one reports failure. In negotiating for China's first computer, they were monitoring the situation almost day by day.

At their meeting with the Vice-Minister later that night, they told him of the price situation that had developed. Mr. Mu thought that the price was fair. Mr. Mu told me later that he had reported that the talks were proceeding nicely and that he and Big Mu were really satisfied with the cooperation that IBM was giving them. Big Mu was particularly happy with the depth of the education programs we were offering. Both Mr. Mu and Big Mu were worried that Mr. Wu's insistence on a discount would upset the impending deal. The minister, Mr. Suen Yu Yu, questioned them at length on these matters and then suggested that they leave the problem with him.

Big Mu later told me he couldn't be sure but he believed that Mr. Suen Yu Yu made a telephone call that night to Mr. Jiang Ze Min of the Foreign Affairs Bureau (remember, he was involved with the dinner at the Italian Ambassador's residence the year before; we believe he was the one who selected the Italian company). He further believes that Mr. Jiang made a telephone call to the head of Techimport. Ultimately a message got down to Mr. Wu.

The next morning, Mr. Wu formally asked us to stay while he worked out the price problem. The Shenyang people, Mr. Mu and Big Mu, came into the room smiling broadly. They actually danced into the room they were so happy. Their revolution was back on track! We continued on other items. The subject of price never came up again!

Many years later during a visit with him in Beijing, Mr. Wu told me that he thought that we had given him a very low price; a price that had no profit in it. If that's true, then his whole price gambit was a big bluff. His hard stance on price almost derailed the deal. I wonder which was it, a bluff, or a fair attempt to get a discount.

No sooner had we gotten over the hurdle of the week, John said to me, "We have to go to Tokyo." I was dumbfounded. Here we were after many months almost at the point of success and suddenly we had to go to Tokyo. What the hell was going on?

Chapter 10 – Executive's Tour

New York Times, September 10, 1977

"OPEN MAO TOMB"

We were really on a roll and could look forward to finishing up the remaining details. Maybe to commemorate that progress, they finally opened Mao's Mausoleum to the public. Maybe it was the other way around; we were gaining agreement because they opened Mao's Tomb. Who know? We had gotten through the price arguments, although stressful, relatively unscathed. We had gotten through the education and the class size struggle without too much blood letting and it looked as if we could breeze through the remaining problems. Of course, we didn't know what Mr. Wu would bring up from day to day, but at least the subjects that were left couldn't be as contentious as the ones we had already finished. So, when John told me that we had to go to Tokyo for a week or more, it was devastating. Leaving the discussions at this point would be a setback. It would be difficult to get back up to speed if there were a hiatus. With all this momentum going for us, an interruption was crazy! Why do we have to go to Tokyo in the middle of all this action?

"Charlie called me from Tokyo and suggested that we be out of Beijing while the executives are here."

John continued. "Remember Charlie was here in the spring to arrange that trip for the senior executives?" We were in the hotel dining room having lunch. He put his fork down and spoke very seriously.

"I remember." That was the time that Charlie and his wife "pre-tested" the China tour that the IBM senior executives were going to make in the fall.

"Well, it's here. It's scheduled for next week. We gotta be out of here." He was deadly serious.

"Why?" I was perplexed. What did that have to do with us?

"We don't want to be porters and runners for these guys. They will insist on meeting all the people we are negotiating with. They will insist on "executive-ing" the talks. Our Chinese friends will invite them to our meetings so that they can manipulate them as well. Since we've been here so long, they will expect that we know a lot more than we do. All in all, we gotta go to Tokyo. If we meet them there, a lot of stuff won't come up." He explained very slowly. He knew what was at stake.

While John and I were having what I thought to be a disastrous conversation, Charlie was having his own troubles in Tokyo. The senior IBM executives insisted that Charlie accompany them to China. Their request was perfectly reasonable. Charlie, of all senior IBM executives, had the most experience with the Chinese; through us, to be sure, but they had none. Charlie was having a devil of a time convincing his bosses that if he, Charlie, was with them, he and they would inevitably be drawn into the negotiations. Charlie also did not want to be a luggage carrier since he would be junior to all the others. The negotiations had just gotten over a tremendous price hurdle. Our Chinese hosts, Mr Wu, and his boss, would rightfully insist on banqueting our bosses (he had already met Charlie during his spring visit) and the conversations at that banquet would drag the senior executives into our talks. We couldn't run that risk and let that happen! Even I could understand that.

On top of that, neither John nor I could figure out why the top three people at IBM, at the same time, would be making this trip.

IBM executives, insofar as we knew, never traveled together. The risk of corporate succession was at stake. Was there something going on that we didn't know about? It was very confusing. For an IBM executive to tour China, something quite "in" at that moment in history, was one thing but all of them at the same time was quite another. We wondered if there was another agenda at play.

We told Mr. Wu that we had to go to Tokyo to check out some of the things we had agreed on and left the next day. We promised to return in about a week. He didn't believe us, but he could do nothing. When we told him, we did not even change seats at the table as we usually did when John had something important to say. Our request for a break, however, gave him the opportunity to repeat for the tenth time the story of the Emperor and remote authority to act. It seems that during a winter campaign a Chinese Emperor sent a General and his army to besiege the Koreans and await orders. The General did that and sent a messenger back to the Emperor for further orders. By the time the messenger traveled back to China and then returned to the General, he found the General's army frozen and starving to death. The moral of the story was that if you send a General (us) to do a task, give him enough authority to complete it. Whenever we said that we had to "check" something with New York or with our management, this story was repeated to us. Never mind that Mr. Wu had to ask his leaders for direction every night; our Emperor was 8000 miles away, his was only eighty feet away.

For John and me, this going and coming was a big job at the wrong time. We had been in our hotel rooms, cum office, for two months. Like any other hotel room/office, it was impossible to just walk out and lock the door. We had to pack everything up in a way that we would be able to find it when we got back. We had to find some place to store the packages. There was no way we could cart all the accumulated paper, manuals, and miscellaneous "junk" of those months back and forth to Tokyo. Even if we could pack the whole thing up in one day, where could we leave it?

Once before, we had a similar situation. Early on, when we came up to a scheduled departure, we usually had a plan of what do to with all the accumulated materials. One time, John took ten cartons of paper to the garage of the Commercial Attaché of the Canadian Embassy whom he had met playing tennis. He was very nice to us. The cartons stayed there for a month and no one touched them. At that time, close to the beginning of the talks, we hadn't accumulated much, just ten cartons. This time, it was a horse of a different color and magnitude.

We took the easy way out. I went down to the hotel cashier's desk and asked for my bill. When they gave it to me, I asked them to change it to add two weeks on to the bill to cover the time we would be in Tokyo. The little lady, without a word, looked at me as if I were crazy. What will these Westerners do next? I wanted to pay in advance for the room even though I was not going to be in it. She called over her supervisor. He asked me if I really wanted to pay for the room when I wouldn't be in it. I said "Yes, and I wanted to be sure that no one else would be in it as well." At $100 per night it was well worth it!

We did this question and answer script once again. He said, "Wait a moment", and went into an inner office. I heard him on the telephone. In about three minutes, he was back. Everything was fine. If I wanted to keep the room and pay for it, even though I wouldn't be there, it was okay with them. Problem Solved!

John and I went to Tokyo. There was an IBM Board of Directors meeting going on. That was the reason why all the senior executives were there as well. We stayed in the same hotel as the IBM senior executives. It was a vacation for us. We had nothing to do but wait. We lived in the lap of luxury and observed the goings-on of the "Big Wheels". I couldn't help thinking as I saw these people that the Board members have it real cushy. They were being paid to attend this meeting on top of all their expenses and the expenses of the tours they were given. From my viewpoint, it looked like they were all very good friends with the IBM executives and it appeared to be a big social hour. It seemed that they were much closer to the executives who selected them than the people they were supposed to represent. Then, what do I know? Of course, Charlie was there trying to organize and superintend their departure to China immediately after the conclusion of the Board meeting..

John and I had contact with them only once. Charlie introduced Frank Cary, CEO of IBM, and John Opal, the President of IBM, to John and I. John worked for Frank Cary when he was President of the Service Bureau Corporation. Charlie knew John Opal from the time they were both Executive Assistants to previous CEO's. From their response, it was obvious they did not connect us with their up-coming trip. Charlie had arranged a briefing session for the people touring China. It was quite an exalted group. The CEO, the President, a Senior Vice President and our boss, Ralph Pfeiffer, one Vice President, Howard Figueroa, and their wives along with George Conrades, Frank's Executive Assistant, to carry all the bags. My daughter Maria joined them to act as their translator for the trip. To this day, I do not understand the reason for Howard Figueroa's attendance. Maybe he was going to carry some bags as well.

Charlie had Ken, our erstwhile consultant from Chase; give them, wives and all, a political and economic briefing about China. We had not used him since we found his negotiation methods differed sharply from mine. I hasten to note that his academic credentials were flawless. Although I thought his presentation was excellent, when I saw some of the audience trying to keep their eyes open, it was obvious that "jet lag" from the New York flight was taking over.

There was only one question raised.

Frank Cary asked Ken "Would the Chinese buy a lot of copiers if I made a good price on them? After all, their written language is ideographs." The only way you could transmit them was by copying, or so he thought. Basically, it was a fair and logical question, even though we had answered it previously.

Ken wholeheartedly agreed. He said, "Sure. I think so." That was the beginning of a major gaffe! His business wisdom that we questioned at the beginning of the year had not changed. We had been asked that very same question just before the briefing had begun. Our answer was "No". The Chinese want computers, not copiers! The Chinese associate the word IBM with computers, not copiers. Apparently, our answer had fallen short of what was required. It seemed there was a warehouse full of Minolta-manufactured copiers with the IBM name on them. We couldn't sell them; they just sat in a Japanese warehouse gathering dust. It would be a great idea to unload them at any price to someone. Hence, the suggested offer to the Chinese.

Cary had asked John. "What do you think about offering these copiers to the Chinese?"

John said. "I don't think so. The Chinese don't want copiers, they want computers." His answer was unequivocal. We couldn't see the Chinese buying two cents worth of copiers; it was computers they wanted.

Frank did not like that answer. "I'm going to ask our consultant." He would ask the expert for his opinion; the same expert that we wouldn't take to China with us. Actually, at a meeting later with the Chairman of the Bank of China, Frank brought up the subject of copiers as our consultant suggested. More on that later.

The only other event worth mentioning was the problem of gifts. The executive group, as befits their station in life, wanted to leave memorable gifts with those Chinese leaders who met with them. When John was asked about gifts way back in the spring, he had agreed wholeheartedly. It was a Chinese tradition. The only condition we relayed to Charlie was to go easy on the value of the gifts; the symbolism, not the value, was important.

In Tokyo, we found out what gifts were planned. Charlie was directed to purchase several Steuben crystal sculptures. There was a gorgeous eagle, a beautiful porpoise and assorted other animals; all hand crafted crystal. They cost a fortune. The big piece was over $5000, the others just under $1000. John told Charlie these obviously valuable gifts were going to embarrass the recipients. In turn, these gifts would embarrass the presenters. John suggested that they give this expensive stuff back and buy some things in Japan for 1/10th the price. Charlie broached the subject with George Conrades, Frank's executive assistant. George had the least experience with China of anyone there. He told Charlie to forget it. The IBM senior executives were not about to give cheap gifts. I guess his symbolism was in the value, not in the process, of giving the gift.

We had suggested that members of the group be equipped with little short wave radios so that they could receive news of the outside world while traveling in China. John purchased four high-quality, high-cost Sony radios. Those radios could receive signals from the moon and beyond. Charlie gave them to the executives. Before we left Tokyo, an accountant asked John (who had put the $4000 for those radios on his expense account) to produce the radios. The accountant had to affix an asset tag to them. He said if he couldn't affix the tag John would have to refund the money. John told him he didn't have the radios any longer. The accountant wanted to know where they were; "You have to pay for them", he said. When told exactly who had the radios, the entire subject was dropped!

Off they went to China. Mr. Wu and company did not attempt to contact them in Beijing. As soon as they were out of Beijing, John and I returned. Later my daughter reported what had happened to the copier deal and the gifts. This is a third-hand version of events; for that reason it may be inaccurate.

Cary and Opal had a meeting with the Chairman of the Bank of China. The Bank of China is probably one of the largest banks in the world. All was going along beautifully; everyone was complementing each other until Cary brought up the subject of copiers. He asked the head of the bank if he would like to purchase some copiers at an attractive price. I was told that the silence that followed was palpable. The bank leader continued the conversation as if he hadn't heard a word. Two big cultural gaffes! The first was making a sales pitch to the head of the National Bank of the Peoples Republic of China about some tool that a clerk would use; the second, referring to price as if the Peoples Republic of China couldn't afford better. I guess everyone assumed that silence was a negative answer. The meeting continued.

Frank presented his host one of the Steuben sculptures in an unopened box as they were leaving. It was a gesture of good will and friendship. There were profuse thanks. He did not open the box. They left. Everyone had been super polite. All was well and good, maybe. Later that night the Steuben box appeared at the hotel quietly and mysteriously. It had been opened, resealed and returned without a message. Nevertheless, the message was understood. Copiers were not mentioned again. Although the largest and most expensive Steuben piece was accepted by the Foreign Minister (who knew of American practices while head of the Chinese delegation to the United Nations), all the other crystal gifts were never offered again. George Conrades, the executive assistant lugged those crystal pieces all over China. They were to be brought back to the U.S. and returned for credit.

But the story doesn't end there. Some days later, in Canton, George got the bright idea that, instead of carrying them on to Hong Kong; he would mail them there from China. He brought that suggestion up while the executives were having breakfast. Frank Cary thought the idea was great, a real time saver. Maria said she didn't think that would be such a good idea, the Chinese postal system wasn't like the one in the U.S. She remembered the condition of my swimming trunks that my wife had mailed to me during the summer. George's package would just as likely never appear, as to appear at all and probably not in the same condition as when posted. Frank asked, "Do you know or are you guessing?" Maria replied, "I don't know, but experience tells me to be very careful."

George piped up. "Hong Kong isn't that far from here." That sealed the deal.

"Well, if you don't know, we'll mail them." Frank said. It was his final word.

Therefore, Maria and the executive assistant took them to the post office and mailed them to the IBM office in Hong Kong. End of story; not really!

Weeks later the boxes re-appeared at the IBM office in Hong Kong. All the crystal sculptures had been reduced to glass powder and shards courtesy of the China National Postal Service. To finish the story, the shattered sculptures were ultimately returned to Steuben for full credit!

These anecdotes aside, several significant unanswered questions remained, especially what motivated this trip in the first place? In a company where executives always traveled separately, this time they traveled together. That alone, raised questions. The trip was obviously a long time in planning. The Board of Directors meeting immediately preceding their travel was scheduled at least 12 months in advance. At that time, a formal invitation from Chinese authorities was required for a visa. In my experience, although there were many people who wanted to visit China, invitations were issued only when the Chinese perceived an advantage issuing one. Charlie had come to Beijing in June to set the detailed itinerary. This was the first major American corporation executive foray into the Peoples Republic. If it was just a tourist visit; why all the executives simultaneously?

One reason could have been the work of Lewis Branscomb, IBM's Chief Scientist at the time. In 1977 he was also serving as chairman of a group called the Committee for Scholarly Communication with the Peoples Republic of China. This group arranged visits to the PRC by important scientists to share information. It would have been quite logical for Dr. Branscomb to arrange this trip for IBM executives in the name of science.

In the years since, I tried to find the answers to some of these questions. I have not been successful.

One last story. Several months later, I was on my way back to China. I had stopped in Houston to visit with a seismic exploration company that was interested in making a bid to China with one of our computers. We were sitting in the Vice-President's office when his secretary called to tell us I had a call from the IBM Chairman's office. We were dumbfounded. I had never received a call from the Chairman's office in my life; the Vice President must have thought that I was a very important person to receive such a call.

George Conrades wanted me. This was the same Executive Assistant who carried the Steuben sculptures around China and then mailed them to Hong Kong.

"Frank is having a reunion party with the people that were in China with him. I thought it would be a great idea if they had some of the Chinese beer they loved. I found out that you were on your way and thought you could bring a case back." In the American way, he used Frank's name as if he were a close friend. I was dumbfounded by the request. I thought to myself, "Is this what executive assistants do?"

Background: He was referring to Tsingtsao Beer, for which China is famous. It's brewed in a German built brewery in Tsingtsao, China which was part of the German colony there. It's sold in China in one liter brown bottles which have a distinctive shape. A case of liter sized glass bottles filled with beer must weigh a ton.

"George, they sell that beer in Chinatown." This was a true statement. Commercial relations with China had improved significantly since we started there. All kinds of Chinese things were appearing in American markets.

"Yeah, but I thought the real beer would be better." His voice was getting insistent. Employees don't argue with executive assistants to the CEO.

"George, it is the real beer.   I would have to carry a very heavy case 8000 miles. There is no way they would let me check it as baggage and if I had it packed for accompanied shipment, it would cost fifty times what the beer cost. And, there is no guaranty the bottles would remain whole." I was desperate. I did not want to carry a case of beer to the U.S. from China.

"Yeah, but it would be the real thing." He was getting desperate too. His idea was slowly sinking in the West, like the sunset.

Now I knew what Executive Assistants did. Later he would be a president of some division in IBM.

"George, I'll have my office find the real stuff in Chinatown and ship you a case. Okay?"

"Will it look exactly like the beer in China?"

`"George, it is the same beer as in China"

"Okay"

I turned around to the other people in the room and shrugged my shoulders. They had heard my side of the conversation. They had Chairmen and executive assistants in their company as well.

A couple of years later, I heard (maybe fifth hand) of another China story involving that executive tour. Charlie's boss Ralph Pfeiffer attended the party celebrating their tour of China. It was the party that George wanted the beer for. In preparation for the occasion, Ralph had the art department at his headquarters prepare a series of photo albums containing selected snapshots taken during the tour. Simple enough, right? Wrong! The artists first arranged to get all the pictures that were taken, including some of mine, even though I had not been on the trip. They had well over two hundred to choose from. It took quite some time.

They selected what they thought were the better ones. Each were fixed up, retouched, and made into presentation type photos. Then they were mounted on special pages with printed captions for each, the where and when of each photo. The pages were put together with covers made of hand tooled leather, appropriately hand lettered with the names of the participants, all five of them. The albums were impressive, so I was told. They were presented at the party and I imagine they were a great hit. Those albums must have been expensive.

Many, many months later, the internal audit department of headquarters told Charlie the recipients of those albums were going to have to pay income taxes on their value. Either that or the corporation doesn't take an income tax deduction for the cost. In the auditor's opinion, the photo albums were so personal the company couldn't deduct their cost as a valid business expense. It could, however, treat them as additional compensation to each recipient of an album. Remember, we're not talking small change here.

Charlie blew his cork! He was going to have to go to his boss to so inform him. I could just visualize it. "You remember the albums, don't you Ralph? They were the photo albums you gave Frank and John at Frank's China party...."

I can't imagine the money would have been significant to these executives. I guess it would have been humiliating to explain all this to his colleagues Ralph was not about to do that, so he ended up paying for them out of his own pocket to satisfy his own internal audit department.

Justice and reason triumphed.

Chapter 11 – Home Run

New York Times, October 22, 1977

"ENTRANCE EXAMS REINSTATED AT PEKING UNIVERSITY"

When we returned from Tokyo, we went right back to the grind. Our workdays in China were quite long and stressful. The feeling of isolation from the U.S. was with us all the time. We awoke very early. While I was shaving, I listened to the Voice of America located in the Philippines at about 6:00a.m. Around 6:30a.m. most weekdays, I got a telephone call from Alice, our contract coordinator in the U.S. She would give me the latest reading on any points that were still open. She would also give me any new wording suggestions for getting over a sticking point. Then down to breakfast with John during which we would rehash what Alice had told me. The rest of the day, except for lunch back at the hotel, was spent at Er Li Go with the Chinese. When we returned in the evening, it was just time to finish dinner before we had to get on the telephone to the U.S. Those calls sometimes lasted until very late. Because of the 12 hour difference in time it was a long work day. We tried to fill the time waiting for these phone calls by listening to tapes we brought with us. We played an Ella Fitzgerald recording of Cole Porter's songs so much, we wore the tape out!

We tried to do other things to offset the grind. From our room we could look down and across the street to an open-air basketball arena. At night, they had lights on so that the play could go on. We were too far up to make out much of the activity, but the idea of attending a basketball game became essential. It was something to do rather than continuing to stare at the ceiling. John, with Maria as his translator, went down one evening. He walked across the street and went right up to the box office. He took some Chinese money out of his pocket and held it in his hand.

"How much are two tickets?" He asked the attendant.

Maria repeated the question in Chinese. John repeated it when the little clerk didn't answer.

Finally, the attendant said, "We have no tickets." Even Maria, who understood what he said, couldn't comprehend why he wouldn't or couldn't sell him the tickets..

"What do you mean, you have no tickets. How did all those people get in?" Maria asked the attendant without waiting for John to respond.

Silence

Finally, "I can't sell tickets to foreigners." I guess he realized John and Maria were not going away until he gave some sort of answer.

John couldn't think of an answer to that one, so he just turned and walked back to the hotel.

The next day, John told Mr. Wu of our disappointment. He nodded but didn't say a word. Later that day, he invited us to go to an ice hockey game.

Stupidly, I said, "Ice hockey, you need ice for that. It's not cold enough yet." How stupid I was. Why in the world would he invite us to an ice hockey game if they didn't have ice? It's just another little example of my Western bias.

Ms Ma proudly answered, "We have a sports arena."

I felt like a fool. I had fallen into the trap again!

They picked us up after dinner that night. We met Chen, Mr. Mu, and Big Mu outside of a large covered arena somewhere beyond the center of Beijing.

Ms. Ma continued her put-down. She pointed out all the details of the arena.

"Chairman Mao dedicated this park at this spot."

"Oh" That particular fact didn't turn me on.

"This arena can be used for basketball when the ice hockey time is over"

That was a little more interesting.

"Last year the China National Table Tennis Championship tournament was held here. We have the best teams in the world"

Now she was really getting to me.

I asked her, "Who built this park?" I knew the answer to that one. The architecture of the sports arena was distinctly Russian.

"The Russians," she answered. I thought that fixed her.

Big Mu told me that we were going to see two of the best hockey teams in China. What he didn't tell me was that both teams were from the Peoples Liberation Army. That accounted for all the uniforms among the spectators.

We went inside a hockey arena that was a copy of Madison Square Garden. It was immense. We had great seats. We were right down where you were in danger of getting hit in the head by a flying puck. The teams went at each other as if it was for the championship of China. I think one of the team's names was "Spartans" but I can't be sure of the translation. The only things missing were the hot dogs, beer and program vendors. They also did not have the immense score board that I associate with these sports. Since I couldn't understand the announcer, I couldn't follow all the plays; but it was exciting anyway. The best part was the fact that another evening went by without any of us going nuts!

We also tried to alleviate the grind by inventing things we could do. Maria suggested that we have a Thanksgiving Dinner party in the hotel dining room. Everyone said 'Great". She spoke to the chef to make all the arrangements. How she got to him was a big mystery. She asked for a turkey, a real turkey with stuffing, and apple dressing. The Chef was an older person. Apparently, he remembered how to roast the turkey, cook the stuffing, and make an apple dressing. He must have cooked for foreigners before the revolution. Maybe the foreigners were Americans, who knows? Thanksgiving Day is one of the more purely American holidays; no other culture, most of all the Chinese, shares it. Most importantly, he said he knew where to get a turkey. These were major accomplishments! I did not think there are any turkeys in northern China, perhaps not anywhere in the rest of China as well. Roasting and baking are not common Chinese cooking skills; sautéing, boiling and deep-frying seem to be the Chinese style. Apples are available, but not the hybridized monsters we get in the U.S. We all waited for the Thanksgiving Dinner; it was exciting! Maria told us that even the Chef was excited.

The day finally arrived. During the meetings that day, we told Mr. Wu and the Shenyang people of our arrangements for the Thanksgiving Day Dinner. That announcement meant we had to stop the talks while we explained the origin of Thanksgiving and the turkey. Our explanations created more questions. We had a "grand old time", one of the few on a clearly personal basis with our counterparts. Then we went back to the hotel for our evening meal/Thanksgiving Dinner party. The waiters in the dining room all knew what was going on. They stood in little groups around the room. They were probably talking about what these crazy foreigners were doing. Finally, the Chef himself all dressed in very clean, starched whites, toque and all, with a silent drum roll, carried the beautifully roasted turkey across the room to our table. We were stunned to find that he had located a turkey in China at all. The turkey was browned all over; the skin was very taut over the turkey frame. If you are used to seeing a big fat brown turkey with enormous breasts and legs the sight of this one would shock you. Although browned beautifully, it also looked like someone had run it to death before cooking. It was skinny and scrawny. This turkey had died of exhaustion. Nevertheless, the Chef had done a magnificent job and we told him so. The Chef carved the turkey like the professional he was. He wouldn't let any of us do the carving; it was dangerous for foreigners to wield the sharp knife. It tasted great! The greatest thing was the switch from Chinese style cooking for one meal. We even gave pieces of our turkey to some other Americans in the dining room!

To cap our Thanksgiving celebrations, Mr. Wu presented us with a totally unanticipated requirement the following day. Mr. Wu announced that their factory executives had to be educated in the use of the computer. This requirement was in addition to the training program we previously had agreed to for the people who would run and maintain the computer. We were shocked!! Nothing like this had been mentioned when we spent the better part of two weeks haggling over the training program. John and I thought it was another ploy to get something for nothing.

We began the discussions. How many executives? What executive levels are involved? What kind of executive, i.e., administration, finance, what? How long should this program be? Every question we posed was promptly responded to. Six executives were named; the plant manager, the plant deputy manager, the plant financial boss, the plant planning manager and the plant operations manager, and one more unidentified executive plus one translator. Somehow had to deal with seven new participants in some kind of education program written into the contract.

The only activity John and I could come up with was some kind of "executive" tour of factories and IBM centers. In the U.S., IBM had two so called executive training centers. There, an executive could attend pre-planned classes on various computer subjects. And, more important to us they were free. We decided to offer Mr. Wu a four week tour around the United States visiting various IBM customers who would show off their computers. The tour would end with one of our ten-day executive programs in our San Jose Executive Training facility.

I presented this plan to Mr. Wu. Judging from the facial expressions on the Shenyang people, we had hit another home run. They were ecstatic; but Mr. Wu threw some cold water on the plan by insisting all this talk be put into the contract. I couldn't commit to something like this while I was in China; it would take a significant amount of planning and scheduling. Mr. Wu was adamant. He wanted IBM's obligation in the contract.

"Mr Wu, I can't put this kind of plan into a contract. You can take my word for it!"

"Mr. Joseph, I believe you. My leaders, however, prefer to see these obligations in writing to avoid misunderstandings later on."

"Mr. Wu, how about this. I will put words into the contract obligating IBM to invite a group of customer executives, not to exceed seven, to a tour of factories in the U.S. for a period not to exceed four weeks for the purpose of demonstrating the uses of computers in those environments. How about that?"

Mr. Wu thought about my proposal for a while. The Shenyang people held their breath. Then he said, as he usually did,. "I will study it and let you know."

The next morning, he opened the meeting and signified his acceptance. We moved on.

`At the negotiation table, the last subjects were the toughest. Whereas the price issue was a relatively standard issue with any purchase, we were approaching subjects unique to computers, embargo and IBM. They involved arbitration clauses and our duty to verify by inspection that the computer was not being used for military purposes. The inspection requirement was forced upon us by the U.S. export licensing requirement. The theory was it would be difficult for a computer user to divert the use of his computer to unauthorized activities if the vendor

(IBM, representing the U.S. government) would suddenly, and without notice, descend upon him to check up. The theory was nonsense. How could anyone know what a computer was processing merely by looking at it? But some clerk in Washington decided random vendor inspections would make everyone so nervous that diversions to military uses would be averted. And, what happens in-between the inspections? Logical analysis was not the key here, inspection was an absolute requirement; no inspection, no license; no license, no sale!

This inspection requirement was so ridiculous it sometimes turned ludicrous. In the Soviet Bloc, a government computer customer in Hungary was so incensed at the requirement that it devised a way to avoid having IBM enter their computer room to look. In 1975, the inspection requirement came down to providing printed reports of the contents of the computer memory. This customer printed out the reports as required. Since they wouldn't let the IBM representative into the computer room, the computer reports were put into a little wagon that was shoved out the door. The little wagon rolled down the hall to where the IBM representative was waiting. He picked up the reports and delivered them to a U.S. consulate. The theory was somebody in the government, somewhere, could read the memory contents and know what the computer was doing with all those zeros and ones. My theory was different. It would be better not to license these kinds of sales at all than to permit them with conditions like this one.

On the Chinese side, their attitude was perfectly understandable. Hey, you people from IBM! You sell us a computer and then tell us that you must come and see what we are doing with it. It's none of your business! Mr. Wu would turn purple whenever the subject came up, and I couldn't blame him. More on this subject later.

The arbitration clause attempted to describe what the parties would do when an impasse on some point of contention couldn't be resolved. Arbitration clauses are standard bill of fare in sales contracts, even more standard in international sales contracts where cultural practices are different. Neither party would want an unresolved issue to remain unresolved; usually both would want to resolve it and move on. Thus, both parties agree to accept the decision of some third party who makes a decision based on the rules of a country that the contracting parties select in advance. That is the normal procedure when a private company sells to another private company. This time, it is a little different. This time we have a private company (IBM) selling to a government; not any government, but to a government that had not yet agreed to any international rules of conduct. In fact, Chairman Mao had obliterated all international rules in China! This contract was different! This contract was more like a treaty!

Mr. Wu, and maybe the whole government, still had major problems with the basic idea behind arbitration and inspection. Inspection involves the acceptance of an inspector. Arbitration involves voluntarily accepting the control of a third party, i.e., the arbitrator. Arbitration involves accepting the rules of another country, i.e., the rules of law. China had no rules of law, they had the Communist Party. Mr. Wu grandly made the point that the Peoples Republic of China wouldn't accept control by anyone else of internal activities in the country. He gave us a history lesson on what happened when China was controlled from the outside. We heard about the British, we heard about the French, and we heard about the Germans. The Japanese occupation was a particular favorite. Historically, great indignities, to use an understated expression, were heaped on China by all the major powers in the world, including the United States. They were terrible stories; stories that made you understand the attractiveness of Communism to the Chinese. That history, however, was not particularly relevant to the commercial sale transaction we were engaging in; we were trying to help.

We discussed the inspection requirement for two weeks. We "solved" it by putting off further discussion until we could figure out a way around the other problem, the arbitration problem. We went around and around for another week on arbitration. It became fairly obvious to all of us that both parties wanted to complete this deal but we couldn't figure out how. I couldn't come up with any word or synonym for arbitration that Mr. Wu would even consider. I tried mediation, adjudication and ten other words. I tried the "I'll call New York" for alternatives. Nothing would budge him. He was making this into a cause celebe.

Mr. Mu and Big Mu were really down in the dumps. From the high point of picking out the best, the fastest computer, to solving the price problem, they had descended into the depths as our relative positions hardened. This whole discussion was completely out of their hands. Mr. Wu was in charge of these matters; they had finished their part of the negotiations. As users, they had absolutely nothing to say on these subjects. Their faces reflected their feelings. Mr. Mu's eyes were glassy; he couldn't stop fiddling with his notebook. He couldn't sit still while Mr. Wu made the same arguments over and over again. Big Mu, on the other hand, became a lump of clothing in the chair. His slump was so pronounced because he was so tall. He became bent over, almost in two; every muscle of his body manifested dejection.

When it became apparent that we were at an impasse, Mr. Wu called for adjournment before John could move into the center seat to begin his exit speech. Mr. Wu knew that would be a clear signal that there was no immediate hope. We had already mentioned that we needed time next day to arrange for a flight back home. Wu immediately invited us to a dinner that night. We thought that he was attempting the old Chinese ploy, "if you can't get them to agree, get them drunk"!

Mr. Wu arrived with two cars that evening. We went in one, while the men from the factory went in the other. Although the restaurant had a name, I couldn't pronounce it. We called it the "Sizzling Platter" restaurant because their specialty was a delicious chicken dish served on a platter that sizzled and sputtered with heat as it was delivered to the table. There wasn't a lot of drinking that night although Mr. Mu had his normal quota.

When we returned to the hotel, we gathered in the lobby to say our goodbyes. We were a somber crowd. Everyone knew that unless our respective bosses came up with some alternative, there would be no contract. If the government of China wouldn't accept arbitration to resolve differences and IBM wouldn't sign an international contract without some form of arbitration, we were deadlocked.

The next day, John and I walked all over Beijing while we waited for the call from Mr. Wu. It came that evening.

"We will meet tomorrow morning as usual." Mr. Wu said to me.

"What happened?" I asked. I was impatient; I didn't want to wait until tomorrow.

"We will meet tomorrow morning as usual." he repeated. Mr Wu had said whatever he was going to say and that was it.

I thought of what had happened over the past couple of weeks. Either John or I was on the telephone every night asking either Alice in the Contracts Department, or Charlie, our boss for a way out of the situation. Sometimes, the response we received from the U.S. was negative. The lawyers and contract people can say "no" in 10,000 different ways. But, there were other times when their help put us over the top. The arbitration argument was one of those. Mr. Wu apparently wouldn't accept anybody telling his government what they could or could not do. He, or they, was paranoid on the subject. I guess that's a holdover from the times when China was occupied by one or another of many foreign powers. The arbitration issue was a "show-stopper" for both parties.

Finally, Charlie had come to our rescue back in New York. He successfully lobbied Nick Katzenbach, the IBM General Counsel, to accept Sweden as the arbitration site and argue later over what country's law (by not mentioning it in the agreement) would be used by the arbitrators. IBM has preferred other countries like Switzerland or, alternatively, the Netherlands for reasons I was not aware of. I only knew that I couldn't get Mr. Wu to accept either of those places. Actually, he wouldn't accept any arbitration in any country. That was the status until the boat became a present.

Mr. Wu opened the next day's meeting with a terse, "We accept Sweden", and that was the end of it. At that moment, I would have loved to remind him of his Chinese General in Korea story he told us over and over when we had to check with New York. I let the moment pass, I was exhausted.

Over the next couple of days, we quickly chose some arbitration outfit in Sweden using some commercial laws to be negotiated at that time. The funny part of all this is we all agreed in the event of a contract dispute, we would allow some judicial body in Sweden to arbitrate under some laws that we would argue about then.

The agreement on Sweden opened the floodgates of approvals. The inspection clause was disposed of two days later. We agreed to change the words "inspection visits" to "assistance visits". However, we worded the visitation requirements as mandatory on both IBM and the Chinese to satisfy the licensing people. I wrote IBM was obligated to make "assistance visits". According to my explanation technology was always changing; therefore, it was essential that we keep them up to date The Chinese were obligated to grant our personnel visas and access for that purpose. Both problems (arbitration and inspection) solved, almost at the same time.

When next we called the U.S., the good news spread quickly. Since neither John, Charlie nor I were corporate officers we could not sign a legally binding contract for IBM. The Board of Directors would name one of us to sign in the name of the company. We had not thought of that little requirement before. Later on, we would get that authority before we went to China. Charlie notified us that he was taking the next plane so that he could sign the contract. That took a couple of days. In about a week, we had the contract all prettied up, Charlie had arrived and we were ready for the signing ceremony.

We arrived at the usual room in Er Li Go before the Chinese, which was a little unusual. We briefed Charlie just before the meeting. We told him to smile, but say nothing, agree to nothing, until after the signatures had been taken. We were afraid that he might agree or disagree with something new, or perhaps reopen something old. We told him to wait for my signal, and then sign. The Chinese trooped in. Mr. Wu led the way, followed by Mr. Ma, the Shenyang representatives and Ms Ma. Mr Ma, as was his custom, was wearing what appeared to be a custom tailored Mao jacket and pants. His dress stood out like a blue spotlight. Everyone was smiling except Mr Wu. He had his normal dour look on. The Shenyang people appeared so happy that they seemed tipsy. They wanted to talk but couldn't with Mr. Ma there. After some chitchat, we sat down. I placed the contracts on the table in front of Charlie. I nodded to him; he signed. Now it was time for the Chinese to sign.

With the pen in his hand, Mr. Ma said, with a completely straight face, "I want to change the quantities in this contract to double everything". He looked right at Charlie as the translation was made.

Charlie's eyes lit up and his mouth started to move. I could tell what he was thinking. Go out to China to sign a $2,600,000 deal and come back with a $5,200,000 deal! John looked at him so hard I thought his head would break. The invisible words flowed between them. "Stick to the script Charles." John always called him "Charles" instead of "Charlie" when real serious things were discussed. John feared that as soon as "Charles" indicated agreement, Mr. Ma would start a discussion about the price.

I said, "Do you mean you want two computers and everything else."

Mr. Ma said, "Yes."

`Big Mu's eyes nearly came out of his head. Nevertheless, he said nothing. Mr. Mu just sat back and smiled a little. Mr.

Wu looked like he was playing poker with a "Full House" in his hand.

Charlie still wanted to say something. I surreptitiously touched his arm.

I said, "Mr. Ma, why don't we do this? Sign this contract, then we will make a copy of it and sign another one tomorrow. Then we can identify the new user and get all of his information." I knew that he knew all about embargos on exports of computers. He knew that we could sign fifty contracts but only get each one licensed for export at a time, one by one to named users for named purposes. He knew all of that.

"No, I want to change this one." Mr. Ma said. I felt he was playing with us.

"We can't do that. We can't contract for an unknown user." He didn't give a damn, but I did. We had an embargo to worry about. Mr. Ma had to know that.

"Well, that's a shame." We had fallen neatly into his trap. The Chinese made a reasonable proposal to double the size the contract; get two computers instead of one; educate another 12 Chinese, etc. We were the ones who had to refuse. It was another one of his gambits to show who was in charge. Having established that, he signed the contract and gave it back to Charlie.

Everybody congratulated everyone else and ten months of work were over! Deng Tsao Ping's industrial revolution for China could continue!

Later Charlie asked, "What the hell was all that about?

John told him that was Mr. Ma having his fun with us. "He knew we couldn't sign a contract without knowing the user. What would we tell the export licensing people?"

We had another banquet that night.

The war wasn't over yet. We still had several related tasks before we could truly celebrate. Although we had a contract, we didn't have a license to export the computer we had just sold. We had to attest, by personal visit, that the Shenyang Blower Works was a civilian activity. We had to go to Shenyang to look.

As if John or I could tell if there was any military involvement there!! We also had to make a schedule and reservations for the hardware and software education; we had to make a schedule and appointments for the United States tour for the factory leaders. When we had all that done, we could really celebrate!

On the Chinese side, a giant movement in their revolution had taken place!

Chapter 12 – Shenyang Tour

New York Times, March 7, 1978

"NEW CONSTITUTION – ECONOMIC GROWTH OVER POLITCAL"

We returned home (contract in hand!) for the Christmas and New Year's holidays. John and I had been in negotiation with the Chinese for ten months! Every paragraph had been parsed several times; each word had been translated into Chinese at least twice, and sometimes three or four times.

Before we left Mr. Wu and John arranged our schedule for the requisite trip to Shenyang in February. The newly signed contract had a provision, as did our application for an export license, which required us to visit the computer site. We returned to Beijing in late January to get to work. In Beijing, under Chinese etiquette we were Mr. Wu's guests. In Beijing, we were in the capital city of a large nation. In Shenyang, we would be the factory's guests. In Shenyang, we were in the industrial capital of north China. It was like Washington, D.C. and Cleveland, Ohio. In Shenyang, we would be much further north than in Beijing. In fact, Shenyang is in the same latitude as North Korea. Shenyang was the headquarters for the 5th Route Army of the Peoples Liberation Army that poured over the Korean border to rout our troops during that war.

After much preparation, Mr. Mu and Big Mu put John and me (with our new translator, Terry) on the overnight train to Shenyang. They took us to the very same train station that the police had evicted us from months previously. Mr. Mu led us to the very same platform where the cop had stopped us the previous summer. Big Mu was at the end of the group. He repeated whatever Mr. Mu said. Some people were carrying large parcels and bundles and we passed several police officers. No one stopped us. As we walked past the gigantic locomotive, John couldn't help reaching up to touch the slick, mirror like surfaces of the pistons. The wheels were at least twice his height. They had white sides. The whole machine radiated enormous power. The exteriors of the railway cars were spotless. Platform lights reflected off the sides of the cars like little stars. Mr. Mu kept us moving at a quick pace until we came to our sleeping car.

If you can imagine what an early Pullman car in the U.S.A. was like, you can picture our sleeper car. Each car had some Chinese character painted on the side. Maybe it was "Pullman" in Chinese. In the states, each Pullman car had a name as well. Unfortunately, that's where the similarity stopped. We had to clamber up the stairs; it was tough because it was a big step and we had a lot of boxes, bags and such. No porter with a little stepping stool was there to get us up to the first step. A porter of sorts was waiting in his little lobby at the end of the car. He did not have a uniform on as Pullman porters do. He was dressed in the same Mao outfit that Mr Mu and Big Mu wore. Theirs were a lot neater than his. He was sitting in front of a little red-hot pot-bellied stove warming his hands. The lobby was warm and cozy. Mr. Mu said something to him and they both laughed. Terry did not translate. Whatever was said, both enjoyed it. Mr. Mu took us further into the car.

Sleeper bunks with some dark curtains lined both sides of a narrow center aisle. There were wooden upper and lower berths. We moved past all the sleeper bunks. So far, it was similar to the Pullman cars. The aisle turned left and ran along the side of the railway car. Two-person sleeping compartments were in this section of the car, again just like the old Pullman cars back home. Mr. Mu showed who was to go in each compartment. John went into one. Mr Mu shoved Terry and me in another. I don't know where Mr. Mu and Big Mu went.

Our compartment was equipped with an overstuffed upholstered bench seat on one side and the standard up and down bunks on the other. The ubiquitous doilies covered the bench seat back. I had visions of the famous 1920's Oriental Express of Agatha Christie fame.

I said to Terry, "Which do you want? Upper or lower?" I pointed to each of the bunks.

"We're sleeping here. Together?" She was incredulous. This was her first trip to China. This was her first working job as a translator. This was her first trip with me. I was old enough to be her father. It's also quite possible that this was her first overnight trip on a train anywhere.

"I guess so. Upper or lower?" I pointed again.

"I'm not climbing up there." She was emphatic.

"I guess I'll take the upper." Fully dressed, I climbed into the upper bunk. The train jerked and we were off to Shenyang. I don't know what Terry did. I had enough of my own troubles.

The one story houses of Beijing went by quickly and then we were out in the countryside. No lights were visible, in fact, nothing was visible, just a lot of "nothing". No one slept that night. We quickly discovered that the porter's little pot bellied stove was the only heat in the car. As we whistled and roared along, the car and the roadbed made very unfamiliar noises. I expected we would hear the rhythmic clakity clack of the rails and the hypnotic sounds of rushing air. Repetitive rhythms were missing, no hypnotic repetition, just a lot of discordant noise. It was all so Chinese.

With no heat we sat, or tried to sleep, fully dressed. Nothing helped. We traveled all night like that. While we passed through the countryside, the moon and then the sun glistened off the rivers and lakes. The sun was well up when the train arrived in Shenyang. As we approached the city, the clear air began to get foggy and the sun ceased to have a definite size. It became a glow instead. At the station, it seemed as if everything was blurry from the dirty air. I could almost taste the pollution. As we left the railroad car and walked down the platform, the shiny and glistening sides of the cars we noticed in Beijing had disappeared. Everything was dusty and dingy. I turned to John and told him, "You're not going to be doing any early morning runs around here. You'll get black lung disease in about a week." He nodded.

They met us with several "Red Flag" limousines, duplicates of the cars used by Al Capone in Chicago during the early thirties. I thought they must have been exported to China, but John insisted these cars were hand built in China. John told me that he measured some things on a couple of them. All the measurements were different. They were built by hand. We saw a lot of them in China. In Beijing, John asked Mr. Wu to inquire whether he could purchase one for export to the U.S. He figured he could make a profit selling such a collector's item. Many months later, Wu came back with a negative answer. Mr Mu and Big Mu greeted some men when we climbed down from the railroad cars. Mr Mu introduced Mr. Won Go Bin, the factory Secretary, whatever that is. He shook our hands while keeping up a stream of Chinese. While shaking our hand, he was pulling us towards some waiting cars. He reminded me of politicians back home who greet people professionally all the time. Other people took all our boxes and bags quickly. We recognized some drivers and other un-named friends from the Beijing discussions. There were several translators; all seemed to speaking at once. We were introduced to Mr. Liu Da Fu one of the translators. We found out much, much later that some of the "translators" were security guards. Not every Chinese was in favor of this relationship with the U.S. I am glad they did not tell us at the time.

They bundled us off to what Mr. Liu, the translator, called the Lioliang Hotel. He told us that the hotel was named after the province or maybe the province was named after the hotel. He wasn't sure which. His explanation sounded odd; we learned to accept these odd things and move on to more important subjects. The Chinese seemed to appreciate our forbearance. Much later, I discovered the hotel was called the Yamato Hotel when it was built and used by the Japanese occupation forces in Northeast China. It was situated on one side of a major traffic circle near the center of the city. I use the term "traffic circle" because that's what it looked like. However, there was no auto traffic. There were some bicyclists going around the circle. There were piles of gray snow all around. Nothing else.

An immense bronze statue of Chairman Mao stood in the center of the circle. It was at least three times life size. Chairman Mao was depicted holding out one hand to welcome all comers (I guess) to Communism while the other one protected some solders, women and children. They must have mass-produced that statue. I saw at least five identical ones. Chairman Mao had died over a year and half before. That statue looked as if it had been there a lot longer than that. A couple of street lights tried to pierce the foggy pollution. The pollution reminded me of descriptions I had read of London in the 17th Century. In the daylight of early morning, the statue was overwhelming! At times, you could only see the outstretched hand eerily piercing the smog without the body behind it.

The "Red Flag" cars pulled up to the front steps of the hotel. Everyone got out and helped us sort out our baggage. Mr. Mu took us into the lobby. He greeted a gentleman who was waiting there and after a couple of remarks everyone laughed. Maybe Mr. Mu said to him, "I've got the foreigners, what do I do with them?" Who knows? We shook hands with the gentleman in the lobby and that was our check in to the hotel. It wasn't very formal.

A grand staircase led up from the ornate, dusty, dingy lobby to the top floor. I saw the top floor when I looked up. There were only three floors in the hotel. My second floor room was in the front and overlooked Chairman Mao. I looked him right in the eye. He was beckoning to me. I could barely see the little wart he had on his cheek. I kept looking out of the window at Chairman Mao. He looked fuzzy. The window had a complete double set of panes. The glass on the inside was very dirty. Everything outside appeared indistinct. On the other hand, since it was winter, the double glazing provided insulation from the outside cold during the night. I also noticed that there was frost on the inside of the window facing the room. That shouldn't be. I examined this phenomenon. The inside window should be warm, not cold. I looked further. There were a great many spaces and holes between the inner and outer window frames. The two panes of glass became irrelevant.

My room was rather narrow, and since the furniture was smaller than usual, everything appeared to be in scale. The furniture was at least fifty years old, possibly made during the Japanese occupation and sized appropriately. There were two big comforters on the bed. The double (?) glazing on the windows made those two comforters on the bed very important!. I thought that was a nice touch. I tried the bed for size. My feet hung over the end.

The room did have a private bathroom. All the fixtures in the bathroom were of Japanese manufacture. A funny thing about the bathroom was the toilet. It appeared to be much higher than normal. You had to climb up to sit down. When I looked closer, I found that it WAS much higher. It was sitting on a square concrete base that was at least six inches high. I looked forward to some high altitude operations on that toilet!

I went downstairs. John, Terry and Mr Liu were waiting.

I whispered to John, "How's your room?"

He answered, "Like yours, I guess." He whispered as well. Now I wonder why we were whispering, no one could understand English anyway.

That wasn't quite the answer I was looking for.

"I mean, how's the bathroom? I have a high-altitude toilet."

"I don't know, I couldn't find the light switch. I tripped on something trying to find the damn thing. I have to get someone to turn the lights on."

So I told him about my bathroom. Even when we were in Japan, we never had a toilet quite like this one.

We were loaded back into the "Red Flag" limos. A new man jumped in after us and sat on the jump seat. He didn't say a word to us or to the translator. Maybe he missed the bus, who knows? Much, much later I found out he was another security guard. These new people constantly surrounded us. Our hosts were very conscious of an unpleasant fact in Shenyang not everyone was on Deng Tsao Ping's modernization train. Some people were vehemently opposed to the very idea of adjusting Communism to western standards! Everywhere we went, particularly outside the factory, we were accompanied by the nameless, silent guards!

Upon arrival at the Shenyang Blower Factory, the car deposited us on the street curb. We were escorted into a courtyard right off the street with a lot of construction material lying around. The frozen mud made walking perilous. Cars would have broken an axle in that mud. A large sign had been hung over the doors of a building entrance on one side of the courtyard. The sign greeted us (IBM) in English and Chinese. The English lettering was a little cockeyed, but we were deeply impressed and moved by their efforts at hospitality

John turned to me and said, "I'll bet you were never greeted like this at home."

"Hell, no, sometimes my customers hid from me. This is something new for me."

We went into the building.

We were shown into a long room lined with overstuffed furniture festooned with doilies. This business with overstuffed furniture laced with doilies was really the thing in China. Some bureaucrat in the central authority in Beijing must have decided to furnish all reception rooms with overstuffed furniture. That bureaucrat also decided that the arms and backs of the furniture should be covered with white doilies. I thought to myself, there is a factory somewhere in China (Factory Number 64!) that is entirely devoted to making doilies and overstuffed furniture. That same person in Beijing apparently also decided that when visitors came, they should be welcomed and entertained in a public reception room. You sit with your guests and "chit chat" without their ever seeing the rest of the place. I experienced the same routine in the Soviet Union.

Down at one end of the long room there was a glass case mounted on a table. The "S.S.Friendship", our model boat, was inside the glass case. It was gratifying, to say the least, to see that boat displayed in their public reception room. Mr. Mu brought us over to the case to be sure that we saw it. He said through the interpreter they were very proud to have that symbol of our trust and friendship. This thoughtful act impressed both John and me. I was particularly impressed. In my jaded way, I always discounted the Chinese use of the words "friendship" and "friends". I figured that the English translation of the Chinese words gravitated to these words because there were no others that fully translated the Chinese thought. Today, I feel I was wrong; these people really felt that way and I am ashamed of my thoughts.

On one side of the room there was a coffee table in front of the central sofa. As we filed into the room, we were directed to the chairs opposite the coffee table while our hosts took seats directly in front of it. After a little "chit-chat," another gentleman joined us. He was tall and good looking, older than the others. We had not seen him before. No one told us his name. He took the center seat on the sofa facing us. He waited while the young Chinese girl filled our tea cups with jasmine tea from a thermos. The smell and the warmth were wonderful. As soon as she left the room, he stood up and took a folded piece of yellow paper out of his breast pocket.

He carefully unfolded the yellow piece of paper. It had many folds and creases. The paper was torn where some of the folds met. That paper must have been used many, many times before, it was literally worn out. He began reading in a monotone. I think it was a monotone, but since it was in Chinese I could be wrong. The new translator, Liu Da Fu, translated in a loud voice, over that of the speaker, who kept right on speaking. We were getting Chinese in one ear while getting fractured English in the other. Simultaneous translation was rare in our experience. The translator usually waited for the speaker to pause before translating. We quickly realized that this was a standard and well rehearsed welcoming speech.

I don't remember all the words, but I do remember he greeted us in the name of the Director of the Factory. He went into a long monologue about what Liu translated as the "Four of Gang". We understood them to be the "Gang of Four" that little group that tried to take over the government when Chairman Mao died. As he spoke, this "Four of Gang", Madame Mao and some others were safely under house arrest by the new management and soon to be sentenced to jail. We were getting the current party line on the political turmoil in China. Most unusual! We had never heard political, particularly internal political, subjects. This was really a first! We were getting the domestic version of the welcoming speech; the speech that was reserved for fellow Communists! In a dozen or more banquets over nine months in Beijing, not once had any of the speeches or toasts mentioned anything political, either theirs or ours. All speeches were the foreigner versions.

Somewhere in the middle of this monologue, the speaker "belched" and continued right on as if nothing had happened. John and I looked at one another. We couldn't laugh. We couldn't react in any way that would be disrespectful of the speaker. It was an effort.

When he finished, the look on his face said, "Boy, am I glad that's over with." We all shook hands with him. We sat down and drank the hot tea. The hot tea was necessary to ward off the frostbite from sitting in the cold for a long time. Then he left for his other duties. We never saw him again. Many months later, I asked, out of curiosity, where he was. After an embarrassing silence, they said that he was gone. "Gone?" I said. "What does that mean?" He was assigned somewhere else. "Why?" I asked. After some more silence, the translator told me that Beijing had appointed him deputy director just recently because of his party connections. He was not an engineer nor had ever worked in a peoples' factory. The local leaders objected; they had replaced him with a local man. So much for centralized planning and control!

Mr. Mu told us he was going to show us the factory and the new computer building. We didn't have to put on our coats and hats, we had never removed them. John and I quickly took our last gulp of the hot tea; at least our insides were warm. We left the reception room and went out into a cold, grey overcast day. After crossing a courtyard, part of which was frozen mud, Mu led us into a building that was longer than two gymnasiums tied together and much higher as well. We stepped through large openings at one end of building. There was no door, just a wall with an opening in it.

We walked down a center aisle consisting of a dirt floor and little raised platforms on either side. There were a few people down at the end of the building standing around apparently doing nothing. Some sat on the dirt floor smoking; others were conversing. All were wearing the standard factory worker's garb, a blue Mao jacket over dirty grey or blue baggy pants. Mr. Mu was wearing the same thing, only his were clean and fitted. Mr. Mu told us through Liu that this was the testing workshop. We had to take his word for it since there was nothing in the room that suggested testing or anything else for that matter. I asked Mr. Mu where the testing was taking place. He said the equipment had not yet arrived, but when it did, it was going to be installed in this building. We walked down the length of the building to where the workers were standing. Mr. Mu nodded to them and they smiled back at him. We didn't know it at the time, but we were witnessing an example of the "work unit" system. These workers, we were told later, had completed their work units for the morning and therefore had time off until the afternoon work period began. As I listened, I couldn't figure out exactly what that work unit was. I saw nothing in that shop that remotely resembled work. Our group moved out of the workshop into the one next door. Again, we moved through a wide-open passage.

This workshop was just like the last one physically. But there was a lot of activity going on. Mr. Mu told us that this was the painting workshop. We could see various pieces of machinery on these platforms on either side of a central dirt floor aisle in various stages of being painted. There were three or four relatively small machines on one side, one massive round machine on the other. The parts of the machines were painted in different colors. Mr. Mu told us that the electrical parts were painted one color, the mechanical parts another etc. All the work was done by hand. Mr. Mu told us that these were the old products of the factory, not the new ones that required computers.

I looked for, but did not see, any mechanical painting equipment. Workers did everything. In this workshop, in contrast with the previous one, the work units required for the morning had not yet been accomplished so everyone was busy.

From this workshop we moved on to the foundry workshop. This one was twice as large as the last one. The dirt aisle was down one side in front of six immense roaring furnaces. Each of the furnaces was open faced with a big round mouth that belched roars and fire as we walked by. The mouths of the furnaces were up high and, as we watched, they tilted the mouth of one down and out poured molten white hot metal into a massive ladle hung from a ceiling crane. The noise was awesome! The heat was sweltering! It was impossible to talk over the uproar. When we got down to the end of the furnaces, we saw workers tearing a mold apart, literally destroying it to get at the casting inside. That particular molding was one side of a compressor housing, or so Mr. Mu told us when we could hear him.

`He explained to us that after the casting had cooled off for a couple of days, they would remove the mold. The molds were only used once, but the sandy material that they were made of was reused over and over after it was cleaned. I thought to myself that had to be a remnant of the old "self sufficiency" days. The castings were cleaned up and all the rough edges from the molding process were removed. The castings went into the machining workshop after that.

We went there next. The machining workshop was filled with monstrous machine tools that scraped, bored and cut the castings from the foundry. We could see four or five of these machines but only one of them was active. Mr. Mu explained that this machine milled or scraped the parts of the compressor that joined together to make an air tight seal between the two sides. It was a giant shaving machine, only it was shaving a very large piece of steel. There were a couple of workers watching this shaving machine. That was it! There wasn't another soul in that tremendous room. I asked Mr. Mu where everyone was. He said he didn't know. Down at the end of the shop there was a very tall machine covered by a canvas shroud. Mr. Mu did not explain what that machine did or why it was covered up.

The last workshop we visited was the gearbox shop. Mr. Mu explained that all the gears and shafts for the compressors were machined here after coming from the foundry. He said that this was going to be the high-tech shop since they were purchasing machine tools that would cut and mill complex shapes that would be required for the new compressors. He likened this work to that which was required to carve a ship's propellers. The minute he said that, I thought of the Defense Department in Washington. They really would be interested in what was going on in this workshop. At the moment, there was only a very old machine in the shop. Mu told us that it wasn't even "NC", whatever that meant. I learned later that "NC" meant numerical control.

We "slogged" over to a building that was just coming out of the ground. Construction must have started very recently. All the other buildings we had been in were built with concrete blocks; this one sported bricks. Standing in front of the hole in the ground, Big Mu proudly told us this was the new computer building.

"Computer Building? Why are you building a computer building?" I asked.

**COMPUTER ROOM (?) UNDER CONSTRUCTION IN
SHENYANG - FEBRUARY 1978**

FEB 1978 - GREETINGS AT SHENYANG FACTORY

BIG MU WELCOMES IBM TO SHENYANG BLOWER WORKS
FEBRUARY 1978

MY WIFE AND I VISITING SHENYANG - SUMMER 1978

"Because of what your earthquake construction expert told us last year. We want to be sure that our new computer remains safe," Big Mu proudly announced. He was in all his glory here. I discovered many, many months later Big Mu's answer was only partially true; the building also housed other things required by the Beijing plan. In fact, we were looking at the first evidence the computer we had just sold them for factory administration was going to be used for something entirely different.

"But a whole new building?"

"Yes" He went on to tell us, "This building will have two floors. The first floor will be devoted to the special environment computer room, as your experts suggested. The second floor will contain classrooms so that we can teach others what we will learn in your schools" I thought to myself, why would a compressor factory need classrooms in a computer building? As it turned out, that was the understatement of a century. We were so naïve!

"Wow"

Big Mu was so proud of the building. "And", he said, "we are building the computer room just like the ones your experts told us about in the U.S. It will have a raised floor, air-conditioning, environmental controls, and a glass wall."

He led us into an area which he said was going to be the computer room. He told us one wall of the room would be entirely glass. There was just a corridor on the other side of the glass wall. The computer would be demonstrated in a showroom complete with viewing platforms. He showed us where the raised floor would be, and as we walked around the muddy hole, his pride was radiating from him like heat from a stove.

After the computer building, the tour was over. Mr. Mu hustled us into the cars that were waiting outside the reception building to return to our hotel.

In the evening there was a welcoming banquet at our hotel. Since there were no other guests in the hotel, it was eerie. When we went down to the hotel dining room for the banquet, our footsteps echoed. Everyone who had been at the negotiating table from the Blower Works was there. In addition, the Chairman of the factory Mr He Ju San was there. The head of the Reception Department, Wong Go Bin, and a couple of other people we had never seen before (some more brand new guys!) were there. Apparently, Mr Wong was also the Secretary of the Factory. We had met him at the railroad station under that title. We must have misunderstood one or the other of the introductions; or, maybe the translator had it all mixed up. We went with the flow! By this time, we were used to having people in our meetings and banquets whom we did not know. We figured that they were friends of somebody who was getting a free meal. In that respect it was like American business lunches. But Americans don't have reception departments.

In the United States, we have administrative assistants, and guest service departments and the like. In China, the Reception Department is responsible for all visitors to the particular plant or department or ministry. They provide for the care and feeding of all guests. They are the arrangers, the drivers, the tour guides and the payers that accompany all foreign visitors Sometimes they have other titles, but the way our friends referred to them was "reception department" I was told some time later that this department also supplied those other unknown people who were guarding us. They were there to be sure we were safe. There had been some concern that someone who objected to having Americans in Shenyang might get violent. I immediately thought of the William Holden incident in Peking some months before.

On one of our early visits, John had noticed the actor, William Holden, in the Peking Hotel dining room. He pointed him out to me.

"Go over and say hello to him" I told John while I gently poked him.

"Nah, leave him alone, he must be here on a tour or something" he replied.

Holden was sitting at a table with another man, who was obviously American by his clothing. A beautiful American woman was with them.

We argued about the identity of the woman. After arguing all day with the Chinese, it was a relief to josh each other about almost anything.

I said, "That must be his wife." I really didn't know if he was even married.

"I don't think so. I read something about him being divorced." John continued eating. He was acting like he saw famous movie stars in the hotel restaurant with him every day. How nonchalant can you be?

"Well then, it's not his wife."

"It sure looks like some actress. Maybe it's Marilyn Monroe in disguise." Now John was joking and pulling my leg. He was facing their table; I was facing away from them.

"You're full of it! Marilyn Monroe is blonde, that woman is a brunette." I slapped my hand on the table in emphasis. Neither of us had seen an American movie in over a year.

"Wait a minute, I know. It's Stephanie Powers." He knocked his knuckle on the table. At first, I had no idea who Stephanie Powers was; then I remembered. We finally decided that it really was Stephanie Powers, the actress. We buzzed back and forth about them and finally went back to eating full time.

The next evening, Maria told us the man with Holden was an American attorney. Maria said she had seen the Chinese news on television and saw the story. After the dinner the previous evening attorney had been stabbed while walking alone on the street in front of the hotel. Some nut had come up to him on the street and let him have it. The Chinese police had the perpetrator. The very next day, Maria told us the man that the police were holding had been put to death. Chinese justice! Swift and Final! So, it was okay to have these unknown guys around us.

The Shenyang banquet table was gorgeous with twelve places set. I was told to sit on one side of the Director of the Factory Mr. He Ju San; John was told to sit on the other. Liu De Fu sat on one side and Chen So Min (a translator from the talks in Beijing) sat on the other side. The same protocol rules we saw at the negotiating table in Beijing were followed here. We could tell the pecking order of the Chinese staff by their distance from the Director. Mr. Mu, Mr. Shu and Big Mu were next to us. They had spent all the time at the table in Beijing with us. Wong Go bin, from the factory reception department was all the way over on the opposite side of the table along with our college translator Terry. The ubiquitous stranger was on that end as well.

The first of twelve courses arrived. Each of the foreigners was served by his Chinese host next to him from the circular serving platform in the middle of the table. After the first course was served and eaten, the toasts began. We had had a lot of experience in Beijing in toasting with a drink called Mao Tai. The particular brand of Mao Tai used here was in a square squat milky white bottle. The bottle was made of fire resistant, crash resistant and explosion resistant glass and it had a red top. A clear 150 proof liquor was inside. You could put a fuse in the bottle and it would be a Molotov cocktail. It was served in small 1 ounce cups or stemmed glasses. There was no way that you could sip this liquor without severely burning your mouth. It had to be drunk in one gulp, quickly passing through your mouth but not touching. In this way the burning sensation was confined to your throat where there were fewer nerves. Mao Tai has the taste, if you could call it that, of the Greek liquor called Retsina. I have no idea how it is made. I hazarded a guess that it was distilled from chopped down pine forests; John's guess was that it was made from distilled discarded turnips.

Our experience told us to be very careful with this liquid lightning. The effect of Mao Tai is logarithmically proportionate to the amount you drink. A little bit goes a long way! The toasts we drank that night were legion. I believe that we set a record.

The first toast was to welcome IBM to Shenyang. That was given by the Chairman, Mr He Ju San.

The second toast was given by Mr. Mu. He welcomed the new technology, whatever that meant.

Big Mu gave the third toast. He welcomed us individually to Shenyang. We were told that we were the first Westerners to visit Shenyang in more than fifty years and I believed them.

The fourth toast was to the beginning of the relationship between the United States and China... I confess that I don't know who gave that one.

The fifth was to the foresight of the Chinese leaders in allowing our contract to go forward. I think John gave that one.

The sixth was to the unnamed IBM leaders for their foresight in agreeing to this contract with the Factory.

Etiquette required that each of these toasts be responded to with an appropriate return toast. Before our brains slipped into automatic drive then neutral and finally oblivion, I am sure that John and I did OK.

I don't remember much after that. I was told we had twenty-two toasts that night, each accompanied with a shot of Mao Tai! I don't remember what we ate. In fact, after the third or fourth glass, I was not exactly sure of much. You kind of get in the swing of things and the rhythm of the toast and answering toast, toast and answer, etc. However, I am sure the dinner selections were the best and finest that the hotel had to offer. Chinese tradition demanded no less. I also remember that some of the older Chinese attending that dinner merely touched their Mao Tai cups to their lips, but did not drink; others poured the Mao Tai into the ashtrays. Through my own alcoholic haze, I think I saw John try the Mao Tai ashtray gambit as well. He was found out when a lighted match was thrown in the ashtray. The Mao Tai blew up and then burned fiercely! I was sure there were some semi-professional and maybe even professional drinkers in that group that night.

We parted as old friends, really old and drunken friends. I went up to my room. It was cold. I lay down; actually I fell down, on the bed, fully clothed. I had the distinct impression of the bed (with me in it) taking off like an airplane and flying around the room. Some of the flying motion made me nauseous so I had to get up to land the airplane and calm my stomach. I went into the bathroom and discovered that the toilet was much too high off the floor for me to maneuver on to it. I tried to get up by grabbing the towel rack on the wall next to the toilet. Since it was so old, or else I was so strong, it came right off the wall. By this time I knew I had to get some fresh air quickly.

I put my coat on and went down through the lobby to the street. The lobby was deserted, and most of the lights were out. The street lights had been turned off and it was really cold, but it felt good. There had to be some oxygen in that pollution. I began to walk around Chairman Mao, going to the right, counterclockwise. I shuffled along with my face buried in my coat lapels. It was pitch black and well below zero. I stumbled each time I stepped into one of the cross streets coming into the circle. My breath literally froze in the air then dropped to the ground. But I was getting the oxygen I needed along with frostbite of the lungs.

When I got about halfway around the circle, I saw a dark shape coming toward me from the other direction. Drunk or not, I was scared. Here I was in the middle of the night, walking by myself in the middle of a Chinese city that hadn't seen a Westerner in 50 years. The security people were all in bed. The shape was walking just like me, hunched up in his overcoat, his breath looking like puffs of light smoke in the darkness. As he got closer, I recognized Mr. Mu and he recognized me. Although neither of us spoke the other's language, we both indicated in sign language we were walking off the Mao Tai that we had drunk that night. We pounded each other on the back and proceeded on our respective ways around the circle. By the time I got back to the hotel entrance, he had gone on home or continued drinking wherever.

During the next couple of days, we toured during the day and banqueted at night. We did not know the agenda until it happened.

One day, after our afternoon discussions, they picked us up at the Lioliang Hotel in big black Red Flag cars. Big Mu told me through the translator that we were going to a show. John went in one car with Big Mu while I went with Mr. Mu, and another unidentified man, in the other car. No matter where we were that night, there was always an unidentified young man with us. No one spoke to him; he did not speak to anyone. He was dressed just like everyone else, blue Mao jacket and pants over several other layers of clothing. No one told us who he was. No one introduced him to us. No one told us why he was there he was just there! Of course, later, we found out he was another security man.

After a short drive, we stopped in front of a large building with columns in the front on top of a short set of stone steps. When we got out of the cars, Mr. Mu began ordering (I think!) everyone around.

He said, and Liu, the translator repeated, "Quickly, we must hurry before the show starts." We quickly ran up the steps.

There were some people there, but when Mr. Mu spoke to them, they quickly moved out of our way.

We went through a rather nondescript lobby and entered a theater from the right rear. The theater was packed. It seemed to me that there must have been a thousand people in there. Every seat was taken, not only in the orchestra, but up in the balcony as well. It seemed as if everyone was talking at once. Only here every one was speaking Chinese. The noise, the hubbub, the atonal babble was awesome.

The talking stopped the instant we entered. It was as if someone had turned off a radio that had been playing at full blast. The silence was as awesome as the noise had been. Then, every person in that theater stood up and turned to face us. As we moved down the aisle they applauded us!

Our mouths dropped open. Every person that we passed down that aisle was smiling his greeting to us. Again, we were impressed beyond words. Our hosts in Beijing had never been able to accomplish this!

I said to John, "Wow, how did they arrange this. All these people can't be workers at the Blower factory! Wow!"

He didn't answer. He was overwhelmed as well.

We went down the aisle to all this clapping until the second row and then moved into our seats in the center of the row. We sat down. The applause continued for another few seconds. Suddenly everybody sat down at once, as if there was some silent command. The theater lights were turned off, the stage lights went up, the curtain rose and the show began.

The acrobats were fantastic! I saw a performance of Russian acrobats at the Moscow Circus, but this was much better. The performers were all over the stage, and in three dimensions. I don't know how to describe all their routines, but each of them kept me on the edge of my seat. It was really something to see.

At the conclusion of the performance, after all the applause for the acrobats had ended, we stood up. As we did, some hidden (at least from us!) conductor turned on the "Silent" button. Total quiet descended on the theater, not one person moved out of his seat, not one word was spoken. It was frightening. I had never seen such civilian discipline like this in my life!

We left our seats and moved back up the aisle to the door that we had entered. Still, no one moved or made a sound. We left the theater. As we entered the lobby again and proceeded down the steps to our cars, the theater erupted into a roar of sound and movement as the audience pushed and shoved to the doors and the street outside. It was as if a cork had been released from a champagne bottle. The people gushed from the theater.

How had they arranged all that?

The third night that we were in Shenyang, we were treated to a dinner in the Blower Works Worker Cafeteria. That's the name that I gave to the place. I have no idea what the proper name was or even if it had a name. I do know that it's the place where all the workers were fed at least two meals every day.

It was pitch black when we entered. . The room was so large and there was so little light that you could only see right up close to where you were standing. I guess they did not want us to see the rest of the cafeteria. All else was gray to black shadows except for two lighted areas. The first was the banquet table where we were going to eat that night. It was all lit up with powerful flood lamps that did not look like they were part of the normal lighting. The table glistened in the darkness of the rest of the room. Behind the table you could see the dark outlines of the factory kitchens with hanging pots and pans. Nearby, there were a bunch of dimmer lights sprinkled over a small area. They looked like random Christmas lights without any pattern.

As we walked across the floor toward the brightly lit table, we heard the U.S. national anthem being played. It was just a little off, a little discordant with a loose note here and there. It had to be live music, a record or a tape would never have sounded like that.

I turned to John. "Do you hear what I'm hearing?"

"Yeah, I hear it. Where's it coming from?"

"I think it's coming from over there" I pointed to the sprinkle of little lights. We headed in that direction. As we got closer, we could see that the lights were coming from little lights on a whole lot of music stands.

"It's an orchestra!"

And, sure enough, now that we were close enough, we could see the musicians. They were very busy and intent on producing the "Star Spangled Banner" in our honor. In the darkness they all looked like the seven dwarfs bending over their work tables.

I moved over to the little man who was standing in front of all the others. He had to be the leader of the orchestra. He was dressed in the standard worker uniform consisting of the faded blue Mao jacket over several layers of other clothing, the faded blue shapeless pants and the blue touring cap. Dressed like that, he was almost invisible in the darkness without the little music lights shining on him. He was playing the shiniest and oldest looking trumpet that I had ever seen. That trumpet had been polished within an inch of its life and it had more dents in it than a Model T Ford.

I looked around at all the other musicians. Each of them had an instrument that was just like the one the leader had. They were old! They were out of tune! They were dented! Each reflected the little lights like little mirrors. But they all sounded great in the middle of that black cavern, 8,000 miles from home.

We listened. At the end of the piece, my eyes were moist. The leader moved his instrument away from his lips and as I took his hand in mine, he broke out into the biggest smile his face was capable of. When he smiled, I could see that he was missing a front tooth. I thought to myself, how do you play the trumpet without front teeth? I had all that I could do to keep from crying and laughing at the same time. I thanked him profusely.

"Thank you, Thank you that was wonderful."

"Where did you get the music that you just played?"

"Oh, we just had it." He answered through the translator. "We practiced a lot when they told us you were coming."

The translator looked at me as if to say, "Why do you want to know?"

"But where did you get the music? Do you know that song by heart?" I really couldn't understand how Chinese musicians in a factory near Manchuria could know how to play the U.S. national anthem.

He shrugged and smiled some more, but didn't answer.

Maybe something was lost in translation but it was evident that he wasn't going to answer. Maybe it was a crime to harbor capitalist music or something like that. Maybe I should not have been asking him so many questions. So I thanked him some more and we moved over to the banquet table.

As usual, each American visitor was placed in his protocol perfect seat. John was seated next to the factory chairman Mr. He Ju San (the big boss) who had a translator next to him, and then I came next with Mr. Mu next to me, etc.

The banquet table was set up just like in a fancy restaurant. From a distance, it looked like the standard banquet table we had gotten used to, a big round table with a raised revolving platform in the middle which carried all the courses from person to person. The only difference was the tableware and dishes. When I looked closely, I saw they were the same ones used for the workers during the day. They were spotlessly clean, but they were also thick, heavy and chipped from use. The Mao Tai was the same and the endless tea was the same, most importantly, the comradery was the same. We all had a good time, but this time, we didn't try to toast one another under the table.

After a little while, we realized that the table was placed near the kitchen to take advantage of the heat. It was real cold that night, but the enthusiasm of our companions and the orchestra did a lot to ward off the cold. Of course, the Mao Tai helped as well.

It was a very moving experience.

Chapter 13 – Waiting for the Computer

New York Times, November 17, 1976

"CHINA HAS PEAK TEST BLAST; U.S. SETS FALLOUT WATCH" "MISS WORLD CROWNED IN LONDON"

At the end of February, 1978, we returned home exhausted from our Shenyang trip. Even though we had a lot of work ahead of us, a little triumph was in order. We had spent ten months talking and lecturing the Chinese on the American way of contracting. Mr. Wu had spent ten months enlightening us on the Chinese Communist business methods. I think everyone came away from that experience with a much better understanding and, more important, a much better appreciation of each other. However, don't get me wrong, my understanding and appreciation falls far short of becoming a believer in the Communist political or governmental line. It's just that I have learned how to deal with it.

The first order of business in the U.S. was to get the export license processing started. Toward that end, I had taken many photographs of the plant. John and I thought that photographic evidence might take the place of verbal records of what we had seen. I had all the film developed and sent it to the Commerce Department in Washington. There were over a hundred pictures. A curious thing happened just after I did that. I received one of the regular visits by a C.I.A. agent. These visits usually occurred right after any of us returned from China. In the beginning, both John and I were asked if we would agree to speak with C.I.A. agents. Maria was asked as well. Both John and I responded, "Sure, I would be glad to help". We certainly did not want to appear unpatriotic. Maria, however, did not choose to be interviewed by the C.I.A.

As it turned out, I always saw the same agent every time I returned from China. I know he came from New York and I remember he always asked to see me on a Friday. Usually he would ask me where I had been and what I had seen. Usually I told him about the Beijing Hotel, the Beijing taxis and our talks at Er Li Go. His eyes would glaze over quickly. Those interviews were never long. However, this time was different. When I told him we had been in Shenyang, he became very interested. Then he asked what I had seen, I told him everything I saw was on film.

"Where are the pictures?"

I said, "In Washington, at the Commerce Department."

"Commerce Department?" he said. His voice echoed disbelief. "Why did you send them to the Commerce Department?" His voice rising.

"That's where our export license application is. The pictures demonstrate the civilian nature of the factory." I expected he would understand what we were doing.

"You shouldn't have done that." he intoned. I immediately thought that I was going to prison. The impression he gave me was that I had done something detrimental to the national security. After all, this man was from the C.I.A. He was a C.I.A. agent!

"Why?" I said in a scared little voice.

"You could have given them to me. We would have given them to Commerce after we analyzed them."

"But you can get them from Commerce yourself. It's the same government."

"No, no! If I turned them in, we would get the credit."

I realized that I was listening to a script out of a manual on bureaucracy. This C.I.A. agent actually believed the nonsense he was handing me! I even believed him for a minute! Since I had reached this level of understanding, I really wanted to finish this interview as quickly as possible. Just to get off this subject, I asked him "Why do we always meet early on Friday afternoon?"

He answered, "To get away from my office early on Fridays. I live close to here."

That did it! I resolved not to meet with these people again. There really was no point to meeting with him. Whatever information he got from me, he could get from John.

In April, the Chinese informed us their group would be coming to the United States in September. Our invitation to their tour of the U.S. was an obligation written into the contract. In fact, obligation or not, we were happy to arrange it. After their hospitality in Shenyang, we felt it was only proper that we show them the same respect they had shown us. The tour members were the Managing Director of the factory Mr. He Ju San, the Deputy Managing Director of the factory Mr. Liu, the Finance Director of the factory (whose name escapes me), and some others. I only found out years later that the "some others" were people from the Technology Bureau of the Beijing Ministry. Liu Dae Foo was their translator. To prevent any translation problems from arising we assigned one of our American students (Chinese majors) to accompany them. In this case, Maria, my daughter, got the assignment.

We arranged for this group to visit major industrial customers; we asked their hosts to demonstrate modern factory techniques in addition to plant visits. This was all in tune with the information we put in the application for an export license. They visited factories in New York, Chicago, Cleveland, and after several weeks ended up in San Jose, California. There they spent three weeks attending a special class in the IBM Executive

Education facility. One of the instructors was a Chinese American, Wilson Wang. He really appreciated his audience and was a big hit with them. The lecturers told them about the latest techniques in computer assisted factory management. One would think that the Chinese factory managers would jump at the chance of implementing these Western techniques. For one thing, it would be in keeping with the Deng Tsao Ping edict to modernize. For another, some of the techniques would probably make the plant more efficient quickly. For yet another, use of any of these techniques would prove to the leaders that the money and the time spent with IBM was useful. To the best of my knowledge, not one of the many ideas that they heard described was implemented.

Most of the plant visits were successful, a few were not. The most common problem we encountered was when the host location used an American of Chinese descent to give the presentations to this group. On several occasions, these local Chinese presented American techniques in a manner that was deprecating to their guests. On one occasion when I was present, I heard the Chinese American (in translation, of course) say things that were rude and impolite to his guests. The point they were trying to make was that America was better than China, particularly in the subject they were speaking about. Whether that was true or false, in my mind, was irrelevant. As for our guests, they deserved better. Sometimes, the presenter used a Chinese vocabulary learned from his mother, kitchen Chinese. That became obvious when he peppered his speech with English words to fill in the gaps in his vocabulary.

We had a particularly stressful scene at IBM's computer chip facility. Furnaces that heat silicon powder to a very hot temperature until it is molten are the main attraction. The molten silicon cools in a controlled way so that a silicon crystal forms. The weight of the finished crystal of pure, almost clear silicon is the determinate for the size of the furnace. The furnaces are designated "50 pound" furnaces, or "75 pound" furnaces, etc. The finished silicon crystals are sliced into wafers used to make the electronic chips that ultimately find their way inside the computer.

The factory executive chose a Chinese American engineer to make the presentations of this process. The engineer gave his talk while standing next to a 50 pound furnace, i.e., capable of producing a silicon crystal weighing 50 pounds. He explained the entire process in Chinese. He did not have a technical Chinese language vocabulary. His talk was interspersed with many English words like "furnace", "powder" and "temperature". After a while, the Chinese translator accompanying the Shenyang group filled in the gaps. At the end of his explanation, he couldn't help saying this furnace was not the latest method of producing silicon crystals. Proudly, he said, "The furnaces are only available in the U.S." To complete the subtle gaff, he went on to say,

2nd TOUR GROUP AT IBM MANUFACTURING SITE

1st SHENYANG TOUR GROUP - SAN JOSE, CALIFORNIA

"We have been working on even larger furnaces to speed up the crystal forming time and to make bigger crystals. In fact, we have a 100 pound very advanced furnace in the next room. I can't show it to you because it's secret".

The silence in the room was as thick as a cushion. Teasing is not polite in China; political teasing most of all! Talking down to people ranks right up there with teasing. Remember, under Communism "Comrade" is not merely a title; theoretically everyone is equal. One of the men in the Shenyang group looked the speaker right in the eye and said,

"Why do you tell us about that if you will not show us?"

The speaker's mouth dropped open. He did not expect a retort from his audience. I stepped up as soon as our translator finished her translation to me. I gently began pushing everyone towards the door of the room. "We have to go. We are late for the next demonstration".

Later that evening, Liu Da Foo told me that the Director was incensed at us for permitting someone like that to speak to them. Liu went on to say that, we had better have a superior demonstration tomorrow so the Director would forget the insults. I had to agree! The speaker's attitude was gratuitous and stupid.

The next day we had a presentation from the director of the laboratory. He hit a home run with his speech!

Meanwhile, back in China, preparations for the students and the computer delivery were moving along handsomely. Six graduate electrical engineers, four system operators and six translators applied for visas. Their schedule took them first to Hong Kong for six weeks for basic training. Some of this group went on to Toronto and then San Francisco while others went directly to New York and on to Los Angeles. Most of them were away from home for up to nine months. None of them had ever been outside the city of Shenyang, China. Each was investigated to be certain that he would return upon completion of their studies. Someone told me, very, very privately, that Shenyang "lost" only one member of their many delegations sent for overseas training. The term "lost" was a metaphor for someone who defected to the U.S. authorities claiming political asylum. The U.S. was in the process of reconciliation with the new government in China while the embarrassment of these defectors kept cropping up. It was a "lose-lose" situation! The "lost" Shenyang member happened to be carrying the delegation's U.S. dollars at the time of his defection in Los Angeles. I was told the other delegation members did not care whether the "lost" member came or went; the loss of their expense money was a far larger consequence. I thank the "powers" that the "lost" member didn't come from our delegations.

Since this education program in modern western technology was a forerunner of many such programs to come, these groups received special attention. In fact, the management tour and the education program became the pattern for thousands of similar events in the years following. The visa officer at the Shenyang Consulate told me many years later that there were over 100,000 Chinese in the U.S. in the years following our contract. 100,000 students is an imposing figure, they were not all, of course, from Shenyang.

The education IBM had contractually agreed to provide to the staff of the Shenyang Blower Works was given all over the world. Some was given in Hong Kong. Some was given in the United States and other classes were held in Europe. The computer maintenance education was held in Toronto, Canada. I visited this group in Toronto. Big Mu was the leader. I couldn't see them during class days because they were too busy. They couldn't stay in a hotel because the combination of the number of rooms they needed and the price was beyond their dollar allowance. The group had rented an apartment with the help of the local IBM education staff. I visited them there.

The apartment consisted of two bedrooms, kitchen and living room. Three men slept in each bedroom and the job of keeping the room clean and tidy rotated among the three. This arrangement was a lot better, Big Mu told me, than a similar one in China. At home, he said, everyone would be sleeping in a dormitory in a large room with many, many beds in it. Here, someone could sleep while others were studying.

There were two very important jobs in the student group. The first was the holding the money for eating and living. Sometimes the leader of the group held this job, sometimes someone else. In Toronto, after the first couple of weeks, the job moved over to the best translator they had, a good idea because the holder of the money was the spender of the money. The translator was the only one who could read the labels in the supermarket. His proficiency in English, however, did not make him a good cook, which was the second most important job.

The "cooker" or chef job rotated among the group. It was impossible to eat meals in a restaurant on the foreign currency allowance given them. Even if they could, they told me the Chinese meals they found in Toronto were not as good as the meals back in Shenyang. The solution to that problem was to cook their own meals. That should be no problem. Westerners perceive that all Chinese men are good cooks; and they are. The people I visited in Toronto verified that perception deliciously.

Big Mu told me the "cooker" job rotated among students and translators. The only one exempted was the translator-banker-treasurer. Whoever had the "cooker" job that week, along with the translator-banker, had to go to the supermarket and purchase their requirements. In addition, they had to stay within the budget. If the translator-banker overspent his budget, the "cooker" for the following week would criticize him publicly. That was bad news! Public criticism was a core Communist punishment. Everyone tried to avoid it at all costs. As a result, no one spent more than the budget, the foods they purchased tended to be the same inexpensive stuff each week. At the end of this training cycle, the group had money left over. The "cooker" was obligated to provide the rest of the students with on-time meals. Sometimes this meant that he had to miss some of his classes to prepare the evening meal.

I asked Big Mu if there was a real good chef among his group. He said that Mr. Pu was the best. Everyone waited patiently until Mr. Pu's turn at being the "cooker" came around. I went over to Mr. Pu, whom I had not met before, to tell him, with the translator's help, I was very sorry that I had not come to visit during his tenure as chef. He positively beamed. I whispered, because I did not want the current "cooker" to hear me. There was no point in hurting his feelings. However, I did announce that we all were going to the local Chinese restaurant tonight to celebrate my visit. There was a collective sigh of approval when the translator finished my invitation.

Information was leaking back to China that our education efforts were the finest. I don't know, but I assumed the leaders of each education group were reporting their progress. I know I tried to make sure that the Chinese were received well. I wanted their perception of the educational experience with IBM to be "the best in the world", further assuming those progress reports went on to the Beijing Ministry. Remember my comments about positive progress reporting as the norm in the Communist environment. Under those rules, my assumptions were probably correct. The students' reports had another effect. When we returned to Beijing for further marketing activities, we were besieged by people and organizations that wanted computers. Our contract, along with the manner with which we were implementing it (and, along with Deng Tsao Ping) had broken a dam. A flood of pent-up "requirements" was about to engulf us.

The first thing we noticed was the absence of Foreign Trade Ministry activity. Before the dam broke, there was no direct contact between seller and the potential user. The contact was always confined to one of the "bureaus" or one of the foreign trade "corporations". This time, the users were making contact not only through the "corporations", but directly as well.

John and I were having difficulty handling all these simultaneous requests. We had just spent the better part of a year handling just one sale. We had several more major contacts to care for. The largest Chinese shipyard called. The major oil exploration "Institute" called. The largest automobile plant was eager to talk to us. The largest wire and cable factory needed a computer. Each one of these potential customers was larger than its largest counterpart in the U.S. We had to interview each one of these contacts. We had to determine if we could get an export license for the potential user. We had to determine if they had sufficient hard currency for a reasonable size purchase. We had to determine if we had sufficient resources to handle a sudden increase in the number of sites all over China, the increase in equipment and the increase in students. We needed help!

Our success, or at least perceived success, with Shenyang and with the Ministry of Machine Building, caused a flood of requests for information and meetings with our new "friends" in China. We wanted to deal with everyone who was a potential buyer, but we had to prioritize who we would talk to first. We thought our first obligation was to the Ministry that gave Shenyang the money for its computer. The only problem was both the automobile factory and the wire factory were under the authority of this Ministry. A Madam Shi Yu Ping represented the automobile factory, while a Madame Jao represented the wire and cable factory. Both women were in the Foreign Affairs Bureau at the Ministry. At our first meetings with these women, Madam Jao was most insistent on stating her requirements. Therefore, Madame Jao got our attention first; the squeaky wheel gets the oil.

On this particular trip, we had a young graduate student, Katie, from University of Michigan with us as our translator. Katie spoke excellent colloquial Chinese. She and Madam Jao hit it off immediately. Madam Jao did not bring a translator with her to our meetings; she was quite happy to have Katie do her translating. That was okay with us; we thought it left her at a slight disadvantage. If it did, she didn't care. Her story was your typical bureaucratic, albeit Chinese style, "Catch 22" tale. She had a fixed foreign currency budget to modernize three factories. These factories all happened to be in Shenyang. She was responsible for the Wire and Cable Factory, the Transformer factory and a much smaller foundry. Madame Jao had $1,000,000 at her disposal. She told us about the money right up front. Before we could ask her about the use of the computer, etc., she quickly followed up with a demand that we sell her the most computers that $1,000,000 would buy. The more usual request we were in the habit of hearing was to sell them the most advanced, the largest computer. My impression was that Madame Jao just wanted to spend her money on a computer, any computer, so long as the label said "computer." The China modernization train was leaving the station; Madame Jao was going to be on it come hell or high water!

We sat with her for many mornings trying to determine which computer model was appropriate. The best solution to this problem was to select a computer that we could simply ship to China without any export license implications. That would mean an older and much smaller unit. We selected a very small machine, a "System 7". Although it was unique for its time, it had only 1/100th the power, my guess, of a modern day personal computer. It had built-in connections for all kinds of terminals and sensors. It was a machine with limited capacity for computing, but maximum capacity for expansion and maximum capacity for collecting data from many different sources. Madame Jao didn't care about all these technical points. Her concern was that whatever we provided had the label "computer".

We went to Shenyang with her to inform her factories they were going to get a computer. We flew to Shenyang for the first time. We had a whole series of eye-opening experiences. First, we had to purchase the tickets. Someone, I think it was Mr. Wu, gave us a paper with the name and address of the Beijing Central Ticket office for the airline. We took Katie along with us. We navigated the taxi situation and the reading skill of the taxi driver adequately. The room where the reservations and ticketing people worked was immense. It seems all public places in China are immense. A wall-to-wall counter, at least 100 feet long, covered one end of the room. Signs hanging from the ceiling over the counter at intervals bore the names of destination cities. Some clerks were lounging around under some of the signs; other positions were vacant. There were only a few people on our side of the counter.

The whole wall behind the counter had little cubbyholes just like in old Post Offices in the U.S. An entire flock of birds could have found homes in all those cubbyholes. There must have been hundreds of cubbyholes. Most of the cubbyholes were empty; some had some paper visible. The cubbyholes began about knee high and went almost to the ceiling. It was impressive.

Katie steered us to the position under the Shenyang sign. She did a lot of "chit chatting" in Chinese. After a while, she turned to us and said "We have seats on the 12 Noon flight tomorrow." While she was relating this, I saw the clerk write something on three little pieces of paper. After he completed the third piece of paper, he turned to the cubbyholes. His fingers lightly touched the edges of the holes as he looked for the one he wanted. When he found it, he took all the paper out. He looked at a couple of pieces of paper, selected three of them. Then he put the selected pieces of paper into the next hole down. The pieces of paper he wrote on at the counter were placed in the first slot along with the remainder of the ones still in there. Then the clerk came back to the counter where we were waiting.

Katie said, laughing, "I think we just saw our reservations confirmed".

"What about the reservations of the people he put in the other box?" I asked.

"I believe they got bumped to the next flight," Katie answered.

"How come we rate so high that we bump someone else?"

"I don't know," she answered.

"Find out what the price is"

She turned back to the man at the counter and did some more "chit chatting" in Chinese. When the sing-songing died down, she said to us, "You're never going to believe this".

"What?"

"There are two prices for every seat. One price is for Chinese. The other price is for foreigners. The foreigner's price is five times the Chinese price. He just told me that was the reason he moved three Chinese reservations to the next plane."

"You have to be kidding!"

"No. If we wanted to buy all the seats at the foreigner price, we could have the whole plane," Katie went on to tell me.

We purchased our tickets and chalked the whole experience up as one more lesson in the continued saga of international relations with China. The next lesson came the very next day.

The flight up to Shenyang was uneventful. Our arrival in Shenyang was not. We landed at what we understood to be the Shenyang Municipal Airport (my label). Our computer shipment was headed for this same airport. The airplane taxied right up to a terminal building. All looked normal through the porthole. When we stepped onto the portable stairs to debark, however, the sight across the tarmac was impressive. There must have been tens and tens of Russian MIG aircraft lined up in front of us. Each little stubby plane had the Chinese insignia on it. The Red Stars painted on the fuselages seemed like a constellation of stars marching down the line. There were so many in that line we couldn't see the end. I turned to John and whispered, "The CIA guy would sure like to be here." He agreed. This was supposed to be the civilian airfield, the Shenyang Municipal Airport, where the chartered airplane with our computer was landing. We proceeded into the terminal. We were met by the welcoming committee and whisked into town very quickly.

Our reception in each factory was muted, to say the least; I could have read it wrong. My impression was that the people in these factories were not enamored of Ministry people from Beijing. The absence of a loving relationship extended even when the visitor had gifts (such as a computer) to offer. To be fair, I was on the side of the factories. The way Madame Jao described it, the computer would be located at the Wire and Cable Factory because it was geographically in between the other two plants.

Display terminals would be located at the other two factories along with a printer for each factory. Communications between the computer and its terminals would be over the local telephone lines. Each factory would have people stationed at the computer site to do the things that their home factory wanted.

I tried to suggest to Madame Jao that it would be better if the Wire and Cable Factory did not share the computer. They could develop their own applications and get the benefits from their own operation. Later, computers purchased for the other two factories could use the programs and experience from the Wire Factory. She would have none of it. I learned from my friends at the Blower Works (our new customer) that the Wire factory people did not want this computer. They wanted one like the Blower Works. Unfortunately, they had no money to make their own purchase. Everything they received came from Beijing and everything from Beijing came through Madam Jao. Central planning is a wonderful thing, Right?

While in Shenyang, I paid a visit to the Shenyang Blower Works to see how their new computer building was progressing. It had been a couple of months since I was last there. I was anxious to see how far they had progressed. I was pleasantly surprised! In the short space of about 6-8 weeks, they had completely enclosed the building, and were busy completing the different rooms on the first floor. The computer room glass wall (Big Mu's glory!) was installed; the raised floor that allowed the computer power and signal cables to connect each unit had been installed; most of the lighting had been installed; the air conditioning and environmental controls had been installed. As I walked around the almost complete, but empty, computer room I kept bumping into little thermometers hanging down from the ceiling panels. There was a lot of them; it seems one was hanging down every two or three feet.

While I talked with Mr. Mu, I saw a short, very old Chinese man shove a little ladder under each one of the thermometers, then climb up the ladder. He held a little clip board in one hand while in the other he reached out for the thermometer. He read the thermometer and wrote something down on a little clip board; he climbed down and repeated this procedure at the next thermometer. This process really intrigued me. I interrupted Mr. Mu to ask him what the little man was doing.

Mr. Mu looked over at the little man. By this time, the old gentleman had done his thing at two other thermometers and was moving on to the next one.

"He is doing our acceptance test for the air conditioning equipment." Mr. Mu told me with a completely straight face. His eyes gave it all away, they glittered. I thought he was pulling my leg.

Mr. Mu went on to explain. "The old man is one of our pensioners. It gives him pleasure to be able to help up with our modernization project. Every half hour, he reads all of the thermometers and gives us a report every day. We check the temperatures that he writes down to be sure they meet the specifications for the air conditioning that your engineer gave us. If the temperatures are right, we will tell Mr. Wu to pay for the equipment."

I was speechless. Talk about killing two birds with one stone. Mr. Mu and his cohorts had devised a way to utilize the endless supply of manpower in China to check on what was to be the most advanced installation in China at the time. I thought to myself, "How Chinese!!"

We signed a contract for Madame Jao's computer. Later on, I got an update on what happened from my friends at the Blower Works. Madam Jao had moved on to greater glories by the time of the computer delivery some nine months later. The Wire and Cable Factory got their computer. They put the unopened crates into an unused room at the factory. The crates remained sealed. I think if I went back there today, the boxes would still be there. On the other hand, maybe not; the Wire and Cable factory was closed down in the late '80s, their products couldn't compete with wires and cables manufactured with modern equipment.

John took care of the Shanghai Shipyards contact. Some time before he went to Shanghai to speak with their representatives, we were invited to the U.S. Liaison Office Naval Attaché's apartment in Beijing for a movie night. The Liaison Office was kind enough to invite other Americans whom they knew to be in Beijing. The movie was "Casablanca". They showed it on the living room wall using an old 16mm projector. The sound was lousy; the film was scratchy. We thought it was great; the alternative to watching any film was staring at the hotel room ceiling!! During an intermission when they changed the reels of film, our host sidled up to John. After the greetings and the thanks, the subject of the Shanghai Shipyards came up. How or why that subject came up, John cannot remember. The Naval Attaché wanted to know if we had contact with them. John told him, "No, not yet" and couldn't help wondering how in the world this guy knew of our conversations with Mr. Wu.

He said, "Be careful, they make submarines down there. When you go, see if you can see the submarine pens."

John was rocked to his core. This naval officer was asking him to play at becoming a junior associate amateur CIA agent. He didn't say a word. The subject changed to the movie. The rest of the evening was very pleasant.

John went to Shanghai and met with their people at the Shipyards. By that time, particularly with the U.S. Navy interested, we now knew that an American computer and the shipyards were incompatible, we expected nothing to come of the meeting. The Chinese seemed to have received the same message from somewhere. The meeting was inconsequential. The talk was about the weather, Chinese food, the ongoing industrial revolution; everything, it seemed, but a computer. The only other thing that John remembers about the meeting was the toilet arrangement. It seems that the toilet was in an extremely narrow alcove with barely enough room for the device. Strange to say, it was facing the opposite wall in the narrowest dimension instead of facing outward in the longest dimension. When John came back to Beijing and told me about it, he thought that was another example of the ethic of the Communist plan. The installer had a work plan dictating the installation of "XX" number of toilets a shift. The plan probably made no mention of the direction the toilet should be facing. He achieved his plan no matter what. There were no quality controls, of course. Quality controls were a modern industrial scheme!

While I was in China, John wanted to hire some people as permanent members of our team. Remember, our Ralph Pfeiffer had originally dictated that we were to remain small and never expand like the abortive IBM Russian operations. John, with a big assist from Charlie, received permission. The first person we hired permanently was Willy, our ever present maintenance expert. He had been in a "borrowed" status for a long time. John then located and hired George Sofronas to join us. George had a lot of experience dealing with Socialist government agencies in the Eastern Bloc countries. Marketing in China consisted of simultaneous marketing in Washington, D. C. Because of the embargo you could easily be blind-sided and fail. George was aware of all those pitfalls.

John assigned George to the China National Petroleum Exploration Corporation. He met a representative of the company a couple of times, a Mr. Shoa. The usual interface from the Ministry of Trade was never present. His conversations quickly determined they wanted a computer to do seismic mapping and interpretation. Seismic exploration consists of setting off a series of explosions in the ground in a pre-determined grid. The resulting sound waves are mapped using a sophisticated computer program. An experienced oilman interprets the computer generated map to determine if there are possible oil deposits. I nearly fell off the chair when George described Mr. Shoa's request. Just to be sure, I asked him to repeat the conversation to me and I asked George how he had responded.

George told me he made some notes and told Mr. Shoa that they could continue the discussion at their next meeting. George's response illustrates the reason John hired an experienced Socialist bloc marketer. George knew the ground rules for this kind of marketing. Do not promise, by word, motion or body language anything until we check it out. George didn't know it, but a similar request had been made of IBM by a Soviet agency several years before. When we reviewed the request with our friends in Washington, they went ballistic. It appeared that the same programming technology used in submarine sonar systems is also used in seismic data processing programs. I have been told the technical name is "parallel processing". The computer processing is extremely fast. A programmer who knows and uses parallel processing can easily transport the algorithms from seismic data processing to sonar data processing. The algorithms are not duplicates; but they are very similar. So, seismic processing was a "no-no" for export unless politicians were involved. On top of all that, the hardware that did sonar or seismic work tends to be very big, very fast, and very expensive, qualities which seem to impress the Chinese Another connection was to Deng Tsao Ping's natural gas, exportable oil grand plan to raise hard currency. We could make a very big sale; the trouble was we could never deliver the computer! What to do with our new friend at the Oil Institute?

George decided to change his tactics at the next meeting. Instead of <u>asking</u> what he wanted to do with his computer, George would <u>tell</u> Mr. Shoa what he could do with it. He would stay away from any suspicious application that might get us into trouble with the export people. He did exactly that. Instead of driving the man away, Mr. Shoa readily agreed with George that he could use the computer for payroll and various other administrative tasks. The important thing was that they get a modern computer from the U.S.A. At that point, George and I had to return home for the Thanksgiving Day holidays, promising to return to continue the discussions.

We returned to Beijing early in December, 1978. We planned to stay for a couple of weeks, leaving in time for the holidays back home. One way or another, George and I wanted to finish with the Oil Institute. We got the surprise of our lives when we went into the building where we were meeting Mr. Shoa. We should have anticipated it. We should have noticed that the dining room at the hotel was unusually full for each meal. The number of foreigners in the hotel had been increasing at a steady pace over the past months. All the previous meetings with our contacts had been in the regular Er Li Go building where there were individual meeting rooms. This time, we went into a vast auditorium in another building. The auditorium floor was divided into little cubicles separated by cloth partitions, just like in a hospital ward in the U.S. Each cubicle had a sofa, covered by the standard beige slipcover and doilies, several pull up chairs, similarly covered, and a coffee table in the middle. It was so small that once in the cubicle you had to leave the cubicle to turn around. Once seated, the meeting participants were right in each other's faces. There was absolutely no privacy. We heard the conversation in the next cubicle; they probably heard ours. The noise of all those voices, though muted, was like the steady hum of a machine.

We got down to his case immediately. Mr. Shoa wanted to know which computer model we were going to sell him. We wanted to know how much hard currency he had to spend. It seemed we began bargaining over the unknown contents of a paper bag. Neither party could tell what was inside the bag. He wanted to know what was inside the bag; we wanted to know how much he was willing to pay for it. He gave in first. He told us that his Ministry had given him $1,000,000 U.S. dollars for this purchase. Their condition was that he had to spend it, or at least encumber it, by the end of the year. Three weeks away! The time limit didn't bother us; we could type up a contract in a couple of days. The amount was the problem.

An export package usually consists of a medium sized computer, spare parts for that computer, training programs for three or four programmers and training programs for two or three maintenance engineers. There was no way we could construct a package (with normal profit) for that amount of money. That conclusion rested on our experience with the Shenyang contract signed twelve months before. The final computer price for the Shenyang contract resulted from many heated discussions with the pricing analysts. The final price needed a blessing from the chief financial officer. There was no "give" in that price at all.

The minimum spare parts complement used in the Shenyang contract was the least number of parts our maintenance people knew was necessary for remote maintenance without a warehouse within reach. There was no "give" in that component of the contract.

Both education programs, programmer and maintenance engineer, were at rock bottom prices on the assumption that we had minimal cost exposure. All the classes were going to be held anyway; all the teachers and space were already assigned. The incremental cost of some more students was minor. There was really no "give" in those numbers.

The entry price for delivery of a modern computer with all the trimmings in China was well in excess of $1,000,000.

We told Mr. Shoa the bad news along with all the details. He was absolutely devastated. His institute had to have a computer; he had to spend that money or lose it. First, he suggested that we contract for the computer alone. Just enough of the computer to use the money he had. Next year, three weeks away, he would ask for additional money for the missing pieces and for the education and spare parts. We did that with Madam Jao at the Ministry of Machine Building, but this situation was much different. The institute had to have a MODERN computer capable of seismic processing, not just any computer.

I answered, "Mr. Shoa, we cannot do that. Based on your hopes for next year, you want us to promise to deliver an incomplete, non-working computer system. My company would never allow me to do that. My government would never let me export a computer like that. That's unreasonable."

Then he suggested we use the Shenyang contract and reduce everything proportionately so that the total would be less than $1,000,000. That way the contract would be complete even though meaningless. He felt he could wave that signed contract in front of his Ministry and keep the $1,000,000. Then, next year, he would get more money to upgrade the contract fully to purchase something that worked.

I didn't even answer that one. He saw the answer in my eyes. He realized he was clutching at straws. No matter how we felt personally, no matter how passionate he was, it was a losing situation unless he could come up with more money now. I suggested we would help him make an immediate request to his Ministry for more money now. He told us that wouldn't work. Other departments in the Ministry were promising to spend their money more quickly. The situation was desperate; he had to spend the money or lose it! He had tears in his eyes. It was terrible for us as well. It was traitorous, as sales representatives, to refuse a sale. Mr. Shoa's situation reminded me of a similar one more than fifteen years ago where my position was more like his.

I worked in an IBM laboratory then. I was assigned to a project to design, build, and test a computer system for use in supermarkets and retail stores. During the month of October one year, my boss asked the project members if anyone could spend a significant amount of money over and above our budget between October and December. The time element was the key, just as with Mr. Shoa's case.

The purchase had to be related to the project, the purchase had to be an addition to our present budget, the amount had to be large and the purchase had to be complete by the end of the year. If I had to define what a "blank check" means in the business world, I would choose this one. One does not get this kind of request too often. Before or since, I never received a request like this one in my entire business career. After a few moments thought, I told him I could spend about $250,000 on a consulting contract to get us some more supermarket and retail store data. At that moment, I had no idea of how or where that was possible. My boss replied, "Okay, as long as you spend it. If you don't spend it, all of it, our credibility goes out the window." (He used a somewhat more colorful term) We both deduced that the Company was forecasting enormous profits that year and wanted to keep them down to levels that were more reasonable. Generating more expenses was a way out. Every project manager in the division of the company I worked for received the same request. There were more than 30 projects in that division at any given time. The sums must have been staggering!

I called Marvin Flax, a friend of mine, immediately. Marvin worked for Booz Allen and Hamilton, a very large and respected consulting firm. I told him what I had promised my boss. I asked if he could help. I emphasized the time constraint and payment conditions attached. I could hear him salivate over the telephone. I suspect, like me, he never received a call from a prospective client like this one. He said that he would get back to me in an hour. He had to speak to his boss. He called me back in fifteen minutes. My take is his boss had never received an offer like mine before either.

We met the following day. He outlined what he wanted to do and what kind of report he would write. He said he wanted to conduct about fifty interviews over the next month. Then he would consolidate the data and begin writing the report. I couldn't understand how he would arrange, schedule and conduct fifty interviews over the next twenty business days, especially since there was a Thanksgiving Holiday in between. He told me emphatically not to worry that was his concern. All I had to do was to help him when asked, stay out of his way and pay his bill on time. I told him if he did not meet the target time, his name (and mine!) was mud all over IBM. Our meeting ended on that note. The end of this story is that he met his target; he delivered his report right after Christmas and gave me his invoice at the same time. I was a hero!

Because of that experience, I had complete empathy for our Chinese friend Mr. Shoa. I knew exactly what he was going through.

Mr Shoa's problem was particularly vexing in a Communist environment. Achieving the plan, any plan, was the only alternative. He had to spend the money or he wouldn't achieve the plan given to his Institute. The fact that he would lose the products the money could buy was bad enough; the embarrassment of not achieving this particular plan was much greater.

Mr. Shoa made one final plea. We excused ourselves. Then he told us that he was going to the foreign trade organization to convince them to purchase some other computer for him. He had to hurry away; he did not have much time to work with. We wished him luck. George suggested we would call him upon our return to Beijing in the New Year. We left the building and went back to the hotel. We never saw Mr. Shoa again. To this day, I wonder whether he got his computer or not, or whether he spent his money or not.

George was disconsolate. He felt he had lost his first sale in China because of what he perceived as IBM's bureaucratic inflexibility. Of course, that was not true, but he felt like it. He got drunk on the trip back home, out of frustration, I think. To a marketing person, refusing a sale to a prospective customer is the ultimate nightmare! Most of the time is spent trying to convince the prospective customer to buy, not to dissuade him.

John had a similar experience. He received a telephone call from Dr. J.D. Pickering a big mucky-muck at the Jet Propulsion Laboratory in California. Dr. Pickering was a founder and leader of the Jet Propulsion Lab. The Lab was "the" institution in the U.S. space efforts. Dr. Pickering had a "satellite photo enhancement" program running on his IBM computers. His IBM computers were large, new and "space exploration" level technology. Dr. Pickering wanted to sell that program to the Chinese for land development uses in the Chinese hinterlands. JPL (Jet Propulsion Laboratory) was a major domestic IBM customer, as were other participants in the U.S. space exploration program. There was no way we would refuse Dr. Pickering anything. Therefore, John went to California so that Dr. Pickering could explain his program. John remembers that it was spectacular; he suggested that an approach be made to the Washington licensing people to see if a license might be forthcoming. This deal required satellite photographs and a large computer for processing; both were still embargoed. Nonetheless, John not only went to California to meet with Dr. Pickering, but also went to China with him. They had a lovely time and the whole thing died a natural death in Washington.

By the end of 1978, the China "market" began to assume the proportions of a giant "one-day" sale at a department store in the U.S. Executives were flocking to Beijing to buy or sell. It was obvious the political scene was changing as well. Leonard Woodcock, the new head of the U.S. Liaison Office in Beijing, was meeting with his counterparts in the Chinese government almost daily. Deng Tsao Ping, still the Deputy Prime Minister, was busy pulling strings all over the government. He was meeting with Mr. Woodcock complaining bitterly that the U.S. was taking too long to open full diplomatic relations with his government.

In Washington, Mr. Brzezinski, the de-facto Secretary of State, was guiding his President, Jimmy Carter, down the path to confrontation with the Soviet Union. The real Secretary of State, Cyrus Vance publicly stated diplomatic relations with the People's Republic were being "considered". Everything came to a head in late December when President Carter formally announced that the U.S. and the People's Republic of China would resume full diplomatic relations on January 1, 1979. The dam burst! All the rules of the embargo went out the window with that one stroke. Normal commercial activities, normal on the American side at least, could commence. The Chinese, however, had some rules of law to establish.

By March 1979 everything was ready at the Shenyang Blower works. All the students had returned, the computer room and the brand new building were finished. The power lines for the building were connected; the new air conditioning (the first in Shenyang) was turned on. The big day had come. The computer, all twelve crates of it, arrived at the Shenyang "Municipal" Airport, the former fighter aircraft base, the airport we had so much trouble with while negotiating and writing the contract. The actual name of the airport was "Airfield #43" or something similar. The military moved most of their airplanes to a corner of the airport. Civilian traffic had, by this time, taken over most of the airfield. There were plans to build a brand new civilian airport but it wouldn't be open for another five years. The day the computer arrived, via a chartered flight from Japan; there were many, many signs of the military presence. It didn't matter to the men at the Shenyang Blower Works. They had the first modern computer in China!

Mr. Mu had received a message a few days before notifying him of the landing schedule. Our traffic people in Tokyo had already notified him of the exact content of the delivery. He knew how many crates there were; what each crate weighed and what was in each crate. Our shipping documents clearly explained the sequence of unloading was the reverse of installation sequence. This was important so that each machine moved once and only once. Mr. Mu also knew that three of our Japanese maintenance engineers had come to Shenyang separately. Their job was to re-install the computer in the new computer building at the factory. The three Japanese engineers were the same ones who had installed, tested, and packed it for shipment in our Japanese factory. We had insisted on this. We insisted on security measures. We tried to remove every risk we could identify. We had done everything, and more, than had been contracted. Now it was Mr. Mu's turn.

The immediate problems of unloading the airplane, loading the crates on trucks, moving the trucks from the airport to the factory, and finally unloading and moving the crates into the computer room in the correct sequence were significant. In the

U.S., these were not problems. In our environment, each of these operations was an opportunity for specialists to do what they do best. We had airlines that handled freight and crates. We had truckers who lift and carry heavy and sensitive equipment. We had delivery companies that moved computer equipment upstairs and down with no apparent effort. We were a highly specialized society. Mr. Mu had none of this.

Mr Mu had called the military commander of the airfield several weeks before the delivery. Colonel Chu had promised all the cooperation necessary. He had told Mr. Mu that he would arrange for a forklift to remove the crates from the aircraft. He had given Mr. Mu the specifications of the forklift to be certain it would be big enough to handle all the crates. He also had warned that everyone would have to stay in the designated areas for visitors. They would be clearly marked by the time the chartered aircraft arrived. He had also told Mr. Mu the aircraft would have to leave immediately after unloading, day or night. It was all military and disciplined. Colonel Chu gave Mr. Mu the name of his subordinate in charge of this operation. Mr Mu thanked him and left. Back at the factory, he checked the forklift information against his crate specifications. It was a good thing that he did. One of the crates was too heavy for the forklift!

Mr Mu quickly arranged for his engineers to examine the problem. The Blower Works was used to moving heavy objects within their factory. They had cranes to move castings and large steel casings from one workshop to the other. Using the old Communist self-sufficiency credo of Chairman Mao, they solved the problem of handling the crates. On delivery day, the factory would send a group of laborers with some wedges and they, with the forklift, would take care of transferring the heavy crate from the airplane to the truck. With the first problem solved, he moved on to the second problem.

The second problem was trucks. The Blower Factory did not have enough trucks to carry twelve crates in one continuous operation. Mr Mu and Mr Shu got on the telephone to their sister factories in Shenyang to rustle up heavy duty trucks. It took some arm-twisting to get the required number. The Director had to contact the Director of the Wire and Cable Factory to get some action. The Wire and Cable people were so annoyed at the Beijing First Ministry of Machine Building over their own computer fiasco that, at first, they were reluctant to help. On the day the airplane was due to arrive, Mr Mu ordered the translator, Mr Liu Da Foo (the translator of "Four of Gang" fame!) to accompany the drivers to the airfield. He was necessary because the documents accompanying the shipment were all in English. Signatures would be necessary and he was the only one who could read and maybe understand the English documents.

A massive convoy of fourteen large flat bed trucks assembled at the Blower Works. Mr Mu did not want to take any risks. If a truck broke down, if a truck was too small or too light, he made sure there would be a replacement instantly available. With Liu Da Foo in the first truck, they started out for the airport. Another of Mr Mu's worries was the road conditions along the way. Many of the roads were unpaved. In the past when they had moved heavy machines, the condition of the road wasn't a concern. The heavy machines were so heavy that the fear was the trucks would harm the roads. In this case, the fear was that the roads would harm the computer. Mr Mu was concerned that the bumping and jumping over unpaved roads would damage sensitive parts of the computer. Liu Da Foo made a note of every part of the road to avoid on the way back with the computers. He was very impressed with his position as the head of this operation.

At the airfield, the military men had everything organized. The Lieutenant (or whatever rank he was) gave each driver a large numbered sign. The driver's number corresponded to his proper sequence for unloading and delivering to the computer room. Since the airplane had been loaded in reverse order in Tokyo, the last crate off the airplane would be the first one delivered. Everything went smoothly. When the extra heavy crate came up in the unloading sequence, the Blower Work's crew put wedges under the <u>fork lift</u> and brought the crate tenderly on to the truck. There was a lot of shouting and screaming to be sure, but all the crates ended up where they were supposed to go. The Army officer then put all the trucks in the proper order for their trip back to town. Liu Da Foo didn't know who organized it, but each driver put a big red flag on his bumper. Off they went, flags flying and snapping in the breeze. Liu directed them past all the road problems. This long convoy of trucks came roaring down the main street of Shenyang. The convoy went around the traffic circle where Chairman Mao's statue pointed them in the direction of the Blower Works. The main street wasn't on their route to the Blower Factory, but Liu wanted to show everyone their new computer even if it was inside fourteen trucks.

The trucks lined up on the street in front of the factory in the proper order for unloading. There was room for only one truck at a time in front of the computer building. There was a lot of shouting and shoving to get each truck in the optimal position for unloading. Each crate was jockeyed off its truck by many hands. They had no forklift. Every inch of space around the pallet had a pair of hands on it. The pallets, on dollies, rolled into the computer room. There, the engineers took over. They removed the crating and the pallet and took the refuse outside to make room for the next crate. That is how it went for the rest of the day. Big Mu did not want to leave any crate outside overnight. Even though all these parts had been in an airplane at 30,000 feet for hours and hours, Big Mu wanted them inside his air conditioned, humidified, climate controlled room. A heart transplant operation could be performed in that room it was so clean! Everyone worked until well into the night. The next morning there was an enormous pile of crating material left in front of the computer building. Every worker on his way to work in the factory stopped by the computer building to see the new computer. They couldn't go inside, but that big pile of crates was enough evidence for them.

The Japanese maintenance engineers took exactly three days to assemble and test the computer. There were no hitches; there were no delays. Nothing was missing. It was a textbook assembly. The men did not even have to refer to the installment manual for help in assembling the computer. After all, they assembled this very same computer in the IBM plant at Fujisawa, Japan the week before! Besides the three men wanted to have some time for sightseeing before they left. Mr Mu was especially impressed. He had purchased many large and complex American machine tools for the Blower Works. He watched the assembly and installation of each one. Most times, the assembly took much longer than planned; most times a significant part was missing or damaged in transit. Not one of these events marred the IBM assembly. The process appeared simple; but this was a highly complex computer. It was an awesome sight!

Our Japanese engineers invited the Chinese engineers to watch and help with the assembly. Willy, our ever-present maintenance man, had briefed the Japanese on how to handle their relationship with the Chinese. Although our people handled the critical parts of the process first, the Shenyang people did many operations. When the final installation test was completed, the Chinese engineers repeated all the tests under the watchful eyes of the IBM engineers. When the second and duplicate testing was complete, everyone in the room cheered. Visitors had been coming and going throughout the testing phase. As the end neared, the room filled up. The Chinese programmers were there. Big Mu was there. Mr. Mu was there. Mr Shu was there. The Managing Director was there. The only significant absentees were Mr. Wu from Techimport in Beijing, the man who wrote the purchase contract for this computer and I. Everyone else who had anything to do with this project was there. When the Chinese engineer running the last test turned around to everyone with his "thumbs-up" gesture, everyone started to talk at the same time. Mr. Mu shouted to Big Mu, "Sign the acceptance paper". He signed. The deal was done!

These three Chinese men from Shenyang, Messer's Shu, Mu, and Big Mu had revolutionized their country without even knowing it!

The Peoples Republic of China had its first modern civilian solid state computer up and running!! At about the same time, some other organization in China set off their fifth or sixth nuclear bomb test. Also, at the same time, to demonstrate the utter absurdity of it all, a new "Miss World" was crowned in London. It was March 12, 1979! Three months and twelve days after the U.S. and the Peoples Republic of China resumed diplomatic relations, IBM broke into the China market with a bang!

I have described the positive outgrowth in China of our efforts to treat the Shenyang contract and people with fairness and equality. Every promise implied or contracted was kept; we gave them more attention than a comparable customer in the United States would have received. One of the payoffs was the intense interest and propositions we received right after the contract was signed and when the computer was installed. During the 24 month period beginning at the time we signed that first contract, IBM almost had a de-facto monopoly on computer purchases by the Peoples Republic of China. But the biggest impact was yet to come.

The Peoples Republic of China had taken over the UN Security Council seat previously held by the Chiang Kai Shek group, the Republic of China in October 1971. The PRC attempted to obtain membership in the UN 21 times before acceptance. The United States objected to their membership, but the vote in October 1971 had overruled the U.S. objection

Once a member, the PRC had to fulfill several internal UN obligations to determine among other things, its membership dues. The major internal stumbling block was the lack of a recent, accurate census of China's population. Although the PRC's State Statistical Bureau was empowered to provide that service, a

Allan Joseph

country wide census had not been done since 1964. That census and the predecessor in 1952 were considered inaccurate and misleading due to major gaps in collecting and analyzing the data. A new national population census was required; as soon as Mao died, a plan for a 1982 census began to take shape. Two actions were taken; first, help from the United Nations Fund for Population Activities (UNFPA) was requested; and, second, help from the United States Census Bureau was requested.

Both appeals for help were answered. The UNFPA responded with technical help, but more importantly, with a promise of money to purchase the computers necessary for the task. The U.S. Census Bureau responded with massive technical help and the invitation of thousands of Chinese to the U.S. for training.

This all happened while John and I were finishing up the installation of the Shenyang computer. The UNFPA contacted IBM for a bid, along with other computer manufacturers. Back in Beijing, we were contacted by the State Statistical Bureau. Their representative told me straight out that the Bureau wanted IBM equipment because of our record with Shenyang installation and would accept no other from the UNFPA. I was amazed at the nerve of the Chinese; China was getting a gift of 26 computers from the UNFPA and dictating the choice of those computers to the donor! On top of that, I couldn't get the idea that the U.S. was the dominant contributor to the UNFPA out of my head!

The IBM representative in New York called to tell me competitive bedding was the only way the UN was going about this purchase. The UN would purchase them in New York for delivery to each of the 25 provincial capitals where the Statistical Bureau had offices in China. Competitive bidding involves two things; neither of which I was adept at. The first was the establishment of a set of specifications only matched by your product. The computers required by the Chinese were run of the mill number crunchers; standard models without any bells or whistles that could be IBM unique. So we were forced to match standard computer specifications over which we had no control.

The second requirement, and more popularly known, was the lowest price. This was the Holy Grail; provide the same equipment as your competitor at a lower price. We could probably handle the price issue if we could get by the standard equipment issue. So we went to work.

At that time, any computer proposal had to be blessed by the Customer Engineering (CE) Department (IBM's maintenance organization). The CE people made certain each machine and each system sold by the marketing departments was technically and functionally perfect. Since, under normal U.S. standards, those CE's were to maintain the machine or system while it was in the customers hands, they wanted to be absolutely certain their standards were met. So, the systems proposed to the UN had to meet those U.S. standards. The fact that the systems were destined for very odd places in China made no difference.

We, in China, were under no such rules. The international side of IBM had their own CE and technical standards, and, in the case of machines sold rather than leased, IBM relinquished their maintenance requirements. The customer was responsible for maintaining his machine; IBM taught them how, IBM sold a cache of spare parts to each customer, the customer, except for backup purposes, was on his own. A turf war on a grand scale was in the making. To make things worse, the configuration requirements on the U.S. side were inflexible and produced a non-competitive price.

The problem hinged on the U.S. CE requirement to have two random access disk drives for each system. The requirement was logical; if one failed the system could operate with the other. If only one disk drive was available and it failed, the entire system crashed and it was almost impossible to rehabilitate it without an available disk drive. On the other hand, if we included two disk drives our bid price was not the lowest and the chance of getting this $26,000,000 contract went out the window.

Our own CE guru came to our rescue. Willy devised a way to theoretically rehabilitate a crashed one disc system that satisfied us. The U.S. engineers refused to accept his solution; but we did. We convinced our management it was worth the effort. We were awarded the $26,000,000 contract; within months of that award, the second disk drive for each of 26 systems was ordered and all was well.

While we were negotiating with the UN for their computer gift to the Chinese, I went to China with a UN Technical Representative, Gunnar (I could never pronounce his last name), to discuss their gift with the Statistical Bureau. We flew to Beijing together. We were met at the airport by a representative of the State Statistical Bureau and escorted through Customs without stopping for anything. No visa stamping, no showing of passports, nothing like any of my previous visits. I was very impressed.

However, after Gunnar and I finished our business together, I went about my other IBM activities. The following week, when I finished my business, I went to the airport. On your way out of China, you must show your entry visa so it could be stamped. I had no entry visa. The desk officer looked through my passport several times without finding an entry stamp. He looked at me; I looked at him. I had no idea what the problem was. I was gestured to the side while the officer handled other departing visitors. After a while, another officer came over to me with my passport in hand. This officer could speak some English; it wasn't long before the problem was explained to me.

The question he posed was simple. How did I get into China without an entry stamp? Where did I come from? What was I doing in China? I had visions of a Chinese jail on rice and water; I would never see my wife and kids again. I told him my story of arriving with a diplomatic group from the UN. The officer left me. I don't know what he did. When he returned, he took my passport to the closest officer's desk and stamped it. I got on the plane, never once looked back.

Chapter 14 – Shangri-La Revisited

In November, 2001, twenty-three years after these events, I visited Mr. Shu, Mr. Mu and Big Mu in Shenyang at their invitation. I also visited Mr. Wu in Beijing. How did this all come about?

While I was living in Connecticut I had a neighbor, John Chou, an American of Chinese descent. He was born in Taiwan, but moved to this country as a young college student some thirty years before. He owns a restaurant nearby where my family and I enjoy wonderful Chinese meals. His chef is an expert at producing authentic Chinese dishes I am familiar with. Every time John met us there, he would ask me if I would like to go to China with him. He is a gregarious person and we became friends.

For a long time, my excuse was, "No, it's too far and too expensive." After all, I had been retired for more than fifteen years and had not been in China for more than ten years previous to my retirement. This answer satisfied him for that moment, but the next time we were in his restaurant, he would ask again. My next excuse was that I had spent a lot of time in China a long time ago and just didn't want to go back again. I've been there. He answered, "But, I'll take you to places you've never been". He was relentless; he would ask me to go every time we were in his restaurant. I began to feel a little guilty that I had not refused outright. Still looking for excuses, I said that I would go, but the price was too high. He said, "We can get round trip tickets for $700.00". That shot my "too high" price argument down. That price was half of what we had paid in 1977.

Out of desperation, I said to him, "I would only go back to China if I could meet with the people I worked with back then in the late 70's." That was all he needed. He asked me for a telephone number to call in China to make a connection with them. His question threw me for a loop. When I was there, telephones were a distinct luxury; only the government offices had them. I had to confess that I had no idea of their telephone number. Even if they had one, how was I to find it? He said, "Look on the internet." He had an answer for every objection I brought up. The thought of finding that telephone number intrigued me.

I spent many an evening searching the internet for a Chinese telephone directory. After many, many false leads, I found what claimed to be an English language telephone directory for China. The Shenyang Blower Works was not listed. Then I went after English language industrial directories where Chinese companies are listed by the products they make. Many hours later, over many evenings and nights of searching, I found <u>one</u> telephone number for the Shenyang factory. I was stunned; twenty-three years ago, the Blower Works was close to the largest factory in Shenyang; they only had one telephone number? I gave it to John. Now I had the upper hand. Every time I saw him, I would ask if he had made contact. I thought I had the upper hand because my mistaken assumption was that he would never find any of the people I worked with. Most, if not all of them, would be either dead or gone on to greater glories. How wrong I was!

The issue with the telephone number really told a larger story. In this global economy in which we live, how can anyone find a telephone number in China? How was any customer who might want to find a product manufacturer in China supposed to go about it? How was the company ever to be successful if no one could find them? Twenty three years ago, you either had the telephone number in advance or else you didn't attempt to telephone to them.

John dialed the telephone number in Shenyang, China from his restaurant in Connecticut. John had to wait until after 10 PM our local time so the call would arrive early in the morning their time. The twelve-hour time difference between China and eastern U.S. had not changed. He simply direct dialed the number! In 1977, we had to plan our telephone calls hours in advance and then get permission to make them. After about twenty unanswered calls over as many nights, someone finally picked up the ringing telephone in Shenyang. In Chinese John asked, "Please let me speak to Mr. Mu Rei Lin, or give me a telephone number where I can reach him". The man who answered had no idea where this telephone call was coming from. The man in China had no idea who was asking him this question. The published telephone number alone gave access to the factory.

In our country, most times the business telephone is answered with the company name along with a question about "How can I help you?" Remember, this is a Communist society. People mind their own business and people simply do not ask questions of strangers. The only clue he had was John's Chinese accent. The accent was from Taiwan, not a northern Chinese accent. The person asked, "Who is this?"

John had to tell him the whole story. First, he had to describe who he was; then he had to tell who I was and why we were trying to reach Mr. Mu. John told me the man on the other end of the line (we never found out who he was) kept saying the Chinese equivalent of "Uhuh, uhuh", and, finally said, "Please wait a minute." John told me it was like a call to his next-door neighbor. He came back on the line a few minutes later and gave John a telephone number for Mr. Mu. John dialed the new telephone number at once. Mr. Mu picked up the telephone, identified himself in Chinese just as we might do in English, and said, "Hello." John was so surprised Mr. Mu said "Hello" a couple of more times. In fact, Mr. Mu spoke in a completely conversational tone. He didn't use the old-fashioned Chinese telephone greeting of screaming into the telephone "Wei, Wei" like the decibels would push the greeting down the telephone line.

John started out by asking Mr. Mu if he remembered me. Mu answered, "Of course." That gave John all the assurance he needed to tell the whole story of meeting me and wanting to go to China, and so forth, etc. He ended the conversation by asking Mr. Mu if he could speak to me. He forgot that I don't speak Chinese and Mr. Mu was not speaking English. Mr. Mu again answered "Of course" in Chinese. John asked Mr. Mu to stay by the telephone; he would get me to call right away.

Though it was after midnight, John Chow called me at home, woke me up, and told me to call Mr. Mu immediately. He gave me the telephone number and instructions how to direct-dial to China his inexpensive way. I said, "Wait a minute, does he speak English?" John, excited by his success, said, "Enough". John later told me he was so excited he had forgotten that his conversation with Mr. Mu had been entirely in Chinese and had no idea of how much English Mr. Mu spoke.

It was 2 a.m., my time, when I called Mr. Mu. As I dialed the long international number, I had a great many trepidations; I couldn't figure out how to begin our conversation. I had been out of business and IBM for a long time; who knew what Mr. Mu's circumstances were? There had been the Tienamin incident. US-China relations had been up and down like a yo-yo for several years. I had read that state-owned factories in China were having a tough go of it in the competitive world. Maybe Mr. Mu was a janitor by this time, for all I knew. In my mind, it also was just as likely that he was the big boss. When the telephone was picked up on the other end, I forgot all those thoughts and just said,

"Hello, Mr. Mu." I used my Chinese greeting which I had learned a long time ago. That almost exhausted my vocabulary.

"Mr. Josep, Good Morning" I was encouraged, Mr. Mu never could get the "ph" sound on the end of my name.

"How are you Mr. Mu.?" I spoke very slowly, enunciating every syllable. It's an American custom to do that. Another custom I learned to avoid was shouting the English words. Shouting assumed volume will help understanding.

"Fine, how are you?"

"I am fine, Mr. Mu. I am thinking of coming to China to visit you and my other old friends." Although that wasn't exactly true at that moment, I couldn't think of another thing to say that would justify calling this man after so long, and from 8,000 miles away. I was rapidly being committed to this trip by the rush of events.

"That is wonderful. We invite you." That statement was a relic of the past. Nowadays, you purchase a ticket, fill out a tourist visa application and you are all set to go. Formerly, in the almost closed world of Communist China, the government had to issue a formal invitation before you ever filled out any application of any kind. That is how a closed country keeps unwanted visitors out. The invitation was the key. For some stupid reason, his words made me feel better.

Mr. Mu, I have two favors to ask of you. Is there some way we can communicate other than by voice. Maybe e-mail or fax? Do you have a fax number?

"Yes, yes, I will give you fax number. I have no e-mail. " There was silence for a couple of minutes. He came back on the telephone and began reading off a telephone number. However, he was reading it in Chinese!

"Mr. Mu, Mr. Mu! In English, please". It took a few seconds for him to stop. It was kind of like the old radio transmissions where you said "Over" to indicate that you were finished with your part of the transmission.

Mr. Mu repeated the telephone number in English very, very slowly. He was mentally translating the number from Chinese into English before speaking the words.

I repeated the number back to him in mixed Chinese and English, using the Chinese words for the numbers that I knew and English for the ones I didn't know. We did this back and forth several times to be sure that I had the correct number.

"Mr. Mu, the second thing is about hotels. We have not been able to get the e-mail address or telephone number or fax number for any hotels in Shenyang. Can you get them for us?"

"We have 3 star and 4 star hotels. Which do you want?"

I answered, "Which stars, Chinese or international?"

He laughed   He knew exactly what I was talking about. International star hotels were just that; usually part of an international hotel chain and usually measured objectively against some common standard of facilities and service. I had discovered long ago that the local bureaucrats awarded Chinese hotels stars as well. In addition to awarding these stars, the same bureaucracy ran the hotels. They usually reflected the hotel management's enthusiasm, rather than the class of hotel service.

He said, "International." That also meant that they were expensive by comparison with the local ones.

"Mr Chow and I don't want to spend a lot of money Are there hotels with one star?" John had made that very plain to me. He did not want to spend a lot of money on an expensive hotel.

"I understand completely".   Mr. Mu's understanding of my request illustrated his facility, even with a limited English vocabulary, to understand, intuitively and accurately, a foreigner's thoughts.

"We invite you to stay at the factory hotel." In the old days, every state-owned enterprise had its own little dormitory/hotel where visitors to the factory/enterprise were put up during their visit. Since there was not a lot of movement around the country, only the very large cities had independent "non-factory associated" hotels. The difficulty was the factory hotels were really dormitories, without private room and bath hotels. After all everyone was equal and it was share and share alike in Communist China. Therefore, there was no need for expensive private rooms.

"That would be fine", I said. I knew that would make John very happy, the factory dormitory wouldn't charge as much as a regular hotel.

Okay, I will send you more information via fax."

We made our goodbye's just a little choked up. Our lack of language only permitted emotional pauses and grunts and, besides, we were men...

As soon as the fact of the visit was established, I began to e-mail some of the people who were with us in Shenyang to see if they wanted to come with us. I tried John Ryan, but he was embroiled in something or other and couldn't go. He told me that he wanted to remember the circumstances and places as he had experienced them; a new look would probably destroy his impressions. I called Willy, our famous maintenance engineer and finally located him in Texas. After our Shenyang experience, he had taken an assignment in Hong Kong, finally moving back to the States several years later. He had recently retired from IBM and the prospect of returning to his triumphs of 23 years ago turned him on. He would be happy to go.

Over the next couple of weeks, many faxes were exchanged. I must admit that while my messages were relatively complete with facts and desires, Mr. Mu's messages were more terse and direct, without a lot of information. I thought that this was a throwback to the old days when everyone, including us, thought every conversation, every communication, was bugged and recorded by someone. At least we acted as if we believed that. Mr. Mu was taking care of all the arrangements in Shenyang. All we had to tell him was when we would arrive. We only had a couple of glitches. Following the style of many years before, I asked Mr. Mu for a government invitation to visit China. In past times, Mr. Wu of Techimport took care of those details; Mr. Mu was never involved. In past times, the central government in Beijing had a bureaucracy to handle such requests. In the intervening period, all those functions moved out of the central government to the local provincial level, at least out of the First Ministry of Machine Building. In fact, the First Ministry had disappeared in the intervening time. I didn't know that. I had no idea that today one could deal solely with a travel agent for tickets, visas and other arrangements. Government details were a matter of little consequence.

Mr. Mu stumbled over my request for an invitation, since someone from the factory had to go to the local provincial government bureau to obtain one. The massive Beijing bureaucracy that handled those things years ago was gone. The authority had passed to the provincial government. Mr. Mu told me the factory had not done that in years and years. Undaunted, he started the process. Ultimately, I did receive an official invitation to visit, but I also discovered that the fee associated with government invitation visas cost $50.00, while the tourist visa was only $10.00. It was rather strange, an invited guest visa costs more than an uninvited tourist visa. In about two milliseconds, John convinced me to go the route of the tourist visa! I still have the invitation.

Another snag came up on my end. I felt that I had to observe my Chinese manners and bring a gift to my hosts. But what should I bring? These were business friends of more than 20 years ago; I had no idea what would be appropriate. I solved the problem by having many enlargements made of pictures I had taken of each of the people I thought I would be meeting with. I hoped they, and maybe even their families, would enjoy seeing presentation quality pictures of themselves as young men. A new problem arose when I realized I did not have pictures of everyone; it would be just my luck to meet the ones for whom I had no picture.

Off we went. Since Willy was coming from Texas, we had arranged to meet when we changed flights in the San Francisco airport. We all made the connection successfully. The non-stop flight to Beijing was boring and debilitating. We arrived at the Beijing airport in the middle of a November night. We had arrived 23 years before on a February night. There was, however, no comparison. We didn't get off the plane on a ramp to the ground. I didn't see the night sky filled with stars in contrast to the blackness all around me. There was no one to greet us when we stepped out of the airplane. There were none of the old protocols.

Instead, there was a large, and I mean BIG, chrome, stainless steel and glass, airport terminal building attached to an endless tunnel that led from the airplane's door. When we came out of the tunnel, it was impossible to see to the end of the building. We must have walked the equivalent of a mile up and down escalators and stairwells for what seemed to be twenty minutes before we arrived at the immigration counters. When we arrived there, we discovered that Mao jackets and pajama bottoms were out; neat clean sparkling uniforms were in. The inspectors were standing around looking everyone over. The room where they were standing was as tall as it was long. If one were courageous enough, a yodel would have echoed endlessly around the walls and ceiling. The whole immigration inspection process was very perfunctory either because of the time or because no one was interested. It was like going to Canada only everyone looked a little different.

The baggage retrieval was a new experience. The conveyor system that held the luggage coming from the plane was as long as a football field. No one had to push and shove to get close to their luggage. There were, however, the few, as in New York, who had to get their bags as soon as they arrived from the airplane. They crowded around the little exit where the bags came out. The rest of us were lined up, a hundred long, at this passenger luggage "feeding trough". Again, the room was so big and cavernous that everything in it, including us, felt small and insignificant. I had the faint feeling that the reason for this grandiose and grand terminal was that Communists wanted people who arrived in their capital to be impressed and overawed upon their arrival.

We successfully navigated though the luggage procedures and went out of the terminal to get our little bus to one of the many local airport hotels. John had made a reservation at the hotel which offered some sort of discount, but that didn't make it bad. When we arrived, we discovered that the hotel was newly constructed. There hadn't been enough time for service and facilities to age. We crawled into bed at about 2:30 in the morning.

The next morning we were up early to catch the 7:00 a.m. flight to Shenyang, a short hour and half away. We had breakfast at a buffet in the hotel. It was so memorable that I have completely forgotten what it was. The only recollection I have was that the coffee was terrible just like the coffee in the Beijing Hotel long ago. There was, however, enough caffeine in it to get us fully awake and going.

Our arrival in Shenyang, on the other hand, was quite memorable. Again, there was a new terminal at a new airport, nowhere near as grand as in Beijing, but still grand in my eyes. It was ten years old and replaced, at least for civilians, the military airport that we had used in 1977. Since we had come from Beijing on an internal China flight we had no immigration or customs formalities to worry us.

Mr. Mu, Mr. Shu, and Big Mu were there to greet us; and a wonderful greeting it was. In the past, we had never touched each other except with handshakes; this time it was with handshakes and hugs. I think we all had little tears in our eyes when we laid eyes upon each other. I recognized both of them instantly, as they did me. It was a thrill to see them again! Big Mu welcomed us to Shenyang in English. It was slow and halting, but it was English for sure. Mr. Mu added his words of welcome in English as well, but his command of the language was a little better than the last time I greeted him. Their faces and ours as well, split in the widest smiles one could imagine. These two men were the same ones I had spent every day with for ten months 23 years before. Though we were business friends, time and distance had worked their magic; we had remained friends.

Everyone spoke at once. "Where is your luggage? How are your wife and daughter?" Remember, both of these men had met my wife several times. These men had watched my daughter translate for several months. Their questions were not merely formal. "How is my wife? How is MayLi?" That was their translation of my daughter's name, Maria. The English "r" sound doesn't exist in Chinese, at least so I have been told.

The blue Mao jackets and pants were gone. The blue Mao caps with the little brims were gone. In their place were normal Western sports coats with harmonizing trousers, white shirts with ties appeared. We looked dingy by comparison. If you removed their heads, you would have thought you were in Keokuk, Iowa, greeting some men who worked in a local factory.

We had enough luggage to fill one of the two relatively small Chinese-built cars they had brought to the airport. We all squeezed into the other car and continued the excited and incomplete conversations and mini-conversations. We traveled down what appeared to me to be a brand new highway. I thought it was new because we passed several working crews fixing something. When I asked, someone said the highway was more than ten years old and connected the new airport with the city. For my benefit, they drove past the old Hotel Lioliang that we had used before. It was all boarded up and had not been used as a hotel for more than fifteen years! Instead of the dull and dingy sky colored grey to black with soot and smog, there was a regular blue one just like we have back home. It was marvelous.

We arrived at a hotel entrance adorned with a door attendant dressed up in a uniform befitting the best hotel in Paris or New York. With a grand flourish, the attendant flung open the doors of our cars and we all fell out. We were all laughing and still trying to carry on a normal conversation between old friends who had not seen one another for a long time. Sentences were not finished before a new one started.

The lobby of the hotel was large and spacious, another new thing for me in Shenyang, China. As we entered, Big Mu asked for our passports and told us he would take care of everything. "Please wait here," he commanded. I had the distinct impression that Big Mu, not Mr. Mu was in charge. He certainly acted as if he were. Big Mu walked up to the registration desk with our passports and began a long conversation with the young woman working there. We stood in the middle of the lobby with Mr. Mu. I learned later Big Mu had all the money budgeted for our visit.

"Mr. Mu, this doesn't look like the factory hotel." I did not remember the factory hotel having marble floors and walls. Nor did I remember a reception and registration counter that ran the entire width of the lobby.

"It is not the factory hotel," he said. That confused me a little.

"Mr. Mu, I thought that you told me that we were going to stay in the factory hotel."

"That is correct. You will stay in this hotel". If you think about his answers for a moment, although terse, both answers were correct if not as verbose as an American answer.

At this point, Big Mu walked back to us from his foray into hotel registration procedure. He had overheard Mr. Mu's comment.

"You will stay in this hotel as our guests. Please do not attempt to pay for anything in this hotel. I have made all arrangements just now with the authorities."

We were stunned. We had expected to stay in the dormitory of the factory. Instead, we were in a high-class hotel as their guests!

I said, "No, No, this cannot be!"

Big Mu interrupted, "Yes, it must be!" Now I was sure. Big Mu was definitely in charge of our visit.

That closed the subject. Big Mu had rarely opened his mouth at the contract talks. He had apparently become or, always had been a leader who was used to being obeyed. Who knows?

Mr. Shu was making a gesture on the side which seemed to indicate we were to agree with all of these arrangements. He put his finger to his lips and made the universal sign for "Shush, shush".

Big Mu went on, "We will wait here for you to clean up in your rooms. Then we will go to the factory to meet all your old friends and the Managing Director." His tone, although very, very friendly and cordial did not invite dissent. As ordered, we left our three hosts in the lobby.

We each went to our assigned rooms to check them out. Mine was a regular Western style moderate to high-level room with all amenities. If you did not look out the window at China and Shenyang, you might have thought that you were in a better class of commercial hotel in Chicago. The bed was comfortable, the bathroom was clean and spacious, the towels fresh and neat. Although a regular tourist might have expected all of this, I certainly did not; my mind was filled with visions of long ago.

John, Willy and I accidentally met in the elevator lobby on our way downstairs to rejoin our old friends. I asked John and Willy about their rooms. Willy had the same impression as I, but John was completely blasé. He had expected nothing less after entering the lobby of the hotel. We had forgotten he had been in China more recently than we had and had seen all the new construction. Willy and I were mentally stuck in the past!

Back in the lobby, we rejoined our friends. Everyone was promptly bundled back into cars. Since the luggage was gone, we could spread out into both. I went in the car with Big Mu. He drove. I nearly fell out of my seat. The last time I had seen him, he was riding a bicycle to and from the contract discussions. I distinctly remember seeing his long lanky legs sticking out of his "pajama bottom" Mao pants as he pumped his way down the street. The car was his, he told me. Another shock! Yours, how could that be? No one, particularly a factory worker, had his own car in Communist society. I didn't know whether to express my disbelief or just continue thinking it. Finally, I couldn't hold back.

"Your car:" I exclaimed in a very questioning tone..

"Yes. The factory give me a car because I am a manager." English verb tenses always give foreign speakers trouble. I guess the Chinese language does not have past, present, and future in it.

That explained it. But it really didn't. The car wasn't his personally, but he had the use of it. In my experience, only major people were given cars to use and usually they got a driver to go along with it. Driving wasn't a very common skill. But here this old friend was merrily driving his car down the main street of Shenyang. To make matters more confusing, as I looked around, there were many others driving cars. They all looked to me like the same men that I was used to seeing pedaling a bicycle in a crowd of other bicyclists. In fact, Big Mu was so intent on telling me about his car that he failed to see the car in front of him at a stop light. Stop lights! Where did they come from? We banged into the rear of the car and came to a jolting halt as Big Mu braked. Wait a minute! Fender Benders! What is China coming to?

Big Mu got out of the car. The driver of the car in front got out of his car. I am sure they were blaming each other for the accident, it sounded as if one of them would kill the other as I watched. They went at each other for a couple of minutes while each one closely examined the damages. I swear I thought I was in the parking lot of the mall near my home. These two Chinese men, who shouldn't have been driving insofar as I was concerned, continued haranguing each other. Then, to my utter disbelief, each handed his calling card to the other. It was like a documentary on highway accident behavior shown at a driving school. Big Mu got back in the   car. He said the damage was nothing. He said the other driver did not know how to drive,. He told him to call the personnel manager at the factory. Off we went to the factory. I couldn't believe my eyes or ears!

We drove into the factory courtyard. It appeared just as I remembered. The new computer building was in front of us; the building with the reception room was to our left; and the factory workshops were behind and to the left of the computer building. The location of the factory offices where the leaders, the accountants, and the administrators toiled was still a mystery. Big Mu parked his car under a sign with some Chinese characters. I asked what the message on the sign was. Without a smile, Big Mu told me that it said "Reserved for the Director of the Computer Center" My mouth must have dropped open. He said, "That's me." This was the guy who had just finished graduate school.

We went into the reception room. My first look made me feel warm and comfortable. Although it was a different reception room from the one I remembered, it was furnished the same as it had been twenty-three years before. The standard set of overstuffed couches and chairs were placed around the perimeter of the room. The standard beige slipcovers were absent however. This signaled to me that we were major visitors. A long time ago I was told the slip covers came off only when entertaining "leaders". The ubiquitous cotton doilies completely covered the chairs and sofas and the standard coffee table in front of each couch. An immense Chinese rug covered the center of the terrazzo floor, so thick you stumbled if you were not careful. Twenty some years before, that furniture arrangement had been frozen in my brain.

The same cast of characters on the stage with me then was seated on the sofas and chairs. As always, the seating sequence reflected their hierarchical positions. Dead center was a younger man with glasses whom I did not recognize. Mr. Mu introduced him to me as Mr. Su, the present leader of the factory. Big Mu explained to me that he was working in another factory at the time we were involved with the Blower Works. Next to him was Mr. He Ju San the leader of the factory at the time our contract was negotiated and signed. He was the veteran who had lost one hand. He used his other hand to grasp mine while he looked me right in the eye. Even though he had to be in his late seventies, his grip was strong, as was his voice in greeting. When we visited the factory early on, Mr. He Ju San as our host had almost exhausted us with his vitality and strength. He had not lost any of it over time. One had to admire Mr. He Ju San very much. He was a survivor. I know that his workers, at least the ones that I knew, revered him.

Mr. He Ju San had led the management group we had taken all over the United States in 1978 after signing the contract. At Chinese insistence, a clause had been written into the contract obligating us to set up a tour for their management. Even though IBM was renowned for executive tours and executive education, during the negotiation we had acted as if their requirement was too much to ask for. John Ryan and I figured that we could keep a score card of gives and takes just like Mr. Wu. The leaders of the factory would see how American factories operated. Aside from providing a trip outside Shenyang and China for people who had never left, we wanted to introduce them to modern factory computer tools and techniques. He was the one who, while in San Jose, California, refused to go to any Chinese restaurant that used old (pre 1956) Chinese characters in their advertised name. The restaurant had to use the new "simplified" characters introduced by the Communists in 1956. Simplification of Chinese text had been around for a long time; it was only the new Communist government that did anything about it. I never could figure out why he was so adamant on the subject until I realized they had a "minder" with them in the delegation. Even though Mr He Ju San and the other group members were tried and true Communists, the Ministry in Beijing had sent along a "minder" to be sure everyone who left China returned to China. That was standard procedure, in those days, for a Chinese group situation. The person they had sent stood out from the group like a "sore thumb". I never knew his name. I remember he was a rotund person of medium height, with the blackest hair I had ever seen.

It was so black and shiny that I asked the group's translator, Mr. Liu Da Foo, if hairpieces were common in China. After a pregnant pause, Mr. Liu Da Foo told me that this gentleman dyed his hair every couple of days. While in the United States, Mr. Liu Da Foo was sent to the drugstore several times to purchase the black hair dye for him!

The Chinese Red Guards, during the chaos of 1968-69, vilified Mr. He Ju San because he was a manager. Big Mu told me that the Red Guards had marched Mr. He Ju San up and down in front of an assembly of workers while wearing a dunce's hat. They accused him of not hewing to the strict Maoist line. A single accusation, whether true or false, whether from someone who knew the facts or from someone who simply didn't like you, was all it took to be dragged, literally, before a workers' committee. The rule was that you were guilty if accused. With all of that, he survived and prospered, at least in a Communist sense. HIS factory was chosen to get the first modern computer in China.

Next to be introduced, or re-introduced, was Mr. Liu; I never knew his surname. Mr. Liu was Mr. He Ju San's successor as leader of the factory. At the time, he was a deputy to Mr. He Ju San, and while in that position we had met him but had not developed the same relationship with him as with Mr. He Ju San. He, like Mr. He Ju San, was retired and returned to the factory to meet us. He greeted us warmly.

The third man I recognized immediately since he had met us at the airport. He was Mr. Shu, the author of the plan that brought all the new Western technology to the Shenyang factory. Mr. Shu sat with us in Beijing during the early months but had left in the middle of our discussions to go to Italy to learn about the new manufacturing techniques at Nuovo Pignone. We never knew that. In fact, in the early days we didn't even know his name. He just disappeared from our meetings.

We greeted each other profusely. He told me that I looked exactly as I had long ago. I knew that was pushing reality just a little. Of course, I said the same about him. The only hint of his age, well into his seventies, was a little grey in his hair. He was retired as well. The mandatory retirement age of 65 was enforced on managers and workers indiscriminately. The grey in his hair struck a chord. I looked around at all these senior men and realized that, except for Mr. Shu and me, everyone had a full head of very black hair. I thought to myself "maybe graying hair was not a Chinese genetic trait". The memory of the Chinese man, the "minder", who accompanied the management group tour to the U.S. followed instantly. I guess that some Chinese men, like some American men, are sensitive about their age and the grey hair accompanying it.

Mr. Shu had tried to convince me that the Chinese words for "teaching" and "learning" were the same. Therefore, he had suggested we substitute one for the other in the contract. I reminded him of that during our introduction and we both had a big laugh. Mr. Shu understood a little more English than before, but I am still not sure we were laughing at the same thing.

The last in the group were Mr. Mu and Big Mu, who, with Mr. Shu, had met us at the airport earlier. We all reminisced a while, asking how is this person? How is that person? It was interesting to note which people asked about which other people. Mr. He Ju San pointedly asked about Katie, the college translator we had sent on his American tour. Obviously, she had impressed him sufficiently that he remembered her name.

I asked after Mr. Liu Da Fu, their translator on that same tour. They told me he was still working at the factory, but no longer as a translator. He had become a sales representative and had traveled all over the world presenting their products to prospective purchasers. We were to see him later. His story is interesting since I remember his lamenting his absence from home, wife and daughter while he was in California. That feeling, I thought then, was so un-like a Communist that it stuck with me. In retrospect, at least in his case, Communists were just like us.. We talked for a while and then Mr. Mu suggested a tour of the factory workshops.

Deja vue. We walked down the center aisle of a vast workshop that had massive machines on each side. Mr. Mu described each machine in detail, as he did twenty odd years before. This time he added a footnote to each one. In his footnote, he mentioned that he purchased this machine tool from Germany or that milling machine from the U.S. or somewhere. He was quite proud; as he should have been, of his purchases of the newest technology. It was apparent from all those foreign machine tools that the Chinese had not yet mastered the manufacturing of these important machines. On the other hand, maybe this workshop was a test bed for imported machine tools. There was not one Chinese machine among them.

I asked him where the machines were that he showed us during our first visits, each one cost in excess of $1,000,000.

"All gone." He said proudly. "We have only the newest equipment". One thing, however, had not changed; only one of the new machines was working! It was near the end of the shop. All the others were standing silent giants. The Chinese "work unit" system was still functioning. The work units for that day had been achieved; the workers had quit working for the day.

We stopped in front of the working machine. Mr Mu Rei Lin told us, quite proudly, that it was a five-axis machine. I had to think for a minute to figure out exactly what that meant. The machine was capable, I guessed, of making things like jet engine blades, or silent ships' propellers; they have curves in them relating to five different radii. Years ago, the U.S. government would never have allowed the export of such high technology to a place like China. In fact, if such capability were known, there were people in government at that time who could easily have been convinced to bomb the factory. How things change!

Regardless of the high technology and Mr. Mu's pride, my overall impression of the workshop was negative. The movement, the bustling of an active factory was absent. There were several workers standing around the active machine, but the machine was doing the work, not the men. All the other machines were standing silent, the dust an inch thick on every surface. Even though this was not an assembly factory where you might see a continuous fabrication line, the factory did not appear to have much production going on. When I asked Mr. Mu about it, he told me that they were waiting for the marketing department to get them some orders. I also asked him about the Nuovo Pignone technology they had purchased and how many of those compressors had been produced. He told me they used far more advanced technology than that "old stuff". He said they had produced only one compressor based on the Nuovo Pignone designs. I was appalled by what I assumed was a tremendous waste of money. However, he quickly told me that they had improved on the Nuovo Pignone designs very soon after they received them. In that sense, there was no waste; in fact, their development had gone right according to plan.

We left the workshops and walked over to the Computer Building. Here, Big Mu took over. He proudly showed us his empire. In the computer room, with its raised floor and air conditioning, there was a set of little personal computers in the front. These were the only machines that were operating, or so it appeared to me. Behind them were several rows of other older computer units. Way in the back of the room, I saw what looked like the computer model we had sold them back in 1977. Sure enough, when I walked over to it, the nameplate was exactly that. The room was a computer museum!

Every level of computer that IBM had manufactured over the past twenty years was there. From the relatively small computer of 1977 to the fastest and largest commercial machine of the 1990's; each had a place in that room. I couldn't believe it! Why, in a factory on the edge of civilization, would their government install every new computer model as soon as it came out?

In a flash, it dawned on me. This was a big computer exhibition laboratory! This was a very large computer education facility! This factory probably used a tiny portion of the computing capacity represented by those machines. There was a much bigger plan at work here! I asked Big Mu about it. He told me that as new computers were announced, they purchased each one in turn. It was apparent they kept the original authority from Beijing regarding new technology and exercised it to the fullest. But still! We are talking about a couple of million dollars each time around. All those turned off computers spelled "closed exhibition hall" to me. Without even looking around the factory for computer terminals and control units for those terminals, we were looking at more than $20,000,000 in that room alone! Big Mu was rightly proud of his accomplishments.

I asked Big Mu about the engineers who had been trained along with him. He told me some very interesting things. The first thing they did after the IBM people had left Shenyang was to program and set up a remote terminal demonstration.

"Remote?" I asked incredulously. "Really remote?" These people were only weeks out of an IBM school at that time.

"Remote, very remote" he said quite proudly. There was a glint of humor in his eyes.

"If I remember, our contract said that the computer must be used only in local mode. That was one of the conditions." That was a very vivid memory. The Pentagon had insisted on it.

There was no answer, nor did I expect one. Big Mu went on with his story. "We set up a terminal in the Ministry of Machine Building in Beijing and demonstrated how we could run this computer from there. All the ministers and bureau chiefs came and watched. It was a very big event for us." His eyes went wide; he was reliving a moment of glory.

"I can imagine." I was still thinking of what the U.S. government would have done if they had known the first computer in China was remotely demonstrated. Remote computer control is a key to controlling missiles of all kinds! I could remember some military man in the Pentagon telling me that if the Chinese ever got the capability of remote computer control for anything, he would see me hanging in Tienamin Square. To prevent that, a major condition attached to our export license, and contract/

treaty as well, was the required bi-annual inspection visits to the computer site. Theoretically, those visits were intended to dissuade the Chinese from doing anything that was not in our original export license application. The Pentagon would have rejected our export applications if there had been the slightest hint that remote computing (like command and control of missiles) would be involved. Now, twenty-three years later I found out that they did a "no-no" <u>in-between</u> the visits. BUT, the U.S. opening of diplomatic relations with China intervened. At that moment, a potential enemy became a actual friend; all previous rules about exports and licenses went out the window. Our contract, however, remained in force. The Chinese contracted to keep that computer operating in local mode. I guess I am still naïve, I don't think that Big Mu was deliberately violating our deal. I think he was told to do that. He was just showing off the technical progress they had achieved. In fact, I thought that the whole Ministry was showing off. If it was just a remote computing demonstration, you could do that from across the street, down the block, across town; why not Beijing?

Big Mu continued. "After we came back from Beijing, we set up a computer programming school for the Ministry of Machine Building. For about four and half years, we ran programming classes for people from all over China. We had people from Sinkiang, Shanghai, Wushi, from all over." I began to think. This sounds like a super reason for the Ministry to get the computer in the first place.

They leveraged one computer, one education program, into a massive computer literacy project!

"What happened to the computer modernization program here at the factory?" I asked.

"We did that too." He said.

"How?"

"We split the six engineers into two teams. While one team was teaching, the other team was studying and installing programs here at the factory."

This was amazing. In a Western company, particularly a new small computer user, the computer team usually concentrated on one subject at a time. They normally had enough trouble installing one thing at a time without taking on any greater obligations, especially outside of their own shop. Big Mu was telling me his team of brand new computer engineers, not six months out of programming school, without any previous experience either in computing or programming or in the factory they worked for, seriously and successfully designed, planned, and installed an information system.

In addition, to make matters even more impressive, in my experience, undertakings of this magnitude were always accompanied by long and involved question and answer sessions with our IBM technical support people. To my knowledge, not one question of any substance was ever asked of our people. It was fantastic! It was also a little scary!

"Did your people get any extra money for this extra work of teaching and so on?"

"No. They did not get anything more than their regular salary." He said.

"What computer applications were put into the factory?" This was getting more interesting by the minute.

"Payroll." He answered.

"And how did it go"

"Fine"

"What about all those advanced factory management and inventory control programs we explained to the management during their tour?" After all, IBM had spent a great deal of time, and a great deal of money showing their management tour group around.

"Well, we tried some of those and found that they didn't fit." Big Mu's face reflected his disappointment.

"What do you mean 'they didn't fit?" This was getting more and more interesting!

"Our leaders who went on the trip to the U.S. were very enthusiastic about using the information tools that they had learned. When we put terminals in the workshop and tried to train some of the workers, they complained that we were changing their jobs and we did not pay for the changes. When we thought we had that problem solved, the workers came up with another objection. The worker committees wanted to stay with their old methods. The leaders decided that we should wait before trying again. We are still waiting."

Worker Committees, as described in the Communist organization manual, are the core organizational units of the Communist Party. Each work unit (or residential unit, for that matter) had a representative committee to deal with themselves and their management and jobs. They sound like labor unions, but here in China they are a lot more powerful. They operate just like small local political party committees here in the U.S. Without their support of any action, planned or actual, the change is doomed. And, so it was in Shenyang. In state-run factories like this one, the worker committee, not the management, decided information technology advances. I am sure, however, if a command came from Beijing, no matter what objections the Worker Committee might raise, the command would be obeyed. Too many leader jobs were at stake!

Big Mu sounded frustrated. As well he should have been. As he explained it, I could tell that the workers' committee was a constant source of irritation for him. My own perception of what he was explaining to me was a repeat of what always happens in the West. When a new computer application is introduced to the staff at a company, it is sometimes rejected when the application affect their jobs, rejection is based on fear of something new, fear of losing your job. Apparently, the same thing happens in China. In the West, however, the management usually prevails.

"Well, after payroll, which is basically a big calculation program, we did some inventory record keeping and a lot of printing jobs, and that was it."

"So, all of our efforts at executive education went down the tubes?"

"Not exactly." Big Mu answered

There was no point in pursuing this line of conversation; it opened up a can of worms for Big Mu. I couldn't help but be struck by the similarities of circumstances here in Shenyang and in the Western world, even though I had expected great differences. While the planners in Beijing had made it possible for tremendous advances in technology, basic Communist management techniques remained the same in these state-run enterprises. While there was a revolution in "technical" things, there was none in "people" things. This conclusion matched the stories that I had read about the demise of state-owned factories in China. Since they couldn't change the workers, they had to close the factories down at a tremendous human cost. In Shenyang alone, twelve thousand workers lost their jobs when the Transformer Factory and the Wire Cable Factory were closed!

After our tour, we went back to the hotel to get ready for the welcoming banquet. The banquet was in the hotel where we were staying. Big Mu called me from the lobby to tell us to go to the mezzanine floor dining facility; he would meet me there. When we got out of the elevator, Big Mu took us down a long blue-carpeted corridor. On each side, doors were open to very large banquet tables. Apparently, the style of banquet restaurants had not changed in twenty-odd years. In our culture, restaurants are single rooms with many, many tables in them. In their culture, good restaurants were many rooms with a few tables in each. However, even this is changing. We ate in several restaurants with western style seating.

We arrived at our room. Upon entering, it was like stepping into a regal dining hall. An immense round table was set up in the middle of a large room. The table was set with the most ornate gold tableware and crystal I have ever seen, especially in China. The table glittered like a Tiffany showcase for gold jewelry. I had no idea if it was really gold or real crystal, but it sure glistened as if it were real. Maybe the secret to the appearance was in the shine and reflected lights. I simply did not expect such a regal looking table; the décor was imperial!

All our old friends, as well as a few new ones were waiting for us. One at a time, Mr. Mu introduced our old friends. The first introduction was to the plant director we dealt with long ago, Mr. He Ju San. He had welcomed us at the factory. Then the two directors who led the plant after Mr. He Ju San had left. Of course, he and all the others had been retired for some time. Mr. Mu and Big Mu were the only people still working from the original group at the negotiating table. There were other men there who had held important posts in the plant at that time, who did not participate directly in our negotiations. I wondered why these men were there. After a moment's thought, I realized these unknown men were there simply because they were friends of the people I <u>did</u> know. They had been invited to join in our banquet, complete with booze, beer and beef. It was a post retirement benefit if you had the right friends. Whoever said Communist business leaders are different?

Almost at the moment we all took our places at the table, a short stocky and much younger person (not real young, just younger than all the others in the room) appeared. We had met him at the Reception Room when we arrived. Mr. Mu immediately brought him over to where I was standing. That action, more than any words, told me that he was more important than all the others were. Mr. Mu introduced him to me.

"Mr. Josep, you remember our Director, Mr. Su" (again, Mr. Mu's "ph" problem)

"Of course. How do you do? I am very pleased to see you again."

Mr Mu translated. Anyway, he spoke Chinese to Mr. Su. Since this part of the greetings script was standard, he really did not have to wait for me, or Mr. Su, to speak. He may have been telling him my life's history for all I knew. If I had to guess, that was exactly what he was doing.

When Mr. Mu was done, Mr. Su turned to me and, through the translator, said,

"So, you are the computer pioneer"

"Well, that's a little exaggerated" I countered. That sentence must have given the translator a problem. He called over the older translator for the evening, Liu Da Foo (our "Four of Gang" translator) for help. They conferred off to the side for a second or two and then our translator spoke to Mr. Su. I think the word 'exaggerated' was not in the Chinese/English lexicon. Mr. Su was used to his conversation being translated, so he patiently waited for the side issues to be resolved. Then he continued.

"We welcome you and your friends to the Shenyang Blower Works. We are sorry that you have been absent for so many years, but we are happy that you have come back. Please sit down; we can talk at the table." This gentleman was used to being obeyed. As he was saying that last bit, he had me by the elbow gently pushing me towards the table. He was in a hurry to get the banquet going. All the others in the room were used to obeying; they immediately moved to their seats. I don't know how all these men knew the exact seating protocol, but they moved to the correct seat in the exact order of the hierarchy. Each of the foreigners was gently steered to his proper seat. We were put in the correct order starting with Mr. Su. Americans, in a similar situation, would have milled around for a little while and someone might even have whispered aloud, "Where am I supposed to sit?

After we sat down, the waiters began bringing food, which they placed on the turntable in the center of our table. As always, the Chinese host next to each visitor explained what each dish was and offered it to his guest. Big Mu began the conversation with the story of how Mr. O'Leary ate nothing but beef stew for five months in the Peking Hotel restaurant. He hoped that Mr. O'Leary had learned to appreciate good Chinese food in the intervening years. Willy had to tell them that after we had installed their system, he had gone on with IBM in Hong Kong for several years. He had overcome his New York suspicion of all foreign food by now. When we had all finished with the initial courses, the serious drinking began.

I always thought that one of the people present at these banquets was actually the stage manager. How else could they keep things flowing, not just the food, but the liquor, the toasts and the conversation as well? This evening was no exception.

I never detected the signal, but at the very moment I laid down my chopsticks for a rest, Mr. Su picked up the glass filled with Mao-Tai and turned to me.

Mr. Su continued from where he left off. "I want to welcome our guests officially to Shenyang and wish them well for their visit with us. I also want to toast our friendship which has lasted for more than twenty years. "Gom Bei". I knew what that meant, "Bottoms Up". Therefore, I dutifully bottomed up. Out of the corner of my eye, I noticed that Mr. Su, although he had put the glass to his lips, had not drunk any of the liquid. I remembered that many of the higher-level bureaucrats with whom we dined also did the same thing, toast but not drink. In fact, at one dinner many years ago, I asked out host why he wasn't drinking. With a smile, he told me that he had brought along a younger associate, pointing to him, to do his drinking for him. There must be a director's school somewhere that teaches directors how to toast and not drink. However, stupid an American that I was, I had to ask Mr. Su why he wasn't drinking. Everyone else was, indeed, with great vigor.

Mr. Su told me this was his second of four dinners that night. He also said he had a digestive problem that prevented him from drinking any alcohol. I could certainly understand both reasons. If he drank early in the evening, he would be in no condition to speak at, or even attend any of the other dinners. The others were with customers, major buyers who were certainly far more important to him than we were. This information brought up another thought. Chinese relationships were very complex. He had honored his predecessors and us by taking the time to come to this dinner for people he did not know and who did not rank as high as he did, particularly since I was retired. The Chinese take these obligations very seriously.

The dinner progressed very well. I don't remember the dishes, but I do remember how beautifully they were presented. There was endless toasting and drinking. In my suspicious mind, perhaps this was the reason so many of these retired people were invited. For whatever the reason, it was a wonderful evening and I was happy that when it was all over I could just get in the elevator and collapse on the bed in my room. Before I left everyone, I noticed that Mr. Mu and Mr. Wong Go Bin were planning the rest of the evening. Apparently, they could handle a lot more liquor than I could. In that respect, Mr Mu had not changed one iota in twenty-three years.

Every night thereafter, for the entire time we were in Shenyang, there was a banquet in another restaurant. However, this was the last time we saw Mr. Su. We saw the retired men at many of these other banquets.

As we were leaving, Big Mu came up to me and asked me if I could come to his office in the morning to discuss a personal matter. I was very surprised and very much intrigued. What kind of 'personal' matter would he want to discuss with me? In all the years, that word was never used!

There were two cars to pick us up the next morning. Normally one car was sufficient to take all of us. Our escort explained that one car was for John and Willy, the other was for me. John and Willy were going on a tour of the city. I went to Big Mu's office at the factory Computer Building.

After the usual greetings, he asked me to sit at his desk and read some documents he had placed there. As I read, I realized that I was reading a letter from the University of California at the Berkeley International Language program accepting someone named MuCong for the coming year. The letter also stated that an advance payment of $10,000 for tuition, room and board was necessary. A check attached to the papers was payable to the

University in that amount. In addition, there were some other documents relating to this MuCong's character and a completed application for a U.S. student visa. There was a letter from the NorthEast Computer Center attesting that MuCong was working there and that proficiency in English was a requirement for the job. This letter went on to say that upon completion of the studies, this person would return to Shenyang.

I turned to Big Mu.

"Who is MuCong?"

"She is my daughter." He replied. My mouth fell open. Daughter!

He continued. "My daughter is 22 years old and wants to go to America to learn English. She is a graduate accountant here. She works in Beijing for an accounting company. She cannot get a student visa to enter your country."

"What is this NorthEast Computer Company?" I asked.

Big Mu said, "Me". He was laughing. That made no sense to me at all.

"You?"

He continued. "This is my company. It was set up when we first started so that we could do many things for the First Ministry in Beijing that wouldn't concern the factory. I am the managing director. We are also the Computer Department for the factory.

The best answer that I could manage was "Oh"

A big "light" went on in my head. He was asking me for some help with regard to his daughter. However, in his Chinese way, he did not know how to come right and ask for it.

"Why can't she get a visa?" I had no idea.

"I don't know. When she goes to U.S. consulate, they just say no visa. She is coming to Shenyang tomorrow to make application again."

"Maybe I can go to the consulate with her tomorrow and explain to the officer she should get one." Bingo! He had led me, or I had led myself, right into the thing that he wanted.

His face broke into a big smile. The offering of help avoided the necessity of asking for it; asking for it brought the attendant risk of refusal and a big loss of face. A potential problem turned into a win-win situation.

The next day while John and Willy toured the city again, I was in Big Mu's office meeting his daughter. Together we went to the U. S. Consulate. She turned out to be a tall young woman, (he was tall also, hence the name 'Big' Mu) and very good looking. I teased Big Mu, saying that she must look like her Mother, but the joke fell flat when he, very seriously, said that was true. MuCong's spoken English was very rudimentary, but understandable. We chit chatted for a while. She told me about her job in Beijing, and about her college. She impressed me as a cultured well-mannered person. Big Mu drove us to the American consulate.

We had to show our passports to get in the long line for visa applications. The security precautions were daunting. The line wound its way around the gates and blocks that prevented anyone from driving right up to the building. Inside the building, we had to wait in two different rooms, just by ourselves, before being allowed to approach the window where the Consulate officer was reviewing applications. Then, just before the last serpentine entry to the application counter, a sign proclaimed in English and Chinese (I guess), that only one person at a time would be permitted on this last step. I asked one of the many guards there, if it would be possible for me to accompany this woman to the counter. The guard replied with a very emphatic "NO" and vigorously pointed to the sign. I tried to explain. The guard told me that if I wanted to speak to the visa Officer, I must wait at the end of the line until all visa applicants were processed. At that time, the visa officer would be happy to answer any questions.

Meanwhile, MuCong went up to the window counter and passed her papers through the bank-style glass windows to the officer. I could see that he asked her a couple of questions; I could see her head shaking in reply. Then he stamped the documents. She returned to where I was waiting.

"What happened?"

"My application was denied." That was not her exact phrasing or words; she did not have all those words in her vocabulary. Nevertheless, the result was clear; her face showed it.

"What did he stamp on your papers?"

She showed me her Chinese passport. On the last page, he had added a stamp entitled "U.S. Consulate Shenyang" to two duplicate stamps already there. They kept a record of each time that passport was shown to the officer; each rejection was recorded. Each time that MuCong made application, the reviewing officer would know how many times she had been there before and how many times she had been rejected.

We sat and waited for the line to be processed. After about an hour, a guard came over to us. She motioned for me to enter the serpentine before the window. I stepped up to the window. It was just like a well-secured teller position in a busy bank. The glass seemed to be inches thick, you spoke into a microphone; application papers slipped under the window. It was scary to think that our Consulate people had to operate from behind such barriers. I identified myself.

The officer was a young man, maybe 30-35 years old and very pleasant looking. He was sitting on a high stool so that he could keep his elbows on the counter. To his left was a long rack. It held many, many stamps. I thought that this was the only office where no writing was ever necessary; they had a stamp for everything. He was holding one in his hand. After some pleasantries, I told him I wanted to find out why MuCong, I pointed to her waiting for me, couldn't get a visa. His answer stunned me!

The officer replied, "We have not issued a student visa to a young single Chinese female applicant in the last two years." He was straight up and down.

I said, "You've got to be kidding! Why not?"

He continued. "We have statistics that clearly prove young, single Chinese women granted student visas never return to China when their education is completed. Student visas turned out to be another way to get around the immigration laws at home. In order to stop that, Washington told us to stop issuing visas."

I thought to myself. For the faults of a few, everyone must suffer. Then I said, "I would be happy to sign that I would be responsible for her and I would make certain that she would return"

Still pleasantly, he replied. "I would be happy to accept your certification. It wouldn't make a difference. Even the Consul General cannot issue a visa."

I was still holding out some hope. "Have there been any exceptions made under special circumstances?"

"Not that I know of. No matter how I personally feel about any individual situation, this Consulate has not and will not issue a student visa." He pointed to his rack of stamps on the side. "You see those stamps?" He didn't wait for an answer. "The student visa stamp is gone. Even if I wanted to sneak one in, which I don't, the stamp is gone." I thought to myself. That is Draconian!

I made some comments about this state of affairs and then left. MuCong had been watching this conversation. She probably thought that my intercession would produce a visa. When I repeated my conversation, her face dropped another notch. I told her there was no way she was getting a visa to the U.S.

Several days later, Big Mu told me that MuCong was going to England for graduate studies in accounting. Big Mu e-mailed me many months later to tell me she applied to the University of Manchester. She had been accepted. Her English visa arrived without fanfare or problems. MuCong would receive her Masters degree in one year. She planned to return to China speaking English fluently, albeit with an English accent.

No matter what we were doing during the day, our days concluded with a big dinner. The first one, as I have described, was in our hotel. After that, the dinner banquets were held in various restaurants. At one of them, I protested that we

American guests were unable to reciprocate their hospitality. I said we would be the hosts at the following evening's banquet. Measured by the uproar that ensued, I had just committed the worst cultural gaff imaginable. Big Mu said, "Impossible." Mr. Shu just shook his head. Even Mr. Wong Go Bin, the supreme politician, mumbled something. Mr. Mu, already in his cups for the evening, said, "You cannot. We have already paid for them."

He went on. "We have budgeted $5,000 U.S. dollars for your visit. We must spend it. You cannot pay!" I had visions of Communist budgets of years ago and the "plans" they represented.

Total silence descended on the table. It was so quiet for a couple of seconds a gulp of air would have sounded like a hurricane. Then everyone tried to speak at once. In the "hubbub" that followed it was obvious that Mr. Mu had committed a faux pas far greater than mine. Even an ignorant American, like me, understood. It was most impolite to tell your guests how much you were spending on their visit. This was not a cultural thing; this kind of etiquette and politeness does cross international borders. Everyone tried to change the subject as quickly as possible. The dinner ended in the middle of this "hubbub".

Big Mu came up to me as we were leaving. He told me that Mr. Mu should not have spoken in that manner. He said that Mr. Mu sometimes gets that way when he has too much to drink. He apologized if Mr. Mu's comments made us uncomfortable. This gentle man was a real gentleman!

Mr. Mu's unfortunate comment gave us cause to think. Some things had happened on our sightseeing tours that, until this moment, didn't ring true. Big Mu had taken all three of us to a Chinese flea market when we asked if there was some way we could purchase some antiques. The flea market, which was not very large, had a lot of inexpensive "junk" laid out on the ground. I selected a little carving. Big Mu asked me "Do you want that?"

"I think so." I answered.

"Let me have it." I thought he wanted to look at it. Instead, he took it out of my hand and went over to the little guy selling it. As I watched, he took some money out of his pocket and paid for it. I really objected to that and I told him so.

"Never mind, it is nothing!" was his answer.

"How much did it cost? I will give you back the money when I get the chance to exchange some dollars."

He said, "Never mind" and turned away.

Big Mu did the same thing with Willy and again with John. However, with John, he had to have an animated conversation in Chinese before John would give him the thing he selected. John told me later in the car that he really objected to Big Mu's laying out the money for him. It was unnecessary. Nevertheless, Big Mu prevailed.

Now, his actions all made sense.

After four or five days, our hosts were running out of local tourist spots. They were taking their hosting business very seriously. Our interest in buying little souvenirs to take back home must have struck a chord. Big Mu asked if we would like to purchase some jade carvings or jewelry. We all jumped at his suggestion. He went on to tell us that one of his programmers was from Anshon, one of the two jade mining areas in China. This man had a brother-in-law there who made and sold jade artifacts.

I thought the next words out of Big Mu's mouth were going to be "I can get it for you wholesale!" or the Chinese equivalent. He actually said the brother-in-law would give a good price for jade. Close enough!

Anshon was relatively close to Shenyang; it was about two hours away by car. If we wanted, he would ask his man to speak to his brother-in-law to make the arrangements. We could also visit an interesting jade museum in the city. Simultaneously, we all answered "Yes".

Off we went. We had to go in two cars again because the little Chinese manufactured cars couldn't hold three Americans and two tall Northern Chinese. I went with Big Mu again. John and Willy went in another car with a driver and the Reception Department host. We would meet at the Jade Museum in Anshon. It was not long before we were on a four-lane highway heading east. Once we were outside the city, it was desolate. I didn't see any buildings, billboards, or even fences. The difference was the lack of fences. In the U.S., there are fences everywhere you look on the highways. Sometimes there are billboards, although not on the newer roads. However, there are always fences. Whether the fences were there to keep you in, or they were there to keep you out; fences are the most visible American icons on the highways. Here there was nary a one. There were few cars as well. The feeling of isolation was overwhelming. Our driver must have been traveling at over 90-100 miles per hour because our other car was nowhere in sight. The Chinese car was neither heavy nor sluggish; we were flying. Even though there was nothing we could hit, I asked Big Mu to slow down just a tad. I told him that I got seasick when I went so fast. He must have thought he was dealing with yet another crazy old foreigner.

Big Mu told me this highway had just been completed to Dalien, although we were not going that far. Perhaps we could go to Dalien another time. He told me that the government was building highways as quickly as they could. In a month or so, another highway would connect Shenyang and Beijing. He said these highways would soon cover China and that was causing another problem. No one could use them. "Look at how empty it is!" Trucks and cars were not as common in China as they are in the U.S., he told me. Although the Army had plenty of trucks and cars, there were not enough in the civilian economy. The government was encouraging foreign automakers to build factories in China to fill that gap. He said that is why you see strange-looking American Buick automobiles in Shenyang

As he was describing this phenomenon, I had visions of the Communist centralized planning I experienced when I was here last. The central planning people got it backwards. The highways came first. While they were deteriorating from no use, plants were manufacturing the cars to use them. That's wrong side up. The cars came first, the highways for the cars followed. On the other hand, I could have it wrong. If the Chinese had a lot of cement, but not a lot of steel, then their sequence made more sense. The moral of this story is not to judge things too quickly.

By some fluke or miracle both cars arrived at the museum at the same time. They must have some sort of internal clock that they synchronize with each other before starting out on a trip. The museum had every kind of jade and every shape of carving you could imagine. The courtyard of the museum had an immense futuristic sculpture of the sun and the stars (so I was told) that was at least 15 feet high and equally wide. It was jade, of course, and the only thing I could think of was "How the hell did they get it out of the ground?" Inside the museum, the carvings were scaled down somewhat from that monster outside in the front.

Some of the exhibits were interesting, but after two floors of ill-lit carvings in colored and well as green jade, I was ready to leave. I asked Big Mu if we were going to see the brother-in-law with the good priced jade. He said, "We are waiting here until the time for meeting the man." That's the reason we had wandered up and down this jade heaven for a while. We are waiting for brother-in-law. Again, as if by signal, we were hustled back into the cars for a trip to downtown Anshon. I say "downtown", but I don't really know if, in fact, we actually went "downtown".

We drove up to a string of stores located on the ground floor of what appeared to be an apartment building. Some people were waiting in front of one of the shops. Big Mu's programmer got out and had a riotous greeting with one of the men. I guessed that we had found the brother-in-law and the store was the place with the good jade price we were promised. There was lot of shaking hands with introductions; none of which I understood. John understood and he gave them back as good as he got.

We went inside a shop. I have no idea what the brother-in-law's connection was with this particular shop. Whatever the familial connections there were, if any at all, Big Mu told us we did not have to bargain with the sales ladies. They would automatically quote their best price up front. The three of us separated and proceeded to make our selections.

I completed my selections first. I selected a carved jade horse for one daughter, a gorgeous set of earrings for the other and a bunch of jade bracelets for the grandchildren. When I went over to the cashier or at least to the woman who looked like she accepted money, Big Mu stopped me. He took the selections out of my hands, continuing across the shop to this woman. I said, "Wait a minute, I have to pay for those." He turned around to me and said, "I will take care. You can wait in the car." I was annoyed. I did not want him to pay for those things; they were personal and had nothing to do with my visit to the factory.

"Big Mu, you can't do that. I will pay for presents I get!" He did not even answer; it was like I hadn't spoken at all.

"Big Mu, I want to pay for those things!" I was getting angry. I think he heard the anger in my voice. He put the jade pieces on the counter, nodded to the woman and turned around to me.

Using his most authoritative voice, he said, "You cannot buy anything in Shenyang! You are guest here! Please do not be angry." That was it.

He then paid for the presents that Willy had selected. John heard all of this, both the English part and the Chinese part that Big Mu used with the woman. He didn't select anything, even though Big Mu told him to do so. Later he told me it would have been an insult to have them pay for a gift. He did not have the same relationship as we did. In the Chinese culture, they were repaying Willy and me a debt; they did not owe him anything.

We, Big Mu and I, had a replay of that scene a couple of days later. I discovered I was unable to fit all the gifts and other materials in the suitcases I brought with me. I stupidly told Big Mu of my problem. He suggested I go to the discount store and purchase a larger suitcase. Since he used all the right pronouns in that offer, I said fine. We went to one of the nine super large warehouse discount clubs in Shenyang. What a revelation that was! Big Mu showed his membership card. The store was immense. It was K-Mart or Wal-Mart doubled. Every consumer product manufactured in the world seemed to be there. There were fruit and vegetable departments, there were dairy departments, there were canned groceries, refrigerators, American candy, radios and TVs, electronics and of course suitcases. I checked out the prices of American products I recognized as we walked down the aisle to the suitcase department.

All the prices I looked at were about 30% cheaper than in the U.S. I couldn't believe it! How could a manufacturer sell something in China cheaper than where it is made? If you factor in the cost of getting the product from the U.S. to Shenyang to the basic U.S. price, it is impossible, or so I thought, to price it less than in the U.S.

I asked Big Mu, "How come all these things are so cheap? The price is less expensive than at home."

He smiled. "That is because you are in China."

I said, "No, seriously. These prices are less than at home." His answer was so simple and I felt so stupid.

"Our government controls all prices."

I was thrown completely by this apparent surfeit of goods and products. After a few days of observing people's apparent freedom, of western style restaurants and all the other visual cues to the Western world, I had completely forgotten that I was in a Communist country. I was in a Communist country that still had the old style government, even though clothed in a new style economy. What better capitalism than Communist Capitalism?

When I made my selection, I carried it to the checkout counter. Big Mu and I had another of those arguments; this time he actually pushed me away.

Somebody decided we needed some sea air. One day they loaded us all into our cars and set out for Dalien. Dalien is located on the China Sea across the water from northern Japan. It was, and maybe still is, a major port for northern China. We started out very early. The foreign guests ate breakfast in the hotel. All our Chinese friends had missed theirs, however, because of the early hour. The factory cafeteria had not yet opened. Dalien was a four-hour journey over a relatively new and major east-west highway. As soon as we were out of the city we foreigners all fell asleep. I awoke when the ride got very bumpy.

We had pulled into the Chinese version of a freeway pit stop. The drivers and hosts were going to get something to eat. "Would you like something to eat"? They had stopped at the most ramshackle hut I had ever seen. There was a large hand lettered (Chinese characters) sign stretching over the door. I assumed that the sign read the Chinese equivalent of McDonald's. When I entered, I thought I was in a time warp. If you ignore the Chinese environment, the shop looked exactly like the Mom and Pop eateries that had sprung up along the new highways in the U. S. when I was a kid. An old man, was also the cook, the greeter, the cashier in this establishment. No matter that it looked like it was going to fall down any second; it was spotless inside. The counter, the tables and the chairs were all different, all hand built. Each of the utensils, the cooking ones and the eating ones were different. It was wonderful!

I wasn't familiar with the home cooking smells of a Chinese breakfast, so I excused myself and went back outside. I asked Big Mu if there was a men's toilet nearby. He pointed to another doorway down the side of the building. I walked down to the door and pushed it open. I wasn't familiar with that smell either, so I passed. If I could only educate myself to all the new odors, I might have taken many photos. The scene was priceless. We were in the middle of nowhere; this pit stop had a 360-degree view of a completely un-littered horizon. Our hosts quickly ate their breakfast and we returned to the highway.

We arrived in downtown Dalien about noontime. Big Mu was looking for a famous restaurant so we could taste a sample of

Dalien cooking, famous for seafood. Apparently, he got the name from a cousin of another guy that works for him. I thought that Big Mu spent his childhood in Dalien. I asked him. He said, yes. He went on to say that his Mother still lives there. He planned to visit her while we were sightseeing after lunch. When we stepped out of the cars, it was like stepping on to a sidewalk in the middle of Miami. The street was very wide, there were no bicyclists, the large multistoried buildings all looked new, and everything was clean. I asked Big Mu why Shenyang didn't look like this.

He said it was because of the Mayor of Dalien. The Mayor was the son of a very high-ranking Communist Party man in Beijing. He came to Dalien because of that connection. He dictated (my word, not Big Mu's) the reconstruction of the central part of Dalien. He could do things right without any fear of criticism, again because of his connections. Big Mu said that nothing happened in Dalien without his approval. In Shenyang, on the other hand, the Mayor had to get agreement from his bureau heads before anything happened. His position was dependent upon their approval, not the other way around. He gave me another lesson on Communist government structure; although I'm not sure what the lesson was. I hoped he was not telling me that dictatorship is good.

We went sightseeing after one of the best meals I ever had in China. The seafood was delicious; the service was beautiful. After lunch, Big Mu went off to visit his Mother. We went sightseeing. After an hour, I can confidently say that Dalien is a beautiful city. The park by the sea is particularly beautiful. We all enjoyed our visit. Our trip back to Shenyang was uneventful. The foreigners slept again.

The rest of the time in Shenyang passed very quickly. However, like all visits, when it's time to go, the hosts were happy to see us go and the guests were happy to get back to regular dinner meals in the evening. Willy and I had a wonderful time with our old friends; John Chow did not have to show me China. In fact, I think that he was just a little over-awed with the reception that we received. Sometime later John Chow told me of the debt he felt for the treatment he had received in Shenyang. In many ways, this visit had been a revelation for me; many things that happened 23 years ago began to make sense.

After Shenyang, we moved on to Beijing. I wanted to visit with Mr. Wu. I wanted to ask him for some facts and impressions from 23 years ago. Finding him was a problem. In 1977-78, we never called him; he called us. We had no way to contact him on our own even with translators. His office was a complete mystery to us. 23 years later the problem still existed.

My only contact was through Big Mu in Shenyang. He told us his subsequent computer purchases were arranged thorough a First Ministry bureau headed by a lady, Madam Shi Yu Ping. After 1978, so many organizations from so many ministries wanted to purchase foreign computers (including IBM's) that a separate bureau was set up to handle all the contacts and purchasing. This lady headed that unit and because of the nature of her bureau, she was very powerful and influential.

With so many orders coming from China, IBM management decided to move the marketing and support operations much closer to China. IBM Japan was chosen to handle all these affairs.

The logic of that decision was easy to follow geography played a big role as well as the fact IBM Japan was already providing logistical and technical support for our China operations. In retrospect, the decision turned to be a major debacle. Cultural considerations had been ignored, not purposely, but unconsciously. Their ignorance came back with a vengeance!

IBM Japan assigned a manager and several support personnel. The manager was an up and coming man well thought of by his managers. He was a typical Japanese manager; dictatorial and molded in the form of the Japanese warriors of the past, the Samurai. I thought they considered women second-class citizens (there were no women marketing or technical personnel at that time) and treated them accordingly.

On the Chinese side several historical events were at play. Chinese women, particularly under Communism, are the equal of men. There is no flexibility in that ideology. A Chinese woman was in charge of purchasing IBM computers. On top of that, the Chinese either remember or are taught about the Japanese atrocities against Chinese and particularly Chinese women during the Japanese occupation of eastern China. This knowledge would tend to have one walk and talk gingerly about Chinese women!

Unfortunately, that did not happen. Madame Shi became so frustrated with her treatment by the Japanese manager she communicated with IBM in the U.S. in desperation. She sent a telex to my headquarters requesting my presence in China. Normally, a request like that would have been slowly, very slowly, handled; IBM was not in the habit of favoring personal sales contacts. However, the China market was exploding and this lady was handling the explosives. I had not had much contact with Madame Shi while I was in China negotiating with Mr Wu. Her tenure began after my departure. So I went back to China in 1981 to see if I could resolve Madame Shi's problem.

I met her in her office in the brand-new Beijing Hotel. The hotel had converted one wing to offices while the other wing was in the process of complete renovation. After some chit-chat, I heard chapter and verse of her troubles with the Japanese manager. In essence, he had ignored her. *The* situation had gotten to the point that she did not want to do business with IBM even though in very other respect we had a sterling reputation. Madame Shi made it quite plain to be she wouldn't conduct her business through a Japanese IBM.

I also interviewed several of the other Japanese marketing and technical support people I could find in Beijing while I was there. They confirmed much of what Madame Shi had described to me. I left Beijing after telling Madame Shi we respected her comments and appreciated her bringing it to our attention. I went to Tokyo to speak with the IBM management there.

It was obvious the Japanese manager had to go. There was no way he was going to change his attitude toward the Chinese, nor could he publicly lose face in Japan by making such a drastic change. So he had to go. I told the IBM Japan President exactly that and that is exactly what happened. Several months later the entire China support team and management was moved to Hong Kong with an American manager.

With all of this background, when we arrived in Beijing I contacted Madame Shi and enlisted her help in locating Mr. Wu. She not only found him, but arranged a lunch with us at the Beijing Hotel.

Mr. Wu looked exactly the same as he did 23 years before. He was retired, of course, and seemed very happy at seeing us after so long. Nothing new was revealed during our lunch. He did comment, however, not once, but several times, that he felt we had lost money on that first sale in order to get it. He offered no proof for his assertion; he just felt it. I had visions of him waving that little red book around containing, he said, U.S. prices of all IBM products. He was convinced we had lowered the price (at his urging) in order to get that business and all subsequent business. I tried explaining our price to him was the regular U.S. price plus 20% for international uplifts. Even though the cost of our 10 month marketing effort cost about $300,000, it was not factored into the price. All exploratory marketing expenses were separately budgeted and accounted for. Even if our marketing costs were factored in, the profit margin was still positive. I explained that when you manufacture hundreds and hundreds of the same product, the cost of any single one is relatively small; he refused to accept my explanation.

Even with our disagreement, we all had a very pleasant time. If I ever return to Beijing, I would like to see Mr. Wu again; he was an important part of my life for a long time.

Chapter 15 – Revolution Revisited

When everything is said and done, I wondered now in 2010 whether there really had been a revolution involving these three men. Mr. Shu, Mr. Mu and Big Mu had successfully come out of isolation. Between the three of them, they had successfully transformed a factory operating almost entirely by hand, to one operating the most modern machine tools and computers available in 1977. Against significant odds, they had successfully dealt with a Western company that, prior to these events, was just as isolated from them as they were from it. Sure, they had selected, purchased and installed the first modern computer in the Peoples Republic of China; sure, they had completely remade their manufacturing operations in a western image; sure, they had taught hundreds of Chinese new computer programming and techniques; but had that been revolutionary? Had their factory profited from all this activity? Had they profited from this major modernization? Had China profited from this deal?

None of these men is working at the factory any longer. Mr. Shu retired first, followed by Mr. Mu in 2002. Big Mu left the factory to work as a consultant. Come to think of it, consultants didn't exist in the Chinese Communist environment of 1976. In fact, I discovered that there was only one person who was involved in 1976 that was still working in the factory. The younger people, those six electrical engineers, had moved within 6 years of the initial installation. Information specialists move around in the West as well. In that respect, their transitory employment was just like the West.

For the first ten years after the computer arrived, the whole installation functioned mainly as a unit of the ministry in Beijing, if not in name, then certainly in fact. By 1990, the factory itself no longer functions as it had. The factory couldn't compete in an open world; their Communist overhead drowned them financially. The factory, without its original computer department, was downsized dramatically. The factory plant moved to another site in Shenyang. The factory made a joint operation arrangement with an American company to stay in existence.

Second, the whole central national planning and control apparatus engineered by the Communist government had been removed or collapsed under its own weight; I don't know which. As China became a player on the world trade stage, it became apparent to the Chinese their state-owned factories couldn't compete. They had cheap labor, that's true, but in any manufacturing operation where labor was not the major component, these massive state-owned plants simply had too much overhead. The Shenyang Blower Works, a technological giant yesterday, is hanging on by its collective fingers. All the other major plants in Shenyang, the transformer plant, the wire and cable plant, have closed. More than 12,000 workers have been put out of work. For every worker holding down a productive job, there are three or four others benefiting from the no-work/welfare operation of Communism.

Mr Mu said to me, "A U.S. Company came here in 2000 and offered to buy the factory."

"Oh", I said. "What happened?"

Mr. Mu continued, with much sadness on his face. "They wanted to buy the factory and promised to keep 1,600 workers."

"I said, "What would happen to the other 4,000 workers?"

"They would be fired." He said. As phlegmatic as he was, even he had been jolted by the revelation that about 75% of the workers were not essential to making the product. Unlike Western economies the prior Chinese system tolerated extensive labor overhead, all in the interest of full employment. Before Deng invented this new "Communist" form of capitalism a massive lay-off could never have happened!

The all-inclusive, self-contained manufacturing operation to produce high technology gas compressors changed forever. The foundry operation that produced the castings of the compressors was "outsourced" to former workers who opened their own much smaller factory with less overhead far out in the countryside. The computer operations that helped them produce molds for foundry castings went with them. The design department along with its extensive computer operations was outsourced to former employee engineers. The painting department also went away. The only original department remaining from the original revolution in 1976 is the milling department. The milling department scrapes, bores, and smoothes the massive parts so that they can be assembled into working machines. This department, along with all its computer-controlled-very-expensive- monstrous machine tools, is today's Blower Works.

Third, even though Beijing central control disappeared, the principle of central control (outside of the factory itself) reappeared with the establishment of a Machinery Bureau at the Provincial Government level. Instead of reporting to Beijing, the factory now reports to the Lioliang Provincial Government. Everything else, including absentee planning, stayed the same. Liu Da Foo, our old translator, is now a salesman seeking orders for custom designed pumps and compressors. Before this, the factory waited for orders to be sent to them from Beijing. In the midst of all this capitalistic activity, the ubiquitous, inefficient and downright wasteful "work plan" still determines the worker's pay and activities. It's a lose-lose situation.

Mr. Mu, the resilient Mr. Mu, survived all the changes until age forced his retirement. When we first met him he was the factory's chief representative for the purchase of foreign equipment. He was very proud to have purchased the most advanced machine tools available at that time, as well as modern computers. His position was so important to the factory that he reported directly to the Managing Director. When we saw him twenty-three years later he was still the factory's chief buyer of foreign equipment and still reported to the Managing Director. His title was Deputy Chief Engineer. He has survived five different managing directors. Staying in the same relatively high position after your boss is replaced is rare, even in the western business world. Every time the head person is replaced, the new person usually picks all the people around him. But that didn't happen here. Maybe that doesn't happen in the Chinese culture to the same extent that it happens in Western culture, but I don't think so. In addition, Mr. Mu was able to keep working beyond the usual retirement age. That is even more unusual. Retirement for women at 55 and men at 65 was immutable in the Chinese Communist world.

I guess Mr. Mu's resiliency is due, in part, to a position in the local Communist Party, the Factory Central Committee. That is a deduction on my part. I have very little information to support my idea. The only logical support for my supposition is based on experience and intuition. What else could it be? I heard about his Cultural Revolution activities; and I saw the deference shown him by co-workers in the factory. During the Cultural Revolution, Mr. Mu was an active participant in the cleansing committees that were ubiquitous at the time. These cleansing committees were feared by everyone. Any accusation was treated as proof of non-Communist loyalty, or worse, anti-Communist thought. Although mere membership in the Communist Party was not uncommon among the people I met, Mr. Mu's activities were those typical of the voluble stalwarts of the party, at least I think so..

Big Mu, on the other hand, profited from his connection, at least at first, to the new revolution. He ultimately suffered, however, from that connection. At first it appeared that he and his computer installation were placed at the Shenyang Blower Works for their benefit. I, along with my peers at IBM certainly thought so. But, look at the evidence.

The end <u>user</u> of the computer, the end <u>use</u> of the computer and the site of the computer was outside of Beijing and, most importantly, outside of the government. IBM's application for a export license was predicated on my fabrication of what computer applications would be used. The Beijing leaders knew or should have known that the U.S. government would never permit the export and the installation of a modern high-speed computer in the government itself. The Technological Bureau in the Ministry purchased a large computer <u>after</u> the embargo was lifted. Before the lifting of the embargo, the computer had to be in a "commercial" type of activity, an environment totally disconnected from the military and the government.

The Shenyang Blower Works was a natural. Even though the factory was owned and directed by the Communist government so was everything else in the country. The products of the Blower Works were connected to Deng's grand plan. The products manufactured there were intended for oil fields and coal mines. The factory couldn't modernize its operations without modern engineering techniques and modern machine tools. Those new techniques were embodied in computer programs and the new machine tools needed computers to run them. Shenyang was the logical place to go. Shenyang was the industrial heart of China at the time.

Once there, a completely separate building to house the computer and its staff, along with many classrooms was constructed on the grounds of the factory, but not inside the factory. Not only was a new building constructed, but it was equipped with every new type of environmental control, every new type of electric distribution, every new type of everything. That should have given us a hint of the use to which the computer was destined; we failed to see it and the Chinese never corrected us.

After the embargo was lifted with diplomatic recognition, every newly announced IBM computer was purchased and installed there. It clearly was a government showplace. There was plenty of room inside other buildings on the factory site, but a new separate building had been built. I know that Mr. Mu and his cohorts from the engineering departments would have liked to spend some more money on new machine tools, and not computer buildings. However, the choice wasn't his.

The computer staff and its leader were selected by the Beijing leaders not by the Shenyang Blower Works managers. Normally, workers were selected from the men and women entering the labor pool each year by the Shenyang Blower Works managers. Mr. Shu and Mr. Mu did not know of or about Big Mu until he was introduced to them as the manager of their new computer installation. Big Mu did not meet his staff until after he was appointed. These actions, which we knew about, should have given us another hint at the use destined for the new modern computer system. The six engineers from the boat factory could have stayed at the boat factory with a computer purchased for that enterprise. But no United States company could sell or deliver a computer to them; the boat factory produced boats used by the Chinese Navy. The leaders knew, or should have known, the U.S. government would never license a computer for a factory directly connected to the military.

After the installation several things happened that demonstrated the role that the Beijing leaders played in this scenario. The first was the remote demonstration of the computer in Beijing. One of the display terminals IBM delivered to Shenyang moved to Beijing. There, it was connected to the computer room in Shenyang over the Chinese telephone system.

It sounds simple, but at that time it was a complex undertaking given the miserable state of the telephone system and the inexperience of the computer staff. What did it prove? Was the factory running better? Was the factory going to run directly by the bosses in Beijing? My belief is it was a demonstration of technical proficiency, a demonstration of the Western modernity desired by Deng Tsao Peng. It enhanced the reputation of the First Ministry not the Shenyang Blower Works. At that time a more potent demonstration of modernization couldn't have been imagined. The Ministry leaders in Beijing couldn't have been prouder of this significant acceleration in Deng's "dance" to capitalism. The reputation of the Science and Technology Bureau was particularly enhanced. The huge congratulations we received during the final contract banquet from the head of that bureau, Mr. Cao Wei Lian, now makes much more sense than before. He and his boss, Mr. Suen You Yu were the puppet masters par excellence.

The establishment of something called the North Development Company, under the direction of Big Mu, also demonstrated the role that Beijing leaders played. The computer served the factory by doing its payroll. The factory design engineers used those engineering programs on the computer. My guess is that all that work used about 10% or less of the available capacity in the computer we delivered. In later years with more advanced computers with much more capacity, even less capacity was directly used by the Shenyang factory.

The North Development Company used a lot more of the available capacity of the IBM computer than the Shenyang Blower Works. The main use of the computer we delivered was the computer school for hundreds and hundreds of workers from factories all over the north of China. Mr. Cao was instrumental in setting that up. Every one of those workers came from a First Ministry factory! That school operated for many years. What benefit, if any, would come to the Blower Factory from educating all those people from other factories?

Later, the North Development Company took on a more public consulting role for other factories under aegis of the First Ministry.

But the situation began to deteriorate after about ten years when the government restructured itself by throwing off the mantle of centralized planning and control for major industries. I guess the budgets that enabled Big Mu to purchase every new computer that came along disappeared along with the Beijing connection. The Shenyang Blower Works computer installation's role as the national industrial computer demonstration site ended. Now their budget came from the Lioliang Provincial government in Shenyang and not from Beijing. The Lioliang Provincial government's interest in computers was a lot different, and a lot smaller, than the big central Ministry in Beijing. By the time I visited in 2000, Big Mu and his computer installation were less important than before. Most of his staff had disappeared; every programmer had been moved to somewhere else, most maintenance men were gone. Their major function of educating and modernizing had been accomplished. Ultimately, he left as well.

For China, the most important result from the unintended (or, maybe it was intended) result of having the most modern solid state computers in the world on display in the middle of the most industrialized area of China. The impact on every young person upon seeing this could only have been, "I can do this myself", and they did. The whole country is one big entrepreneurial factory looking to compete with anyone and everyone.

The next question is what happened to the IBM Corporation as a result of this seed implantation in 1976-1978. The impact of the Chinese cultural obligation to "friends" and people and companies that "befriend" them is legendary. As a result of the reputation we built during those early years, IBM has enjoyed a tremendous success in China. IBM has three large plants in China with over 6,000 employees there. Those plants manufactured laptop computers for the world-wide markets; they manufacture

IBM servers that drive many computer networks in, Asia, Europe, and Latin American and, of course, they manufacture the IBM personal computer sold in Asia and Europe. In 2004, that whole operation was sold to a Chinese company that did not exist 15 years before! In addition to the manufacturing operations, IBM has 15 sales offices in China with approximately 4,000 sales and service employees. Revenue in 2004 was in excess of $10 Billion US Dollars. By any measure, IBM has profited mightily from our ten-month effort beginning in 1976; the Chinese subsidiary has and probably will continue to experience a 30% annual growth rate.

So, was there a revolution? My answer is "Yes!" But not the one we thought we were engaged in. The revolution did not take place just in the Shenyang Blower Works; it took place throughout North China. During the three years after we signed our contract with Messer's Wu, Shu, Mu and Big Mu, tens and tens of computers were installed and running in a country that for decades before had hardly seen a foreign person or publication, let alone a solid state computer.

Of course, this little installation in Shenyang wasn't the sole cause of that momentous shift; Deng Tsao Ping's plan and the U.S.A.'s relaxation of trade barriers and embargoes played there parts. Hundreds and hundreds of trained people are using those computers for productive tasks. For a society whose mental energies were devoted to "self-sufficiency", the brain-multiplying effect of computers was monumental. For China, the effect was akin to the invention of the wheel or the taming of fire. The political climate wrought by these changes in the economy has yet to appear. These three men in Shenyang were the forerunners of a societal change that is not over yet!